Youth Violence and Delinquency

Recent Titles in
Criminal Justice, Delinquency, and Corrections

Youth Violence and Delinquency

Monsters and Myths

Volume 2
Juvenile Justice

Edited by

MARILYN D. MCSHANE
AND FRANK P. WILLIAMS III

Praeger Perspectives

Criminal Justice, Delinquency, and Corrections

Westport, Connecticut
London

Library of Congress Cataloging-in-Publication Data

Youth violence and delinquency : monsters and myths / edited by Marilyn
D. McShane and Frank P. Williams III.
    p. cm. — (Criminal justice, delinquency, and corrections, ISSN 1535-0371)
    Includes bibliographical references and index.
    ISBN 978-0-275-99112-8 (set : alk. paper) — ISBN 978-0-275-99113-5
(v. 1 : alk. paper) — ISBN 978-0-275-99114-2 (v. 2 : alk. paper) —
ISBN 978-0-275-99115-9 (v. 3 : alk. paper) 1. Juvenile delinquency—
United States. 2. Juvenile justice, Administration of—United States. 3. Victims of
juvenile crime—United States. 4. Juvenile delinquency—United States—Prevention.
I. McShane, Marilyn D., 1956- II. Williams, Franklin P.
    HV9104.Y6854 2007
    364.360973—dc22   2007003047

British Library Cataloguing in Publication Data is available.

Library of Congress Catalog Card Number: 2007003047
ISBN-10: 0-275-99112-1 (set)
            0-275-99113-X (vol. 1)
            0-275-99114-8 (vol. 2)
            0-275-99115-6 (vol. 3)

ISBN-13: 978-0-275-99112-8 (set)
            978-0-275-99113-5 (vol. 1)
            978-0-275-99114-2 (vol. 2)
            978-0-275-99115-9 (vol. 3)

ISSN: 1535-0371

First published in 2007

Praeger Publishers, 88 Post Road West, Westport, CT 06881
An imprint of Greenwood Publishing Group, Inc.
www.praeger.com

Printed in the United States of America

The paper used in this book complies with the
Permanent Paper Standard issued by the National
Information Standards Organization (Z39.48-1984).

10 9 8 7 6 5 4 3 2 1

Contents

Preface

CHILDREN IN THE ARMS OF THE LAW

The 12-year-old boy in his baggy tailored shirt and oversize prep school pants seems lost at the courtroom table. Perhaps as part of defense strategy, he struggles to see over the table, dwarfed next to his lawyers. The youth is on trial for the shooting of his father two years ago, when he was 10, on Prozac and caught in a bitter divorce drama. Grilling potential jurors, the district attorney hammers home the legal age of intent in this state, the age of responsibility, and the age at which you can be tried for murder and face up to 40 years in combined juvenile and adult prison—that age is 10.

Many of the jurors silently shook their heads. They have raised children, they have grandchildren, and they know that children often say and do things, even serious things, without realizing the consequences, without recognizing the finality of gunshot wounds. Yet those jurors most troubled by the proceedings ahead were summarily dismissed, one by one, leaving a stoic assembly of law-and-order adherents unflinchingly ready to administer the verdict. How did we get to this point? Have we lost sight of the principles that once compelled us to separate juveniles from adults, to seek rehabilitative interventions, and to adjust the harsh court terminology to at least appear more family friendly, more youth oriented, and more optimistic?

The average juvenile case today is a much less dramatic incident. The statistics reflect the frequency of larcenies, drug possessions, and possession of stolen goods. What is more remarkable about youth crime is the likelihood that offenses will be committed in groups or at least by pairs of offenders. And, although some youthful violations seem mostly harmless, such as underage smoking or drinking, incidents of drag racing that kills your teenage passenger or costly vandalism most often unites public sentiments into waves of concern about coddling and overindulgence.

Still, changes in law and policy often occur quickly, literally overnight, and without the benefit of the careful scientific research and theoretical analysis that might help us better isolate effective strategies and interventions. The more we learn about juvenile delinquency, the more we realize that myriad social influences, environmental factors, and available resources change the way we approach the problem and address it.

The collection of readings offered in this volume illuminate some of the secrets from the often-mysterious realm of courts and law. Principles vary from state to state, as do traditions and practices in administering juvenile justice. But trends in philosophy and sentiments about the weight of punishments and the accountability of parents seem to be pervasive themes in our contemporary culture.

CHAPTER 1

Contemporary Juvenile Justice Reform Movements: Theory, Policy, and the Future

Michael P. Brown and Jill M. D'Angelo

We may be witnessing juvenile justice reforms that are as historically important as when the first juvenile court was established in 1899 and when, during the 1960s and 1970s, juveniles were afforded many of the same procedural protections guaranteed defendants in criminal court. The reforms to which we are referring have been unfolding for several decades, but the last 15 years or so have revealed two relatively coherent reform movements that are diametrically opposed. One reform movement is to "dismantle" the juvenile justice system. We refer to this as the dismantling reform movement, and its focus is on social control, retribution, and deterrence. A central element of the dismantling movement includes the provision to transfer adolescents from juvenile to criminal court. The other reform movement, the revitalization movement, is consistent with and generally supportive of a separate system of justice for juveniles. Its focus is on restoring the principles upon which the juvenile justice system was established. Although the revitalization reform movement does not propose the elimination of the legal provisions that were extended to juveniles approximately 50 years ago, it reasserts the developmental differences between adolescents and adults and seeks to provide services that prevent delinquency and rehabilitate offenders.

These reform movements exist alongside each other within local jurisdictions and across the country. All juvenile justice systems have characteristics resembling both reform movements, but one movement tends to be more influential than the other. The predominate reform movement today is to dismantle juvenile justice. There continues to be support, however, for the reemergence of the original notions of juvenile justice.

These competing reform movements, which have polarized the general public, practitioners, and academicians, reflect a justice system that is in transition. Instead of advocating one reform movement over another, we take a critical position and contend that neither reform movement provides an effective, comprehensive response to juvenile crime. Elements of each reform movement, however, could be integrated with other time-tested practices to construct a juvenile justice system that instills positive behavioral changes and provides for public safety.

The purposes of this chapter are to examine these competing reform movements and to propose a course of action that improves the juvenile justice system. To do this, we first present Bernard's theory of juvenile justice reform.[1] Second, with Bernard's framework in mind, we explain the reasons for the establishment of the juvenile court and the principles upon which it was established. By doing this, we see how the juvenile court was a core element of one of the most important justice reform movements in the history of the United States. Third, we use Bernard's reform model to examine the catalysts of the contemporary reform movements. Fourth, we describe and provide examples of the dismantling movement and the revitalization movement. Finally, as juvenile justice reform continues to unfold, we propose a juvenile justice system that is better able to balance the needs of juveniles and the needs of society, and incorporate the principles of restorative justice.

A JUVENILE JUSTICE REFORM MODEL

In *The Cycle of Juvenile Justice*, Bernard indicates that reform movements have a discernable cycle. The model he proposes begins with justice officials and the public believing that the number of delinquent acts has increased to a high level. To address these acts, there are many punitive sanctions but relatively few lenient treatments. In this scenario, justice officials may feel as though they must choose between a harsh punishment and doing "nothing." Consequently, while serious offenders meet with a proportionate sanction for their offense, minor offenders may not be punished for their misdeeds. These misdeeds go unpunished because proportionate sanctions are unavailable and officials believe that a disproportionate response may cause the delinquent to enter further into a delinquent lifestyle.

The second stage of the cycle is characterized by the continued belief that delinquency remains at high levels and that the reason for this problem is, in part, due to a lack of appropriate sentencing options, which Bernard calls "forced choice." That is, because justice officials are forced to choose between punitive sanctions and doing "nothing at all," high levels of delinquency persist; both punitive sanctions and doing nothing increases delinquency.

The third stage of the cycle is juvenile justice reform. The answer to the persistent problem of delinquency is to initiate reform that involves the introduction of treatments that would be proportionate to minor offenses. These sentencing options constitute a "...middle ground between harshly punishing and doing nothing at all."[2] Then all there is to do is wait, while justice officials eagerly anticipate a reduction in juvenile delinquency.

The fourth stage involves another reform movement. In this stage, delinquency has not been reduced as expected. In fact, delinquency continues to be seen as high, and the cause for the problem is perceived to be the lenient sanctions introduced during the most recent reform movement. Delinquency is high not because of the lack of available sentencing options but because the justice system response has been inadequate. Consequently, this stage is marked by serious offenders receiving even more punitive sanctions than before and minor offenders receiving harsh sanctions as substitutes for those treatments that once served as the middle ground between punitive sanctions and doing nothing. Eventually, punitive sanctions constitute the majority of justice system responses and the availability of lenient sanctions becomes restricted. The cycle continues.

Bernard points out that three fundamental beliefs provide insight into his reform model. First, justice officials and the public believe that delinquency is exceptionally high. Second, a belief exists that current juvenile justice policies are not only inadequately responding to delinquency, but they are actually exacerbating the problem. Third, a belief exists that the juvenile justice system must be reformed to reduce delinquency.

But what explains why one reform movement is adopted more readily than another? Sometimes proposed reforms may be seen as being new and innovative responses to long-term problems. This perception is often held because decision makers are ill-informed of what has been tried in the past and why it failed to perform as expected. At other times, an old idea is repackaged as something new, when in fact no substantive differences have been made in what is proposed from past practices. Because much of what is proposed to respond to delinquency is not new, history repeats itself.

According to Bernard, the reasons why one reform movement is accepted more readily than another are found in two additional beliefs systems. These beliefs are grounded in ideas or assumptions about what causes delinquency and how best to respond to it. Put another way, those things that are believed to be the causes of delinquency influence how society responds. If one believes that delinquency is a selfish act committed for one's benefit, then one may be more likely to advocate for sanctions that seek to deter and punish. Conversely, if one believes that delinquency is a cry for help, a way to get attention, or a function of social forces beyond the control of the offender, then one may be more likely to fashion a sentence to meet the needs of the offender.

THE BEGINNING OF JUVENILE JUSTICE REFORM

Early nineteenth-century America experienced rapid and dramatic social and economic changes as a result of immigration, industrialization, and urbanization. These changes were wide-reaching and by the mid-nineteenth century, much to the efforts of the child savers movement, adolescents were seen as a unique group.[3] They were not simply considered miniature adults, but rather developmentally different from adults and in need of custodial care, supervision, and guidance. These ideas became ingrained into our larger culture, changed social expectations, and redefined the government's responsibilities as they pertain to youth. Concern over child welfare, coupled with mounting pressure for the government to intervene in the lives of juveniles who were poor and destitute, and genuine alarm over what appeared to be a growing juvenile crime problem[4] were social indicators of still more changes to come.

One is left to wonder whether citizens at that time appreciated the dramatic changes that were to come for the justice system. The House of Refuge movement in the early 1800s marked the beginning of a separate system of justice for juveniles. It was the first juvenile court in 1899, however, that ignited truly revolutionary changes in the American justice system. In less than three decades, juvenile courts had been established in nearly every jurisdiction in every state.

The juvenile court was a social experiment on a grand scale. Rooted in the *parens patriae* philosophy, the juvenile court would act in the best interest of a child. "Justice" was to be personalized to meet the unique needs of each child that came into contact with the court. Therefore, prevention and rehabilitation were the primary goals of the juvenile court. As U.S. Supreme Court Justice Fortas wrote,

> The early reformers were appalled by adult procedures and penalties, and by the fact that children could be given long prison sentences and mixed in jails with hardened criminals. They were profoundly convinced that society's duty to the child could not be confined by the concept of justice alone. They believed that society's role was not to ascertain whether the child was "guilty" or "innocent," but "what is he, how has he become what he is, and what had best be done in his interest and in the interest of the state to save him from a downward career." The child—essentially good, as they saw it—was to be made "to feel that he is the object of the state's care and solicitude," not that he was under arrest or on trial. The rules of criminal procedure were therefore altogether inapplicable. The apparent rigidities, technicalities, and harshness which they observed in both substantive and procedural criminal law were therefore to be discarded. The idea of crime and punishment was to be abandoned. The child was to be "treated" and "rehabilitated" and the procedures from apprehension though institutionalization, were to be "clinical" rather than punitive."[5]

As a government entity, however, the juvenile court had a responsibility to strike a balance between the best interests of the child and providing public safety.

In practical terms, this is a difficult balance to achieve. But being consistent with its original intent, the juvenile court would seek societal protection through the rehabilitation of the child. It would not resort to seeking punishment and retribution, which was the traditional response to law-violating youth until that point in time. Rather, rehabilitation was considered the appropriate justice system response because children were products of their environment. They were seen as victims of society, victims of improper care and custody at home, and victims of their circumstances. As such, children were considered to be not as accountable for their behavior as adults. Furthermore, most youths were considered amenable to treatment, and juvenile court sentences were to reflect individual needs and circumstances.

As originally conceived, juvenile court decision making would not be confined by procedural safeguards defined in the U.S. Constitution. Vast discretion was a necessary element for individualized justice. Additionally, it was believed that children would not need to be protected from a court that was acting as a benevolent parent, interested in the child's best interest. Extending procedural rights into the juvenile court represents yet another important reform movement in the history of juvenile justice. Although that discussion goes beyond the scope of this chapter, it is noteworthy that conventional notions of procedural fairness affect the functioning of all justice policies. This fact was perhaps most dramatically witnessed with the establishment of procedural safeguards that restricted discretion within the juvenile court, especially with regard to waiver procedures and statutes.

CATALYSTS OF THE COMPETING REFORM MOVEMENTS

The contemporary juvenile court reform movements reflect the convergence of a constellation of factors that are largely consistent with Bernard's model of justice system reform. These factors include a rise in delinquency, the concern that juveniles have become more dangerous, the reemergence of gangs and drug-related violence, and changes in attitudes about the types of justice system responses that are appropriate in juvenile court.

Juvenile delinquency began to rise during the latter half of the 1980s and did not show signs of subsiding until 1994. For about a decade, juvenile involvement in crime, in general, and increases in violent juvenile crime, in particular, brought widespread public fear. Although there was only a 7 percent increase from 1985 to 1994 in arrests for property index offenses, for the same time period, arrests for violent index offenses increased 73 percent.[6]

This increase in arrests translated into increased court activity. There was an increase of 41 percent in the total number of cases processed in juvenile courts.[7] For that same time period, person offense cases were up 93 percent, including a 144 percent increase in homicide cases, a 134 percent increase in aggravated assault cases, and a 53 percent increase in robbery cases. Total property offense cases were up 22 percent, with a 69 percent increase in automobile theft cases and a 46 percent increase in vandalism cases. Total drug offense cases were up 62 percent.

Talk of the emergence of the superpredator[8] put people on edge and instilled deep trepidation about juvenile crime at that time and what the future might hold. Part of this concern was fueled by the belief that delinquents were younger than in the past and that they were committing more serious violent offenses. A study by Butts and Snyder reported that although there was a 47 percent increase in person offense arrests among those 15 and older from 1980 to 1995, there was a 94 percent increase among those under age 15 for the same time period.[9] In other words, the rise in violent arrests for those under age 15 was twice that of those 15 and older.

If all of that was not enough, Esbensen aptly points out that youth gang activity also reemerged in the 1980s and 1990s, and the mass media brought a glamorized, yet violent and spontaneous, depiction of gang life into America's living rooms.[10] The reality of gang violence took on relevance for many people, no matter where they lived. Gangs were said to have made their way out of the inner city into the suburbs and rural areas; from the coasts to the Midwest. Reinforcing those fears was local television news that regularly reported gang activity and Hollywood productions that portrayed young people as violent, drug-crazed criminals in such films as *Colors* and *Boyz N the Hood*. Additionally, increases in adolescent involvement with the use and distribution of drugs often involves carrying handguns for protection and intimidation, which is likely to be associated with the rise in youth violence.[11]

Whether our perceptions of juvenile crime are driven by media images, irrational fear, personal experiences, or the best available data, what we believe to be true mitigates our opinions about the purposes of juvenile justice. Focusing on public opinion surveys conducted during the 1980s and 1990s, the literature suggests mixed findings about what the juvenile court should do with juvenile offenders. For example, a national survey conducted in 1982 indicated that nearly 75 percent of the respondents believed that the primary goal of juvenile court was rehabilitation.[12] When justice professionals were asked how best to respond to juvenile criminals, however, more than half responded that punishment worked better than rehabilitation.[13] Yet, more than 80 percent of the same sample indicated that it would be irresponsible to ignore attempts to rehabilitate them.

Bernard's reform model provides unique insight into a survey conducted by Schwartz, et al. The findings of that study suggest a critical reason why juvenile justice is in a state of flux. Schwartz, et al., found that nearly 100 percent (from 97 to 99 percent) of respondents were supportive of punishment for serious juvenile personal, property, and drug offenders. At the same time, however, only slightly fewer respondents (from 88 to 95 percent) were supportive of rehabilitation for the same juvenile offenders. This rehabilitation is perceived to be accomplished by placing offenders in punitive programs or facilities with rehabilitation as a primary goal. As for the rest of the juvenile offenders? Rehabilitation was the best response. The public seems to be of two minds, and it does not see a conflict between punishing the worst offenders while simultaneously preparing them to be productive, contributing adults.[14]

THE COMPETING REFORM MOVEMENTS

We begin this discussion of the competing reform movements by focusing on the dominant movement, which is, in many ways, dismantling the juvenile justice system. We will describe the movement's characteristics in detail and show how it has transformed "justice" for an increasing number of adolescents. We then do the same for the revitalization movement.

The Dismantling Movement

The dismantling movement has a coherent set of principles that drive decision making and policy development. How these principles are implemented in the form of policy is influenced by such things as political jostling. Although the outcomes are not entirely predictable, they are by no means uncertain either.

The central theme of the dismantling reform movement is the process of recriminalizing delinquency. This process is the opposite of what occurred when the juvenile court was established, as juveniles were diverted from criminal to juvenile court. Hence, recriminalization is an "effort to return a part of the juvenile justice system to a period that existed prior to the creation of juvenile courts."[15] Although Singer argues that recriminalization does not eliminate the need for juvenile justice,[16] Feld suggests that elimination of the juvenile court may be the best course of action.[17] But this difference is not a discriminating factor of the dismantling movement. Rather, as Stevenson and associates state, "The sweeping changes in public policy affecting the juvenile court's delinquency jurisdiction have been the responses to concerns about serious, violent, and chronic offenders and the perceived leniency of juvenile court sanctions toward these juveniles."[18] Consequently, we have witnessed changes in the way juveniles are processed that increase the likelihood that they will come into contact with the criminal justice system.

This change in the justice system may be understood in light of van den Haag's oft-cited comments about the elimination of the legal boundaries between violent juveniles and adults. He stated,

> There is little reason left for not holding juveniles responsible under the same laws that apply to adults. The victim of a fifteen-year-old mugger is as mugged as the victim of a twenty-year-old mugger, the victim of a fourteen-year-old murderer or rapist is as dead or raped as the victim of an older one. The need for social defense or protection is the same.[19]

The assumption is that the seriousness of the act is an indication of adult competency and, therefore, culpability. There is also the assumption that adolescents who commit serious crimes are not amenable to treatment. There are two issues to be addressed here. First, there seems to be the belief that chronic or violent delinquents are beyond the hope of rehabilitation. Second, there is also a fundamental lack of confidence in the justice system to rehabilitate and protect society.

Consequently, during the first half of the 1990s, 40 states changed their transfer statutes to make it easier to prosecute juveniles in criminal court.[20] This was accomplished by adding offenses to the list of crimes for which juveniles could be waived and by lowering the age at which they would become eligible for a waiver. Of the three methods by which adolescents may be waived to criminal court—that is, judicial waivers, exclusionary statutes, and prosecutorial waivers—exclusionary statutes and prosecutorial waivers tend to place public safety above the best interests of the child. Exclusionary statutes (i.e., automatic waivers) now exist in 38 states; prosecutorial waivers exist in 15 states.

The exclusionary statute for the state of Alabama is similar to statutes in other states, and it stipulates that a child meeting statutory age or offense criteria must be "charged, arrested, and tried as an adult." Juveniles are excluded from the jurisdiction of the juvenile court if they are 16 years old and charged with capital crimes, drug trafficking, or a class A felony. The exclusion also applies if they are charged with any felony in which the accused is alleged to have used a deadly weapon, caused death or serious injury, or used a dangerous instrument against such people as law enforcement officers, corrections officers, parole or probation officers, juvenile court probation officers, prosecutors, judges, court officers, grand jurors, jurors or witnesses, and teachers, principals, and other employees of Alabama public schools.

The prosecutor for the Commonwealth of Virginia is given the following guidance:

> ...Following a finding of probable cause to believe the child was of the proper age [that is, fourteen] and committed the offense alleged [murder; felonious injury by mob, abduction, malicious wounding, malicious wounding of a police officer, felonious poisoning, adulteration of products, robbery, carjacking, rape, forcible sodomy, or sexual penetration with an object], the juvenile court must certify the charge, together with any ancillary charges, to the grand jury, after which its jurisdiction is terminated. On the other hand, in such a case the Commonwealth attorney may also elect not to give notice, and either seek a discretionary waiver or proceed with the case in juvenile court.[21]

One aspect of the dismantling reform movement is the notion that "once an adult, always an adult." Some 31 states have a special transfer category that stipulates once an adolescent has been transferred to criminal court, she or he will be subject to criminal proceedings in future cases.[22] Some states stipulate that "once an adult, always an adult" only applies when the charge ends in conviction or subsequent charges are felonies. For example, Ohio's law stipulates that—

> Once a juvenile has been transferred to adult court and convicted of (or pleaded guilty to) any felony, he or she is thereafter deemed not to be a "child" in any subsequent case.... Future complaints against such a juvenile must be filed initially in juvenile court, but the court's only role is to confirm the previous conviction/invocation and order a mandatory transfer to adult criminal court upon a finding of probable cause.[23]

In some states, such as Delaware, the determination of nonamenability to treatment through a discretionary waiver is the criterion of the "once an adult, always an adult" provision.

Although the major focus of the dismantling movement involves transferring certain juveniles to criminal court, it also involves substantive changes in the juvenile court itself. This change is palpable and can be seen in the purpose statements of many juvenile courts today. In recent years, for instance, the states of Kansas, Wisconsin, North Carolina, Washington, and Oregon changed the primary purposes of its juvenile court from one oriented toward rehabilitating juveniles to one prioritizing public safety and holding juvenile offenders accountable.[24]

Blended sentencing is an attempt to marshal the benefits of rehabilitation programs of the juvenile justice system and, at the same time, take a more punitive approach to juvenile offenders. The state of Texas has one of the more punitive forms of blended sentences. Under this sentencing scheme, the juvenile, with no minimum age limit, may be sentenced up to 40 years to a Texas Youth Commission facility until the age of majority and then, at that time, the offender may be transferred to the Texas Department of Criminal Justice.[25]

Minnesota takes a somewhat different approach to blended sentencing by stipulating, in part, that for an—

"extended jurisdiction juvenile" (EJJ) prosecution in juvenile court, a juvenile may receive both a juvenile disposition and a stayed adult criminal sentence. A juvenile of at least 14 who is accused of a felony (and thus is eligible for certification) is subject to EJJ prosecution if the prosecutor requests EJJ designation and presents clear and convincing evidence that the designation "serves public safety" and any juvenile of at least 16 who is accused of a felony committed with a firearm or an offense that would result in a presumptive commitment to prison under applicable laws and sentencing guidelines (and thus would qualify for Presumptive Waiver to adult court) is subject to EJJ prosecution if the prosecutor either designates the case an EJJ case or files an unsuccessful motion for certification. Although an EJJ prosecution takes place in juvenile court, the juvenile has a right to be tried before a jury.[26]

Such blended sentences serve as a bridge between the dismantling movement and the revitalization movement.

The Revitalization Movement

When separate justice systems were originally established for juveniles and adults, they reflected the presumption that adolescents were less culpable than adults for their behavior.[27] The founders of a separate juvenile justice system intuitively understood that adolescents were developmentally different from adults and, therefore, should not be held to the same standards as adults. What was believed to be true in 1899 is now supported by research findings. Compared with adults, adolescents are less capable of processing information and making choices, especially in stressful situations;[28] less capable of assessing risks;[29] more vulnerable to peer pressure;[30] and less able to consider long-term behavioral consequences.[31]

Even neuroscience research using diffusion-tensor Magnetic Resonance Imaging shows that the brain of an adolescent is less mature than that of an adult, which tends to explain juvenile impulsivity and the general lack of restraint.[32]

This is not to suggest that some juveniles should not be transferred to criminal court.

The 1966 *Kent v. United States* decision that established standards for the transfer of juveniles to criminal court reflects the understanding that, while some juveniles may be waived to criminal court, this should occur only after considering issues pertaining to the development and maturation of the adolescent. On the issue of culpability, the court stipulated that the youth's level of "sophistication and maturity" should be taken into consideration in the transfer decision. Judicial waivers (or discretionary waivers), which exist in 46 states, generally require judges to consider the juvenile's age, level of mental maturity, and capacity before transferring the case to criminal court.[33]

The revitalization movement stresses the importance of transfers that consider not only age and offense seriousness but also a host of other issues pertaining to the juvenile's ability to benefit from the services offered through the juvenile court. Hence, the revitalization movement advocates for the use of judicial waivers (i.e., discretionary waivers) that consider the psychological and cognitive characteristics of adolescents. Because not all judicial waivers do this, it is important to make this distinction.

A survey of all 50 states and the District of Columbia indicates that only four states exclusively use judicial waivers to transfer juveniles to criminal court. The other states use a combination of different types of waivers. Two of the four states, Missouri and Hawaii, consider the adolescent's malleability to treatment. The other two states, Tennessee and Texas, do not.

Missouri's juvenile justice system is considered a model for other states to emulate. Its waiver statute stipulates the following:

> ... in the case of a child of at least 12 accused of a felony, the juvenile court may order a hearing to consider whether to dismiss the delinquency petition and transfer the child for adult prosecution. (However, the court must at least hold a hearing to consider transfer where the child is accused of one of a number of listed offenses—first or second degree murder, first degree assault, forcible rape, forcible sodomy, first degree robbery, or distribution of drugs— or has committed two or more previous felonies.) Before the hearing, a written report on the child's history, record, offense, rehabilitation prospects, etc., must be prepared for the juvenile court's consideration. Following the hearing, the court may dismiss the case to permit adult prosecution if it finds that the child is not a proper subject to be dealt with under the juvenile law, taking into account a number of determinative considerations (including "racial disparity in certification") specified by law. An order of dismissal to permit adult prosecution must be supported by written findings.[34]

Like Missouri, the state of Hawaii requires the following:

> In all cases, the court must find at a minimum that there is no evidence that the minor is committable to a mental institution.... [and] In the case of a

minor accused of committing any felony after his 16th birthday, besides the requisite finding that the minor is not subject to commitment in a mental institution, the court must also find—on the basis of a "full investigation and hearing"—that either (1) the minor is not treatable in any children's institution or facility in the state or (2) the safety of the community requires that the minor be restrained beyond the period of his minority.[35]

Conversely, Tennessee's judicial waiver indicates the following:

> ...Following a hearing, a child meeting age/offense criteria may be transferred to adult criminal court if the juvenile court finds that there are reasonable grounds to believe that (1) the child committed the offense alleged, (2) the child is not committable to a mental institution, and (3) the interests of the community require that the child be placed under legal restraint.[36]

Except for juveniles who require institutionalization for mental illness, community safety is placed above the interests of the juvenile in Tennessee. Texas' judicial waiver statute stipulates the following:

> ...The juvenile court may waive its exclusive original jurisdiction over a child who meets age/offense criteria if it finds, after a full investigation and hearing, that (1) there is probable cause to believe the child committed the offense alleged and (2) because of the offense's seriousness or the child's background the welfare of the community requires a transfer for criminal proceedings.[37]

The emphasis on rehabilitation is based on the belief that underlying problems are the causes of delinquency, and the juvenile court is equipped to effectively address those problems. But that is not to say that holding juveniles accountable is beyond the scope of the revitalization movement. The waiver statutes for Missouri and Hawaii stress the rehabilitation function of the juvenile court, which seeks to hold adolescents accountable for their behavior. This is likewise true of Missouri's blended-sentence statute:

> In sentencing a juvenile who has been transferred for criminal prosecution, the court may impose both (1) a juvenile disposition and (2) an adult sentence, execution of which is suspended pending successful completion of the juvenile disposition. If the juvenile thereafter violates a condition or commits a new offense, the court may continue the juvenile disposition or revoke it and impose the adult sentence, as it sees fit. When the juvenile reaches the age of 17, a hearing must be held, after which the court must (1) continue the juvenile disposition (if the Division of Youth Services is willing to retain custody), (2) place the juvenile on probation, or (3) revoke the suspension and transfer the juvenile to the Department of Corrections. The Division of Youth Services must petition the court for a hearing if it seeks to release such a juvenile at any time before his 21st birthday, or if it determines that the juvenile is beyond the scope of its treatment programs. In either case, the court must hold a hearing and choose between (1) placing the juvenile on probation or (2) revoking the suspension and transferring the juvenile to the Department of Corrections.[38]

CONCLUSION

Juvenile justice reform movements are a consequence of evolving attitudes and beliefs about adolescents, who they are, what they can understand, and ultimately their level of culpability for illegal acts. Bernard's reform theory provides insight into the contemporary reform movements. Perceptions of an increase in delinquency, ineffective programming, and the popularity of retributive and deterrence-based responses to delinquency give insight into the dominant perspective, which is dismantling the traditional juvenile justice system.

But the dismantling and revitalization reform movements appear more complex than what Bernard's model is able to explain. For example, it was not just a perceived rise in delinquency that fueled contemporary reform movements, but also the perception of an increased level of seriousness of the acts committed by juveniles. Hence, the dominance of the dismantling reform movement may be a function of perceived vulnerability and the lethality of criminal victimization. A second issue is related to the first. That is, the popularity of the dismantling reform movement may be related to the perceived amenability of the offender to treatment. If juveniles are seen as more dangerous, perhaps even amoral and antisocial, they also may be seen as less treatable. This perception again feeds into feelings of vulnerability. One final point on the reform movements, that is, Singer's notion of how recriminalization provides more legal options to deal with delinquent and criminal acts,[39] sheds light on the popularity of waiver statutes, "once an adult, always an adult" provisions, and the growing popularity of blended sentences.

Juvenile justice reform movements have often taken a "silver bullet" approach to delinquency. They attempt to approach a complex, multidimensional issue with a simplistic explanation of delinquency and an equally simplistic approach to curtail a diverse array of delinquent acts. This characterization reflects a system that needs to be revitalized. An improved juvenile justice system requires a reform movement that is grounded in time-tested programs. It is a reform movement that should be driven not so much by political agendas as by what we know about best practices. Although politics will always be a part of any reform movement, such influences must be reduced.

Successes are rarely isolated. Demonstrated success improves public confidence, and resources tend to increase with these results. Bilchik proposes the means by which legitimacy is restored to juvenile justice, and this approach constitutes a comprehensive strategy to reduce delinquency in general and violent offenses in particular.[40]

Bilchik begins with two fundamental premises. First, effective juvenile justice systems hold offenders accountable, help offenders become responsible and productive citizens, and make the larger community safe. These objectives include the adolescent in the larger community and are consistent with the principles of restorative justice. Second, "... effective juvenile justice interventions are swift, certain, consistent and appropriate."[41] This approach is accomplished with effective prevention programs, early intervention programs, graduated sanctions, and assessments to improve system administration and operation.

For those juveniles who enter the system, assessment processes that determine the risks and needs of each juvenile are needed. These assessments are then matched with appropriate programming. Such programs and services need to be comprehensive and involve not only the individual offender but also the offender's family. For those who fail treatment and other programs, graduated sanctions should be used to reinforce the idea that one is accountable for unlawful behavior. A full range of graduated sanctions involves aftercare programming and waivers to criminal court. Detention should be reserved for preadjudication use, when juveniles are a risk to themselves, to others, or to ensure court appearances. Ultimately, effective programming requires a support system that includes an array of public and community resources.

The dismantling reform movement continues to have momentum today. Although it is the dominant movement, signs indicate that the revitalization movement may be slowly gaining influence. The recent *Roper v. Simmons* decision[42] is perhaps the most decisive break from the dismantling movement in over a decade, and it is an explicit recognition of the developmental differences between adolescents and adults. Is this a step in the direction Bilchik proposes? Was *Roper* the first example of integration of divergent practices that will strengthen the juvenile justice system? Or was *Roper* simply an aberration?

NOTES

1. Bernard, 1992.
2. Bernard, 1992, p. 4.
3. Platt, 1969.
4. Ferdinand, 1989.
5. *In re Gault*, 1967.
6. Snyder & Sickmund, 2006.
7. Butts, Snyder, Finnegan, Aughenbaugh, & Poole, 1996.
8. DiIulio, 1996.
9. Butts & Snyder, 1997.
10. Esbensen, 2000.
11. Blumstein, 1995.
12. Schwartz, Guo, & Kerbs, 1993.
13. Cullen, Golden, & Cullen, 1983.
14. Schwartz, et al. 1992.
15. Singer, 1996, p. 1.
16. Singer, 1996.
17. Feld, 1998.
18. Stevenson et al., 1996, p. 9.
19. van den Haag, 1975, p. 174.
20. Torbet & Szymanski, 1998.
21. Griffin, 2005.
22. Griffin, Torbet, & Szymanski, 1998.
23. Griffin, 2005.
24. DiFonzo, 2000.

25. Griffin, 2005.
26. Griffin, 2005.
27. Zimring, 2000.
28. Scott & Grisso, 1997.
29. Finn & Bragg, 1986.
30. Steinberg & Silverberg, 1986.
31. Scott & Grisso, 1997.
32. Beckman, 2004; Sowell, Thompson, Holmes, Jernigan, & Toga, 1999.
33. Sanborn & Salerno, 2005.
34. Griffin, 2005.
35. Griffin, 2005.
36. Griffin, 2005.
37. Griffin, 2005.
38. Griffin, 2005.
39. Singer, 1996.
40. Bilchik, 1998.
41. Bilchik, 1998, p. 2.
42. *Roper v. Simmons*, 2005.

REFERENCES

Beckman, M. (2004). Crime, culpability, and the adolescent brain. *Science, 305,* 596–599.

Bernard, T. J. (1992). *The cycle of juvenile justice.* New York: Oxford University Press.

Bilchik, S. (1998, May). *A juvenile justice system for the 21st century.* Washington, D.C.: Office of Juvenile Justice and Delinquency Prevention.

Blumstein, A. (1995). Violence by young people: Why the deadly nexus? *National Institute of Justice Journal* (August), 2–9. Washington, D.C.: National Institute of Justice.

Butts, J. A., & Snyder, H. N. (1997). *The youngest delinquents: Offenders under age 15.* Washington, D.C.: Office of Juvenile Justice and Delinquency Prevention.

Butts, J. A., Snyder, H. N., Finnegan, T. A., Aughenbaugh, A. L., & Poole, R. S. (1996). *Juvenile court statistics 1994.* Washington, D.C:. Office of Juvenile Justice and Delinquency Prevention.

Cullen, F. T., Golden, K. M., & Cullen, J. B. (1983). Is child saving dead? Attitudes toward juvenile rehabilitation in Illinois. *Journal of Criminal Justice, 11,* 1–13.

DiFonzo, J. H. (2000). Parental responsibility for juvenile crime. *Oregon Law Review, 80,* 1. Retrieved July 27, 2006, from http://www.law.uoren.edu/org/olr/archives/80/80_Or_L_Rev_1.pdf.

DiIulio, J. (1996). *How to stop the coming crime wave.* New York: Manhattan Institute.

Esbensen, F. (2000). Preventing adolescent gang involvement. *Juvenile Justice Bulletin.* Retrieved July 24, 2006, from http://www.ncjrs.gov/html/ojjdp/2000_9_2/contents.html.

Feld, B. C. (1998). Abolish the juvenile court: Youthfulness, criminal responsibility, and sentencing policy. *The Journal of Criminal Law and Criminology, 88*(1), 68–136.

Ferdinand, T. (1989). Juvenile delinquency or juvenile justice: Which came first? *Criminology, 27,* 79–106.

Finn, P., & Bragg, B. W. E. (1986). Perception of the risk of an accident by young and older drivers. *Accident Analysis and Prevention, 18*, 289–298.

Griffin, P. (2005). *Transfer provisions. State juvenile justice profiles.* Pittsburgh, PA: National Center for Juvenile Justice. Retrieved July 22, 2006, from http://www.ncjj.org/stateprofiles/.

Griffin, P., Torbet, P., & Szymanski, L. (1998). *Trying juveniles as adults in criminal court: An analysis of state transfer provisions.* Washington, D.C.: Office of Juvenile Justice and Delinquency Prevention.

Platt, A. (1969). *The child savers: The invention of delinquency.* Chicago, IL: University of Chicago Press.

Sanborn, J. B., & Salerno, A. W. (2005). *Juvenile justice system.* Los Angeles: Roxbury.

Schwartz, I. M., Guo, S., & Kerbs, J. J., et al. (1993). The impact of demographic variables on public opinion regarding juvenile justice: Implications for public policy. *Crime and Delinquency, 39*, 5–28.

Scott, E., & Grisso, T. (1997). Symposium on the future of the juvenile court: The evolution of adolescence: A developmental perspective on juvenile justice. *Journal of Criminal Law and Criminology, 88*, 137–189.

Singer, S. I. (1996). *Recriminalizing delinquency: Violent juvenile crime and juvenile justice reform.* New York: Cambridge University Press.

Snyder, H. N., & Sickmund, M. (2006). *Juvenile offenders and victims: 2006 national report.* Washington, D.C.: Office of Juvenile Justice and Delinquency Prevention.

Sowell, E. R., Thompson, P. M., Holmes, C. J., Jernigan, T. L., & Toga, A. W. (1999). In vivo evidence for post-adolescent brain maturation in frontal and striatal regions. *Nature Neuroscience, 2*, 859–861.

Steinberg, L., & Silverberg, S. B. (1986). The vicissitudes of autonomy in early adolescence. *Child Development, 57*, 841–851.

Stevenson, C. S., Larson, C. S., Carter, L. S., Gomby, D. S., Terman, D. L., & Behrman, R. E. (1996). The future of children. *The Juvenile Court, 6* (3), 4–28.

Torbet, P., & Szymanski, L. (1998). State legislative responses to violent crime: 1996–97 update. *Juvenile Justice Bulletin.* Retrieved July 16, 2006, from http://www.ncjrs.gov/pdffiles/172835.pdf.

van den Haag, E. (1975). *Punishing criminals: Concerning a very old and painful question.* New York: Basic Books.

Zimring, F. E. (2000). Penal proportionality for the young offender: Notes on immaturity, capacity, and diminished responsibility. In T. Grisso & R. G. Schwartz (Eds.), *Youth on trial: A developmental perspective on juvenile justice* (pp. 271–289). Chicago: University of Chicago Press.

CASES CITED

In re Gault. 387 U.S. 1 (1967).

Kent v. United States, 383 U.S. 541 (1966).

Roper v. Simmons, 543 U.S. 551 (2005).

CHAPTER 2

Are We Tough Enough?
Trends in Juvenile Sentencing

Attapol Kuanliang and Jon Sorensen

Before the emergence of a separate system for juveniles, children and adults were treated alike in the justice system. Juveniles were subject to the same criminal proceedings as adults. The only choice typically available to the criminal court was to send convicted juveniles to adult prison or to release them without any sanction.[1] In 1825, the New York House of Refuge was established as the result of the idea that convicted juveniles should be incarcerated separately from adults. The philosophical rationale was that younger offenders, unlike most adult criminals, could be turned away from a life of crime with proper treatment. By the close of the twentieth century, the first juvenile court was founded in Chicago, in Cook County. Progressive ideas about the care and treatment of juveniles rapidly spread, and along with it, separate juvenile justice systems were created throughout the United States.

Under the original rationale of the juvenile court, sentences for individual juveniles were indeterminate. Judges held vast amounts of discretion over the sentencing of an offender, with decisions rooted in the rehabilitative ideal and focused on the best interests of each child. In the 1960s, however, a fundamental shift in sentencing practices was under way because of a lack of faith in rehabilitation and the realization that the juvenile court was not functioning according to its original plan.[2] Early on the criticism focused on the arbitrary nature of the decision making that violated the due process rights of juveniles. Beginning with *In re Gault* in 1967, these legal decisions caused changes in the court's focus from informal treatment to formal legal procedures, thus transforming the court from its original intent. A preoccupation with offense in the new sentencing procedures detracted from the needs of the child. Instead of concentrating on how best to rehabilitate the young offender, the new legal procedures encouraged courts to focus on the current offense, age of the offender, and prior record to determine what sentence to impose. Concern for the juvenile was no longer directed toward the child's future and how to prevent further offending, but rather on his or her past and how to punish inappropriate behavior.[3]

More recently, criticism has been directed at the juvenile courts for being "too soft on crime." This criticism has spurred legislation and policies that change sentencing and other juvenile procedures. During 1970s, the general public demanded increased offender accountability and more punitive sentences for juvenile offenders, a demand heeded by politicians.[4] This movement signaled a shift in sentencing philosophy that has moved juvenile processing further away from treatment toward the punishment of juvenile offenders.

SENTENCING REFORM

One of the first efforts at reform was the 1971 Juvenile Justice Standards Project, jointly sponsored by the Institute of Judicial Administration (IJA) and the American Bar Association (ABA). Members numbered about 300 professionals from across the nation, including prominent representatives of every discipline connected to the juvenile justice system: law, medicine, social work, psychiatry, psychology, sociology, corrections, political science, law enforcement, education, and architecture.[5] The project developed comprehensive guidelines for juvenile offenders that based sentences on the seriousness of the crime rather than on the needs of the youth. Ten years and 23 volumes later, the IJA-ABA Juvenile Justice Standards were completed. From that initial premise, several fundamental principles flowed with logical precision, as follows:

- Sanctions should be proportionate to the seriousness of the offense.
- Sentences or dispositions should be fixed or determinate as declared by the court after a hearing, not indeterminate as determined by correctional authorities based on subsequent behavior or administrative convenience.
- The least restrictive alternative to accomplish the purpose of the intervention should be the choice of decision makers at every stage, with written reasons for finding less drastic remedies inadequate required of every official decision maker.
- Noncriminal misbehavior (status offenses or conduct that would not be a crime if committed by an adult) should be removed from juvenile court jurisdiction.
- Limitations should be imposed on detention, treatment, or other intervention prior to adjudication and disposition.
- Visibility and accountability of decision making should replace closed proceedings and unrestrained official discretion.

- Juveniles should have the right to decide on actions affecting their lives and freedom, unless they are found incapable of making reasoned decisions.
- Parental roles in juvenile proceedings should be redefined with particular attention to possible conflicts between the interests of parent and child.
- There should be a right to counsel for all affected interests at all crucial stages of proceedings and an unwaivable right to counsel for juveniles.
- Strict criteria should be established for waiver of juvenile court jurisdiction to regulate the transfer of juveniles to adult criminal court.[6]

At the beginning of the twenty-first century, juvenile court judges remain quite concerned about these proposed standards. Their basic concern is that these standards attack the underlying philosophy and structure of the juvenile court. Judges also are concerned about how these standards would limit their authority. They see the influence of the hardliners behind this movement toward standardization and believe that the needs of children will be neglected in the long run. These judges also challenge the idea that it is possible, much less feasible, to treat all children alike.[7]

Nevertheless, the standards and juvenile justice sentencing reforms have been adopted across the nation. Laws in many states were changed during the 1970s and 1980s to focus on the "just deserts" of the offender, highlighting punishment for the current offense rather than treatment of the real needs of the child. The current reforms fit within a more general cycle of emphasizing retribution over rehabilitation, but are nonetheless striking for their apparent extremism.[8] Evidence strongly suggests a trend toward arresting more juveniles, processing them more quickly, incarcerating them for longer periods of time with fewer opportunities for rehabilitation, and, in general, treating violent or chronic juvenile offenders as adults.[9] Regardless of the cause, these reforms frequently have been undertaken despite lack of information concerning their potential effects and efficacy and despite severe fiscal constraints.[10]

New York State was the first to act on them through the Juvenile Justice Reform Act of 1976, which went into effect on February 1, 1977. The Act orders a determinate sentence of five years for class A felonies, which include murder, first-degree kidnapping, and first-degree arson. This initial term can be extended by at least one year. The juvenile, according to the Act, should be placed in a residential facility at first, but may serve the remainder of the five-year term in a nonresidential program under intensive supervision.[11]

In 1987, a special type of sentencing legislation was enacted in Texas, titled the Determinate Sentence Act.[12] Legislators hoped to create a system of juvenile sentencing that provided more severe punishment of serious, violent, or chronic offenders. These offenders were not eligible for transfer to the criminal justice system or were eligible for transfer but typically would not be viewed as appropriate for transfer. The creation of determinate sentencing essentially introduced a third sentencing option that bridged the gap between juvenile and adult justice, thereby giving rise to one description of Texas as having three justice systems—a juvenile, criminal, and juvenile-criminal justice system.[13] Apart from minor changes, this legislation remained largely unchanged until 1995, when it was renamed the Violent or Habitual Offenders Act. At the same time, the legislature renamed Title 3 of the Family Code as the "Juvenile Justice Code" and introduced into it the concept of punishment. Two major changes were implemented: (1) the number of determinate sentence-eligible offenses was increased from 5 to approximately 30, and (2) the conditions under which parole or transfer to the adult prison could occur were modified.[14]

With such widespread changes in public sentiment and laws relating to juvenile sentencing, one would assume that juveniles are currently being treated much more harshly in the juvenile justice system. However, systems such as the juvenile justice system have often proved resistant to external directives to change. What exactly has been the impact of these changes? How severely are juvenile law violators currently treated in juvenile courts? Before examining the effect of such changes on the actual sentencing of juvenile offenders, the basic procedures of juvenile justice case processing are reviewed.

JUVENILE COURT PROCEDURES

Juveniles may be referred to the juvenile justice system by law enforcement officers, parents, relatives, school officials, and probation officers, among other people. After the referral, a decision is made to file a petition or to handle the case informally. Juvenile petitions are official documents filed in juvenile courts on the juvenile's behalf, specifying reasons for the youth's court appearance. Filing a petition formally places the juvenile before the juvenile court judge in many jurisdictions, although juveniles may come before the court in less formal ways.[15]

After the petition is filed, the case proceeds to intake. Intake is a screening procedure usually conducted by a juvenile probation officer during which one or several courses of action are recommended. In most jurisdictions, intake results in one of five actions:

- Dismiss the case
- Remand youths to the custody of their parents
- Remand youths to the custody of their parents with provisions for, or referrals to, counseling or special services
- Divert youths to an alternative dispute resolution program
- Refer youths to the juvenile prosecutor for further action and possible filing of a delinquency petition[16]

Cases that are referred to the juvenile prosecutor may be formally processed by the juvenile court. After hearing the evidence presented by both sides in any proceeding, the judge decides or adjudicates the matter in an adjudication hearing. The stage after adjudication is referred to as disposition; it is the sentencing step of the juvenile proceedings.[17] Although several dispositions are available to juvenile court judges, they can be divided into four types: (1) residential placement; (2) probation; (3) other sanctions, such as community services, referral to an outside agency, or treatment programs; and (4) release.

Dispositions of Delinquent Cases

The Office of Juvenile Justice and Delinquency Prevention (OJJDP) reported that in 2002 courts with juvenile jurisdiction handled an estimated 1,615,400 delinquency cases, 24 percent involving offenses against persons, 39 percent property, 12 percent drugs, and 25 percent public order. In about 42 percent of these cases, a delinquency petition was not pursued. Of the generally less serious cases, the most common disposition was dismissal followed by probation and alternative sanctions. Out-of-home placements were voluntary and rare. In one-third of all petitioned delinquency cases in 2002, the youth was not subsequently adjudicated delinquent. Two-thirds of these cases resulted in dismissal, while the remainder, as with the nonpetitioned cases, resulted in some other sanctions, probation, or only rarely voluntary out-of-home placement.

The more serious cases tended to result in delinquency adjudications or, in rare cases, waiver to adult courts. Among the cases adjudicated delinquent, the most common sanction was probation, accounting for nearly two-thirds of the dispositions. Less than one-quarter (23 percent) of cases adjudicated delinquent resulted in placement outside the home. Even among adjudicated delinquents, then, out-of-home placement is an unusual sanction. Although these results may be somewhat unexpected given changes in the law and rhetoric, it is possible that this pattern represents a tougher sanctioning system than existed previously. It is to that possibility that we now turn, examining trends in dispositions over a 15- to 17-year period.

Trends in Juvenile Delinquency and Sentencing

From 1990 to 1999, crowded detention and confinement facilities and delinquency cases involving detention increased by 11 percent, or 33,400 cases.[18] Regardless of the growth in volume, however, the percentage of cases detained from 1985 to 2002 was essentially the same (20 percent). With 1990 as the peak year for most offense categories (23 percent for all cases), the 12-year tendency has been a decline in the percentage of cases detained. Throughout the 1990s, the number of adjudicated cases resulting in out-of-home placement (e.g., training schools, camps, ranches, private treatment facilities, group homes) increased 24 percent, from 124,900 in 1990 to 155,200 in 1999.[19] As a result, approximately 39 percent of all juvenile detention and confinement facilities had more residents than available beds.[20] Out-of-home placements dropped to 144,000 in 2002, but the problem of available bed space remained.

Between 1985 and 2002, the number of delinquency cases processed by juvenile courts increased by 41 percent. When looking at the type of offense, the number of drug law violations increased by 159 percent, offenses against persons and public order offenses each increased by 113 percent, but cases involving property offenses declined 10 percent.[21] Part of the explanation, then, for the overcrowding in juvenile detention and confinement facilities may simply be the result of more cases entering the juvenile justice system, even though the juvenile crime rate has not increased over the past 10 years.

To determine whether stiffer sanctions resulted from changes in the law, the first stage of case processing to be examined is whether petitions were filed more often in delinquency cases during more recent years. Figure 2.1 confirms that the use of formal processing increased for cases between 1985 and 2000, especially for drug and serious offenses. For both the categories of drug offenses and offenses against persons, such as aggravated assault, the likelihood of formal processing increased 18 percentage points, from 43 percent to 61 percent and from 54 percent to 72 percent, respectively. Property offenses were also handled formally more often. For certain types of property offenses, the percentage handled formally was as high as person offenses, including burglary and motor vehicle theft, which resulted in formal processing in more than three-fourths of the cases. This may be compared with larceny-theft and vandalism cases, wherein 43 percent and 51 percent, respectively, were handled formally.[22] Of those cases petitioned, the proportion adjudicated delinquent remained fairly constant from 1985 through 2000—generally between 60 and 70 percent of petitioned cases of all types adjudicated delinquent.

Another decision with serious implications made during the early stage of case processing is whether to waive jurisdiction and transfer youths to adult criminal courts. Wavier policies were one of the main issues causing controversy in the movement of the juvenile justice system away from its

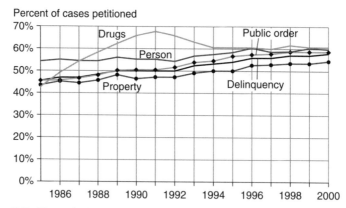

Figure 2.1. Formal Processing of Four General Offense Categories, 1985–2000
Source: Puzzanchera, Stahl, Finnegan, Tierney, & Snyder, 2004.

original philosophy emphasizing rehabilitation. However, the waiver process accounts for only approximately 1 percent or less of all juvenile cases. The number of delinquency cases judicially waived to criminal court in 1994 was 70 percent greater than the number waived in 1985 (see Figure 2.2).

This increase, however, was followed by a 48 percent decrease between 1994 and 2001, with a slight upturn in 2002. As a result, the number of cases waived in 2002 was 1 percent less than the number waived in 1985.[23] One probable reason for the decline in the number of judicial waivers after 1994 was the large increase in the number of states that passed legislation excluding certain serious offenses from juvenile court jurisdiction and permitting the prosecutor to file certain cases directly in criminal court.[24] Even so, youthful offenders under the age of 18 make up less than 2 percent of the incoming adult prison population in a given year.[25] The question of the punitiveness of sanctioning in such cases has been questioned because juveniles who are tried as adults tend to serve shorter sentences, on average, in the adult system than youths adjudicated in the juvenile justice system.[26] Moreover, juveniles placed in adult prisons have a more difficult time adjusting, are more frequently victims of older inmates, and, as a result, place higher demands on prison resources.[27]

The main issue with sentencing in the juvenile justice system concerns the type of disposition received by the juvenile. The most serious disposition in the juvenile justice system is out-of-home, or residential, placement. OJJDP reports that the number of cases adjudicated delinquent that result in out-of-home placement increased between 1985 and 2000. This increase was more than 200 percent for drug offense cases and nearly double for person and public order offense, but decreased overall for property offense cases. In fact, residential placement for all juvenile offenses has been decreasing since 1997 to 2000.[28]

Despite the increasing number of out-of-home placements between 1985 and 2000, the percentage of cases adjudicated delinquent that

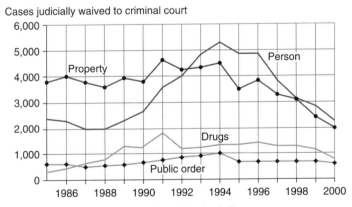

Figure 2.2. Cases Judicially Waived to Criminal Court
Source: Puzzanchera, Stahl, Finnegan, Tierney, & Snyder, 2004.

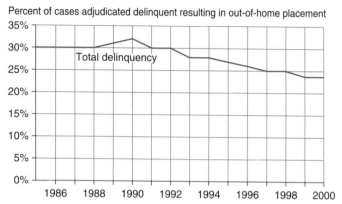

Figure 2.3. Percent of Cases Adjudicated Delinquent Resulting in Out-of-Home Placement
Source: Puzzanchera, Stahl, Finnegan, Tierney, & Snyder, 2004.

resulted in out-of-home placement decreased by approximately 7 percentage points from 30 percent in 1985 to 23 percent in 2002. That is, although the raw number of commitments increased, the percentage of adjudicated cases resulting in commitments decreased (see Figure 2.3). This suggests that the number of cases entering the front end of the system had a greater influence on the final increase in juvenile institutional populations than did newly hatched sentencing policies.

The growth in probation, the most prevalent form of juvenile disposition, has far outstripped that of institutionalization. The number of juveniles who are under probation supervision increased 103 percent between 1985 and 2002. Since 1985, drug offense cases had the largest percent increase (267 percent) in the number of cases adjudicated delinquent that received probation, followed by public order offenses (218 percent), person offenses (198 percent), and property offenses (28 percent).[29] Although more cases may have entered the system, resulting in formal processing, the outcome softened for a larger portion of these cases.

CONCLUSION

The findings presented in this chapter suggest that the "get-tough" movement on juveniles was more rhetoric than reality. Although some transient increases were experienced with waivers, this option was reserved for less than 1 percent of delinquent cases. Furthermore, research has shown that youths waived to the adult system frequently serve less time than similar cases processed in the juvenile justice system. Determinate or juvenile-adult blended sentences have become more common across the states, but the back door remains open ensuring that the vast majority of juveniles receiving these blended sentences serve only the juvenile portion.

This chapter best illustrates the way in which systems react to, or resist, external directives to change. Although the sentencing of juvenile offenders now occurs with more due process and may be slightly more structured, it has not resulted in the draconian sentences for which some pundits and politicians had pushed. Rather, the most common sanction remains probation, and the proportion of formally processed cases resulting in out-of-home placement actually decreased during the latter part of the twentieth century. That the use of probation increased and out-of-home placements decreased during an era of toughening laws illustrates not only the juvenile justice system's resistance to change, but also the level of internal commitment to the philosophy of treatment over punishment.

NOTES

1. Bernard, 1992; Mack, 1909/1999.
2. Ainsworth, 1991; Feld, 1998; Moore & Wakeling, 1997; Urban, St. Cyr, & Decker, 2003.
3. Urban et al., 2003.
4. Feld, 1993; Singer, 1996.
5. Shepherd, 1996.
6. Shepherd, 1996.
7. Bartollas & Miller, 2001.
8. Feld, 1995; Mears, 1998; Polier, 1989.
9. Snyder & Sickmund, 1999.
10. Bureau of Justice Assistance, 1996.
11. Bartollas & Miller, 2001.
12. Mears, 1998.
13. Dawson, 1988.
14. Dawson, 1996; Mears, 1998.
15. Torbet & Szymanski, 1998; Butts & Snyder, 1997.
16. Hodges & Kim, 2000.
17. Siegel & Senna, 1997.
18. Harms, 2003.
19. Puzzanchera, 2003.
20. Sickmund, 2002.
21. Snyder & Sickmund, 2006.
22. Puzzanchera, Stahl, Finnegan, Tierney, & Snyder, 2004.
23. Snyder & Sickmund, 2006.
24. Puzzanchera et al., 2004.
25. Austin, Johnson, & Gregoriou, 2000.
26. Fritsch, Caeti, & Hemmens, 1996.
27. McShane & Williams, 1989.
28. Snyder & Sickmund, 2006.
29. Snyder & Sickmund, 2006.

REFERENCES

Ainsworth. J. E. (1991). Re-imagining childhood and reconstructing the legal order: The case for abolishing the juvenile court. *North Carolina Law Review, 69*, 1089–1100.

Austin, J., Johnson, K. D., & Gregoriou, M. (2000). *Juveniles in adult prison and jails: A national assessment.* Washington, D.C.: U.S. Department of Justice, Bureau of Justice Assistance.

Austin, J., Johnson, K. D., & Weitzer, R. (2005). Alternatives to the secure detention and confinement of juvenile offenders. *Juvenile Justice Bulletin.* Washington, D.C.: Office of Juvenile Justice and Delinquency Prevention.

Bartollas, C. & Miller, S. J. (2001). *Juvenile justice in America* (3rd ed.). Upper Saddle River, NJ: Prentice Hall.

Bernard, T. J. (1992). *The cycle of juvenile justice.* New York: Oxford University Press.

Bureau of Justice Assistance. (1996). *National assessment of structured sentencing.* Washington, D.C.: Bureau of Justice Assistance.

Butts, J. A., & Snyder, H. N. (1997). *The youngest delinquents: Offenders under age 15.* Washington, D.C.: Office of Juvenile Justice and Delinquency Prevention.

Dawson, R. O. (1988). The third justice system: The new juvenile-criminal system of determinate sentencing for the youthful violent offender in Texas. *St. Mary's Law Journal, 19,* 943–1016.

Dawson, R. O. (1996). *Texas juvenile law* (4th ed.). Austin, TX: Texas Juvenile Probation Commission.

Feld, B. C. (1993). *Criminalizing the American juvenile court.* Chicago: University of Chicago Press.

Feld, B. C. (1995). Violent youth and public policy: A case study of juvenile justice law reform. *Minnesota Law Review, 79,* 965–1128.

Feld, B. C. (1998). *Juvenile and criminal justice systems' responses to youth violence.* Chicago: University of Chicago Press.

Fritsch, E. J., Caeti, T. J., & Hemmens, C. (1996). Spare the needle but not the punishment: The incarceration of waived youth in adult prisons. *Crime & Delinquency, 42,* 593–609.

Harms, P. (2003). *Detention in delinquency cases, 1990–1999* (OJJDP Fact Sheet). Washington, D.C.: Office of Juvenile Justice and Delinquency Prevention.

Hodges, K., & Kim, C. S. (2000). Psychometric study of the child and adolescent functional assessment scale: Prediction of contact with the law and poor school attendance. *Journal of Abnormal Child Psychology, 28,* 287–297.

Mack, J. W. (1909/1999). The juvenile court. *Harvard Law Review, 23,* 104–122. [Reprinted in B. C. Feld (Ed.), *Readings in Juvenile Justice Administration* (pp. 13–19). New York: Oxford University Press.]

McShane, M. D., & Williams, F. P., III. (1989). The prison adjustment of juvenile offenders. *Crime and Delinquency, 35,* 254–269.

Mears, P. D. (1998). Evaluation issues confronting juvenile justice sentencing reforms: A case study of Texas. *Crime & Delinquency, 44,* 443–463.

Moore, M. H., & Wakeling, S. (1997). *Juvenile justice: Shoring up the foundations.* Chicago: University of Chicago Press.

Polier, J. W. (1989). *Juvenile justice in double jeopardy: The distanced community and vengeful retribution.* Hillsdale, NJ: Lawrence Erlbaum.

Puzzanchera, C. (2003). *Juvenile court placement of adjudicated youth, 1990–1999* (OJJDP Fact Sheet). Washington, D.C.: Office of Juvenile Justice and Delinquency Prevention.

Puzzanchera, C., Stahl, A. L., Finnegan, T. A., Tierney, N., & Snyder, H. N. (2004). *Juvenile court statistics 2000.* Washington D.C.: National Center for Juvenile Justice, National Council of Juvenile and Family Court Judges.

Shepherd, R. E. (1996). *JJ standards: Anchor in the storm.* American Bar Association. Retrieved July 23, 2006, from www.abanet.org/crimjust/juvjus/cjstandards.html.

Sickmund, M. (2002). *Juvenile residential facility census, 2000: Selected findings* (OJJDP National Report Series Bulletin). Washington, D.C.: Office of Juvenile Justice and Delinquency Prevention.

Siegel, L., & Senna, J. (1997). *Juvenile delinquency: Theory, practice, and law* (6th ed.). St. Paul, MN: West Publishing Company.

Singer, S. I. (1996). *Recriminalizing delinquency: Violent juvenile crime and juvenile justice reform.* New York: Cambridge University Press.

Snyder, H. N., & Sickmund, M. (1999). *Juvenile offenders and victims: 1999 national report.* Washington, D.C.: Office of Juvenile Justice and Delinquency Prevention.

Synder, H. N., & Sickmund, M. (2006). *Juvenile offenders and victims: 2006 national report.* Washington, D.C.: Office of Juvenile Justice and Delinquency Prevention.

Torbet, P. & Szymanski, L. (1998). State legislative responses to violent juvenile crime: 1996–97 update (NCJ 172835) *Juvenile Justice Bulletin*, November. Office of Juvenile Justice and Delinquency Prevention.

Urban, L. S., St. Cyr, J. L., & Decker, S. H. (2003). Goal conflict in the juvenile court. *Journal of Contemporary Criminal Justice, 19,* 454–479.

CASES CITED

In re Gault. 387 U.S. 1, 1967.

CHAPTER 3

Boys to Men: Transferring Juveniles to Adult Court

David Myers

Throughout much of the 1990s, policy makers and the general public voiced strong support for transferring greater numbers and types of serious and violent offenders from juvenile court to adult criminal court. Years of rising juvenile violent crime rates, combined with sensational media accounts of youth involved with guns, drugs, and gangs, fueled a nationwide concern about youth violence and a perceived generation of young people gone out of control. Critics suggested that the century-old juvenile justice system was ill-equipped to handle this problem and, therefore, something drastic was needed to save society from these dangerous adolescents.

In response to this situation, by the mid-1990s nearly all states had passed legislation designed to strengthen the procedures and sanctions available for handling serious and violent juvenile offenders. The general perception had emerged that juvenile courts were too lenient, violent youths were beyond hope for rehabilitation, and the adult criminal system would be a more appropriate place to hold serious youthful offenders accountable for their actions. In adult court, it was thought, more certain and severe punishment would be imposed, which in turn would have a beneficial impact on juvenile crime.

Unfortunately, legislative efforts to send more juveniles to adult criminal court often were not guided by systematic research and careful planning. The topic of treating juveniles as adults has produced much debate, and during the past 20 years, a number of researchers and scholars have questioned the effectiveness of this practice. By assessing the information and evidence that is available, I attempt to bring better understanding to this controversial approach to juvenile crime, which continues to be important in the operation of both the juvenile and adult justice systems.

CONTEMPORARY CONCERNS ABOUT YOUTH VIOLENCE

During the past several decades, youth under the age of 18 have accounted for roughly one-third of all serious property crime arrests and less than one-fifth of all serious violent crime arrests in the United States.[1] Furthermore, of the total population of juveniles in America, only about 6 percent are arrested each year, and fewer than 1 percent are arrested for a violent offense. Despite these figures, from the mid-1980s to the mid-1990s, a disturbing trend occurred that heightened public fears and greatly contributed to legislative changes in juvenile justice.

Between 1985 and 1994, overall juvenile violent crime arrest rates increased by 75 percent, and the juvenile murder arrest rate alone more than doubled.[2] These increases in offending corresponded with a similar upswing in violent crime victimization among youth, and firearm use appeared to be a key aspect of these trends. Moreover, based on the projected growth in the juvenile population for the early twenty-first century, many were predicting a coming storm of youth violence in which young "superpredators" would be wreaking havoc on the nation's streets. Alarmed politicians and commentators warned that we needed to "get ready" for the onslaught of these morally deprived youth who were immune to juvenile justice system sanctioning.[3]

These descriptions of current and future superpredators were influential on public policy. From 1992 to 1995, 47 states and the District of Columbia passed laws that sought to address the youth violence epidemic, and the basic theme of these legislative efforts was "getting tough."[4] Juvenile court hearings and juvenile offender records became more open and accessible, police were granted authorization to fingerprint and photograph specified youths, and the discretion of juvenile judges was reduced through mandatory sentencing. The most popular change, however, occurred in the area of jurisdictional authority, as virtually all states enacted or expanded provisions to facilitate transferring (commonly referred to as "waiving" or "certifying") serious and violent juvenile offenders to adult criminal court.

In legislatively proclaiming that youths who are charged with certain crimes should be treated as adults, policy makers were encouraged by a variety of public opinion polls showing about 75 percent of those surveyed were in support of adult court processing for serious and violent youthful offenders.[5] Although these same surveys revealed little support for placing adolescents in the same correctional facilities as adult criminals and a limited desire to send increasingly younger offenders to the adult system, "adult time for adult crime" became a familiar battle cry. Although this approach to juvenile offending typically is viewed as a contemporary response to an emerging problem, it actually has a lengthy history that is important to consider in assessing the effectiveness of this practice.

SEPARATING THE MEN FROM THE BOYS

The term "juvenile delinquency" frequently is used in our society during discussions of why children and youth break the law and what should be done about it. In general, young people are thought to be distinctly different from adults, including children who commit crime. This is such common knowledge that relatively few people would know that the concept of delinquency is actually less than 200 years old, and throughout a great deal of American and European history, children were not treated much differently from adults. In fact, good evidence shows that, although young people have exhibited higher levels of law-breaking behavior down through the ages, it was not until the 1800s that these same behaviors became a major cause for concern, and the concept of delinquency was born.[6] This implies that delinquency is a relatively recent social invention and one that varies significantly from time to time.

Before the 1800s, Americans generally relied on traditional common law that did not allow children younger than 7 years old to be tried or found guilty of a crime. Between the ages of 7 and 14, young people were assumed to be innocent and unable to fully understand the nature of their behavior, unless a judge or jury determined otherwise. Beyond the age of 14, individuals were viewed as adults, but exceptions could be made. This framework began to change, however, as beliefs about childrearing and childhood behavior evolved and urbanization spread throughout the country.

By the early 1800s, authoritarian Puritan ideals increasingly were being challenged, and appropriate childhood behavior began to be viewed more as a product of love and affection, rather than of fear and submission. This corresponded with an emerging concept of adolescence, whereby youth who had been viewed previously as adults came to be seen as more child-like and not yet set in their ways. The growth of major cities, such as New York, Boston, Philadelphia, and Chicago, also raised concerns about poverty and the negative effects of poor living conditions, particularly on children and adolescents from immigrant families. By the 1820s, juvenile delinquency was not only being used to describe the behavior of children and youths who broke the law, but also was being applied to poor young people who appeared to lack adequate parental supervision and guidance and were prone to a deviant life on the streets.[7]

Attention being paid to juvenile delinquency soon spurred the creation of correctional institutions (known as Houses of Refuge) that were designed to confine and rehabilitate delinquents separately from adult criminals. Based on subsequent legal challenges and growing concerns about the harsh treatment and substandard living conditions characteristic of many juvenile institutions, by the late 1880s, the "child-saving" movement had intensified and social conditions became an increasingly important issue to target for change. Nowhere else was this progressive movement more evident than in Chicago at the turn of the century, where a reform effort lead by the Chicago Women's Club culminated in the establishment of the first formal juvenile court in 1899.

In distinguishing itself from the adult criminal court, the juvenile court was to emphasize and employ a unique philosophy (known as *parens patriae*) and procedure. The modern concept of childhood was to be embraced, stressing the notion that children should be treated differently from adults. Hearings were to be of an informal nature, with due process rights given little attention, to serve the "best interests" of children and provide appropriate rehabilitative services. A distinct language was to be used, denoting caring and concern, rather than punitive punishment. Finally, coercive treatment was to be employed, often through community-based programs and organizations, in an effort to reform "salvageable" children and youth.

Transformation to Criminal

Drawing on Chicago's model, the use of juvenile courts spread rapidly throughout the United States. Although no uniform juvenile justice system was implemented, the implementation of juvenile courts was celebrated as a major achievement, and a great sense of optimism existed with regard to the court's potential for preventing and reducing delinquency. Almost immediately following the creation of the juvenile court, however, debates arose about which children actually belonged within its jurisdiction. In addition to the common practice of diverting younger offenders from juvenile court processing, early juvenile court judges were given the discretion to waive older and more serious delinquents to adult criminal court. Thus, the notion of treating serious and violent juvenile offenders as adults is in no way a new development, but rather one that can be traced over the course of several centuries, both before and after the creation of juvenile courts.[8]

It is interesting that from the outset, juvenile courts seemed to wash their hands of young people who were perhaps the most in need of help. Fearing that laws establishing juvenile courts would be struck down as unconstitutional, juvenile judges did not always assert the original and exclusive jurisdiction provided to them. This allowed another mechanism of transfer to develop, one in which prosecutors' decisions to handle cases of certain adolescent offenders in adult court often were not challenged. Although juvenile court laws and transfer procedures varied from state to state, overcrowded caseloads, issues of constitutionality, and concerns about placing more serious and violent youthful offenders in the company of other children in institutions continued to influence the use of active and passive juvenile transfer throughout the first half of the twentieth century.

By the mid-1900s, supporters of juvenile justice had established that judicial waiver was an essential part of juvenile court operations and was to be used in certain cases in which adolescents were not amenable to the court's rehabilitative efforts and posed a serious threat to public safety. Furthermore, at this time, critics were becoming increasingly vocal about the lack of procedural safeguards granted to youth in juvenile court. During the "due process revolution" of the late 1960s and early 1970s, several U.S. Supreme Court cases established that juveniles could not be denied fundamental due process rights in the pursuit of "individualized justice." For example, in the initial landmark case of *Kent v. United States* (1966), the Court ruled that before being waived to adult criminal court by a juvenile court judge, a youth had the right to a formal hearing to examine the reasons for transfer and the right to counsel at that hearing.

Although initial criticisms of the juvenile court focused on constitutional rights and procedural fairness, a second wave of criticisms and reforms in the 1970s and 1980s was directed at changing the goals and structure of the juvenile justice system.[9] Critics became focused on the growing perceived ineffectiveness of rehabilitation and rapidly rising crime rates. As with the youth violence epidemic of the 1990s, assertions were made that juvenile courts were too lenient, and some commentators even argued that these courts had outlived their usefulness. Similar to changes in ideology that previously occurred in the adult system, juvenile courts began to shift toward a more punitive philosophy that emphasized accountability, deterrence, and incapacitation. It was hoped that these modifications would be an effective response to the increasing public concern about juvenile crime.

Interestingly, calls for abolishing the juvenile court and corresponding juvenile justice reforms in the early to mid-1980s came at a time when juvenile crime, including serious and violent offending, had stabilized and even declined for a period of several years.[10] This preceded the dramatic increase in juvenile violent crime arrest rates from the mid-1980s to the mid-1990s that fueled modern transfer legislation. Since 1994, arrests for serious and violent juvenile offenses have decreased steadily to levels observed in the early 1980s, and concerns about terrorism and homeland security have replaced worries about the onslaught of juvenile superpredators. Waiver laws and policies implemented in the 1990s are still in place, however, and some proponents have credited them for the recent downturn in juvenile offending. The size of the juvenile population still is predicted to grow over the next 25 years, and with funding and other resources directed elsewhere, it is entirely possible that youth violence will reemerge as a significant social problem. It remains important to consider, then, whether transfer to adult court should be perceived as the principal solution.

Methods and Use of Transfer

Today, there are three primary ways to remove a youth from juvenile court jurisdiction: judicial waiver, prosecutorial wavier, and legislative waiver. All states have one or more of these mechanisms in place, and during the past 25 years, virtually all have revised their laws to lower the minimum age for transfer, reduce juvenile court judge discretion in waiver proceedings, expand prosecutorial discretion to file juvenile cases in adult court, and statutorily exclude serious and violent youthful offenders from juvenile court jurisdiction.

Judicial waiver remains the most common transfer provision, whereby a case originates in juvenile court and a juvenile court judge is granted the authority to make the key decision in the transfer process.[11] Only five states currently do not allow for some form of judicial waiver. Although popular in law, relatively few juveniles actually are transferred to adult court under this procedure. Nationwide, judicial waivers peaked at 12,300 in 1994. In more recent years, as youth violence declined and states shifted to other transfer mechanisms, annual judicial waivers have numbered around 7,500, representing about 1 percent of all cases referred to juvenile court.[12]

Sometimes referred to as concurrent jurisdiction or direct file, prosecutorial waiver allows a prosecutor to file certain charges in either juvenile or adult court, generally based on the offense alleged and the juvenile's age and prior record.[13] Prosecutorial waiver is used in 14 states and the District of Columbia and is probably the most controversial method of transfer because of the wide discretion granted to a typically "crime-control–oriented" court official who may be lacking in background information on a particular case. Current and complete national statistics are not available on the use of prosecutorial waiver, but in states that employ this technique, juveniles transferred to adult court by a prosecutor likely outnumber judicially waived youth by a wide margin. In Florida, for example, prosecutors waive around 5,000 cases per year. It is therefore not unreasonable to estimate that prosecutorial waivers nationwide are double or triple the number produced by judicial waiver.[14]

Finally, legislative waiver (also known as statutory exclusion) places eligible youth into the adult criminal system at the time of arrest, thereby removing the initial discretionary powers of juvenile court judges and prosecutors.[15] Legislative waiver laws, popularized in the 1990s and currently active in 29 states, are a strong indicator of the shift in juvenile justice from an individualized treatment philosophy to a more retributive approach. The most commonly excluded crimes are murder and other violent offenses, but youth charged with various repeat felonies, such as burglary, sometimes are targeted. As with prosecutorial waiver, complete national statistics are not available on the use of legislative waiver. However, in 1996, police directly referred more than 81,500 juveniles to adult court at the time of their arrest, a figure that declined to 51,000 by 2001.[16]

The above estimates of juveniles transferred to adult court do not consider the many thousands of youth under the age of 18 who are prosecuted each year in the 13 states that have set the upper age limit for juvenile court jurisdiction at 15 or 16, rather than 17.[17] If these offenders are taken into account, the available data suggest that in the mid-1990s roughly 250,000 young people under the age of 18 were prosecuted in adult courts nationwide, representing 20 to 25 percent of all juvenile offenders at this time.[18] Although this total figure undoubtedly has dropped in more recent years, it would appear likely that up to 200,000 juveniles under the age of 18 continue to be prosecuted in adult criminal courts under the various laws and procedures available today.

Who Gets Transferred?

During the past few decades, a substantial amount of research has focused on the demographic, legal, and social characteristics of transferred youth.[19] In general, these studies have sought to identify key offender traits to provide an understanding of the types of offenders affected by waiver laws and to assess procedural fairness. Most of what is known about the characteristics of transferred offenders has been revealed in studies of judicially waived youth, because many fewer studies have been conducted on juveniles processed through prosecutorial or legislative waiver.

Harsher juvenile court sanctions tend to be associated with older youthful offenders (rather than younger ones), and research consistently has shown that older youths are also more likely to be sent to the adult system. Nevertheless, the increasing use of legislative and prosecutorial waiver in recent times does appear to have increased the number of younger juveniles who are transferred. In addition, virtually all studies that examine the race of waived offenders find that nonwhites (primarily African Americans) are highly overrepresented, usually making up 50 to 95 percent of the juveniles transferred to adult court. Although this hints at racial bias, a smaller number of studies that have considered offense seriousness and prior record (along with race and other factors) have found these legal factors generally explain minority overrepresentation in transfer to adult court.

Similarly, a variety of studies using local, state, and national data indicate that about 95 percent of waived youth are male. Offense seriousness and prior record likely explain much of this gender disparity in juvenile transfer, but the low number of females available for research on this topic often leads to male-only samples and analyses, which leads to the possibility of a gender effect on the likelihood of waiver. Nonetheless, the typical juvenile transferred to adult court has been shown to be older, male, and nonwhite (usually African American). Although socioeconomic status is not a well-measured or frequently studied characteristic in waiver research, few would argue with the statement that transferred juveniles are also typically poor, inner-city offenders.

As noted above, offense seriousness and prior record are two important factors to consider in assessing who is most likely to be transferred to adult court. Somewhat surprisingly, studies using data from the 1970s and 1980s indicated that the largest percentage of transferred youth had been charged with property crimes, but these offenders did tend to exhibit lengthy prior records. Studies conducted since the early 1990s, however, show that this situation has changed. Fueled by the youth violence epidemic and corresponding legislative changes, by the mid-1990s, juveniles charged with person or violent offenses accounted for the largest percentage of waived youth. Contemporary research tends to confirm that, if all else is equal, the more violent the offense and the more extensive the prior record of offending, the more likely a juvenile is to be transferred to adult court.

The Case of Nathaniel Abraham

The characteristics and circumstances surrounding the case of Nathaniel Abraham provide a good illustration of much of the information presented to this point. On October 29, 1997, Abraham shot and killed 18-year-old Ronnie Greene outside a convenience store in Pontiac, Michigan.[20] He apparently did not know Greene, who was shot from about 300 feet away with a stolen 0.22-caliber rifle. Abraham was arrested two days later, tried on murder charges, and convicted. He then received a lengthy sentence of incarceration in a correctional facility. Aside from defense claims that the shooting was accidental, the facts of the case essentially were indisputable, and this type of murder often would not generate anything more than local interest. The convicted killer, however, was less than 5 feet tall, weighed about 65 pounds, and was 11 years old when the shooting occurred. Despite these characteristics, he was prosecuted as an adult defendant.

As perhaps the youngest murder defendant ever to be tried as an adult in American history, Abraham was prosecuted under a new and unique state law that enabled youths under the age of 14 to be charged as adults for certain serious and violent crimes, but the proceedings actually took place in juvenile court.[21] Although older youths remain more likely to be transferred than younger offenders, expanded waiver laws like Michigan's do increase the number of younger defendants who are tried as adults. Abraham was an African American male who committed a very serious offense, with a deadly weapon, and despite relatively little prior juvenile court involvement, he exhibited an alarming history of behavior that resulted in numerous contacts with police and problems at school.

Based on his gender, race, offense seriousness, and history of problem behavior, Abraham represents a somewhat typical juvenile offender who is treated as an adult in this country. At face value, only his young age stands out as unusual, but the statute under which he was charged did not set a minimum age for prosecution as an adult. Other characteristics of this particular defendant, however, seemingly played an important role in the offense and the eventual case outcome.[22]

Born in 1986, Abraham was raised by a single mother, along with an older brother and sister. He began exhibiting a pattern of difficult behavior at a young age, apparently suffered from attention deficit disorder and emotional impairment, and received only a few counseling sessions in an effort to treat these problems. In addition, he grew up in an economically distressed and drug-infested neighborhood, despite living in one of the wealthiest counties in America.

At age 13, Abraham was convicted of second-degree murder for the killing of Greene. Under Michigan's law, the presiding judge had three sentencing options to consider. First, Abraham could have been sentenced strictly as an adult, for which state sentencing guidelines recommended 8 to 25 years in a state prison. Second, he could have been sentenced solely as a juvenile, which would require his release from a juvenile correctional facility by the age of 21. Third, a "blended sentence" could have been imposed, which would have involved placement in a juvenile facility followed by transfer to an adult facility if rehabilitation was not achieved by age 21.

After much deliberation, Judge Eugene A. Moore chose the second alternative of a juvenile sentence, and Abraham was committed to a training school until the age of 21.[23] In doing so, Judge Moore stated that children and youth like Abraham must be held accountable and responsible for their actions, but he also reflected on the history of American juvenile justice and the need for society to do a better job preventing delinquency and rehabilitating young offenders. He asserted that treatment services are more extensive and comprehensive in the juvenile system; the juvenile system has a higher success rate than the adult system; and adult prison should only be used as a last resort, because incarceration does little to address future criminality and presents the opportunity for brutalization. In other words, the judge in this case made an important and symbolic decision that was influenced not only by the characteristics of the offense and offender, but also by his views on differences between the juvenile and adult systems and the actual effectiveness of treating juveniles as adults.

THE IMPACT AND EFFECTIVENESS OF TRANSFER

The basic rationale for the practice of sending hundreds of thousands of youthful offenders to the adult criminal system is that the juvenile court appears unable to serve the needs of certain young people, and therefore, the adult court should take over their cases. The perceived inability of the juvenile court to handle these cases may be based on a lack of faith in juvenile correctional facilities, a belief that harsher punishment is needed than can be provided in the juvenile system, or the view that some offenders are too dangerous to remain outside the criminal system. Despite the modern shift in juvenile justice philosophy from the rehabilitative ideal to a more punitive orientation, the decision to transfer a case still generally denotes that a youth is beyond whatever treatment capacity remains in the juvenile justice system.

Over the past 20 years, in an effort to assess whether the expected benefits of transfer to adult court actually materialize, a growing body of research has examined the impact and effectiveness of this practice.[24] A fairly large number of studies have considered the case processing outcomes of adolescents in adult court, and some have evaluated differences in case outcomes between similar youths processed in the juvenile and adult systems. Other researchers have investigated the treatment and sanctioning effectiveness for serious and violent young offenders in juvenile and adult correctional facilities. Yet another group of studies have assessed the general and specific deterrent effects that may or may not be realized through modern waiver laws.

What Happens in Adult Court?

Proponents of transferring juveniles to adult court frequently emphasize the perceived advantages of greater accountability and stronger punishment. Overall, research that has assessed how well these goals are being met has produced some surprising and mixed results, along with some findings more in line with what would be expected.[25] For example, studies to date suggest that in the early stages of case processing, a majority of transferred offenders are released on bail before final disposition of their cases, and violent youth in adult court are actually more likely to be released than are similar offenders in juvenile court. Many waived youth are set free with little or no supervision by their family or the adult court, and they are likely to experience lengthy case processing time, which puts them at risk for new offending. Those who do remain in custody in adult jails appear more likely to experience a variety of adverse consequences (e.g., violent victimization and lack of treatment and educational services), which also may affect the future criminal behavior of these detained youth.

Research that has focused on the likelihood of conviction for transferred offenders generally has found high conviction rates (in the range of 65 to 95 percent) in adult court. The best-designed studies employing comparison groups of similar offenders in juvenile and adult court have produced mixed results, with relatively little difference found in the likelihood of conviction between the two systems. Some evidence suggests that violent offenders are more likely to be convicted in adult court than in juvenile court, but this finding is explained greatly by the fact that the juvenile court often serves a solid screening function, and cases with the greatest likelihood of conviction are the ones typically sent to adult court. Little to no evidence supports the notion that adult courts do a better job holding youthful offenders accountable in the first several stages of case processing. In fact, under modern legislative and prosecutorial waiver laws, adult courts often do provide the case screening previously conducted by juvenile courts using judicial waiver. This results in numerous cases being dismissed, while many others are "decertified" or "reverse waived" back to juvenile court for further case processing.

Concerning punishment severity, early research on the sentencing of transferred juveniles unexpectedly revealed a "leniency gap" in adult court, with probationary sentences being imposed on many youth who did not appear to be viewed as serious offenders in the adult system. More recent studies indicate a change in this pattern, at least for violent offenders, who, when convicted, tend to receive sentences of incarceration that are longer than those imposed on similar youth in juvenile court. Even those findings must be tempered, however, with the recognition that in these studies the juvenile court often was serving the screening function mentioned above (which placed the "most-deserving" offenders in adult court). Furthermore, in some jurisdictions actual time served in the adult system may be different (shorter) than the sentence originally imposed.

Although case processing time is a concern and point of emphasis in the juvenile system, adolescents in adult court typically experience lengthy periods of case processing. During this time, they may be released into the community with little or no supervision, or they may remain detained in adult jails. Regardless of whether they are released or detained, many waived youth are initially presented with little or no opportunity for treatment of their drug and alcohol, mental health, or other problems. Whether these needs can be subsequently and effectively addressed through adult court sanctioning is another important issue to consider.

Prospects for Punishment and Rehabilitation

Those who argue in favor of "adult crime, adult time" generally assert that criminal court processing is needed to ensure that adequate punishment is imposed on serious and violent youthful offenders. Research findings may have been unexpected with regard to the case processing outcomes of adolescents in adult court, but many of these youth do receive sentences of incarceration that sometimes are quite lengthy. Moreover, for offenders who stay in juvenile court, a more punitive philosophy exists than was in place throughout most of the twentieth century. A central question, then, pertains to the effectiveness of this punishment-oriented approach to juvenile crime and whether the sanctions and services provided to youth in the adult system have a greater beneficial impact than those given to similar offenders in the juvenile system.

Despite the popularity of the "get-tough" movement and the ever-increasing use of incarceration as the prime method of punishment during the past 30 years, throughout the 1990s there was renewed interest in correctional rehabilitation among politicians, practitioners, and the general public. The extraordinary monetary cost and limited crime reduction generated by large-scale imprisonment could no longer be ignored; the "toughest" intermediate sanctions (e.g., disciplinary-style boot camps) were not producing the anticipated beneficial effects on offender behavior and prison populations; and increasing concern was being voiced about minority overrepresentation in correctional facilities. Furthermore, contemporary studies suggested that treatment and rehabilitation programs actually could be effective in reducing recidivism (repeat offending), if they were properly implemented and offenders were matched with appropriate programs that addressed their specific needs.[26]

Although the general prospects for rehabilitation have been revived in recent years, punitive and incarceration-based strategies remain at the center of criminal justice system operations, and being tough on crime still dominates political platforms. In terms of juvenile justice, however, much more attention has been given to studying and understanding the causes and treatment of serious, violent, and chronic offending. Several books, in-depth reviews of modern research, and meta-analyses of earlier studies were published and revealed important relationships among risk factors, protective factors, and delinquent behavior, as well as provided evidence of effectiveness for a variety of prevention, early intervention, and rehabilitation programs being offered to at-risk children and known delinquents. Essentially, juvenile justice was being revived in a way that emphasized doing things differently from the crackdown and get-tough approaches.

Overall, during the past decade, those in the field of juvenile justice and delinquency prevention have stressed the use of scientific research to (1) guide policy and practices; reduce risk factors and enhance protective factors in families, schools, and communities, and for children and youth; (2) provide treatment and rehabilitation programs that focus on risks and needs assessment; (3) match high-risk youth and offenders with structured services to improve behavioral and social skills; and (4) supply well-designed community-based programs, smaller and more treatment-oriented correctional facilities, and enriched aftercare services. Much scientific evidence exists to support these practices, and at the same time these approaches have been taken, delinquency and youth violence have declined to levels representative of the early 1980s (the start of the "get-tough" movement in juvenile justice).

On any given day, more than 100,000 juveniles under the age of 18 are housed in residential correctional facilities, including roughly 15,000 youths who are incarcerated in adult jails and prisons.[27] They are predominantly male, and most are minorities, as disproportionate minority confinement continues to be a characteristic of both the juvenile and adult systems. Overcrowding, victimization, and poor living conditions still exist in some juvenile facilities, but solid evidence has been generated (from the research mentioned above) that indicates juvenile correctional programming can effectively treat and reduce the recidivism of serious and violent youthful offenders. In fact, juvenile prevention and intervention programs have been found to have the greatest effect when they are directed at the highest-risk youth and more serious offenders. Similar positive results have been obtained in institutional (secure) and noninstitutional programs.

Juvenile and adult correctional facilities and programs are different in several fundamental ways.[28] First, adult criminal justice populations are obviously much older, on average, than juvenile justice populations. Older offender ages are correlated with greater physical size and strength, longer and more violent criminal histories, and more experience within the justice system, meaning that youths transferred to the adult system are exposed to a different type of peer than typically exists in the juvenile system. This exposure often takes place during an extended period of time.

Second, juvenile and adult facilities and programs exhibit basic organizational differences. For example, adult institutions tend to be much larger, many times holding between 500 and 1,000 inmates, or about 10 times the average number held in juvenile institutions. Although overcrowding and disproportionate minority confinement are evident in both the juvenile and adult correctional systems, these problems tend to be more pronounced in adult jails and prisons. Moreover, institutional size and overcrowding have been linked to levels of facility violence and other adverse consequences, and contemporary research on treatment and rehabilitation indicates that smaller and more structured facilities (particularly in the juvenile system) provide more effective services.

Third, staffing patterns are markedly different between juvenile and adult institutions and programs. Adult facilities generally place a high priority on custody and order, with a large majority of personnel hired to address these areas. In a custody-oriented atmosphere, offender perceptions of oppression, alienation, and danger have been found to be higher. Conversely, in juvenile facilities, staffing for education and treatment programs is given higher priority, and inmate-to-staff ratios are much more favorable. In addition, in treatment-oriented programs, relationships with staff and other program participants tend to be more positive, and those in treatment are more receptive to the ideas of change and remaining law-abiding upon release.

Several studies have shown that when compared with offenders placed in juvenile institutions, adolescents in adult facilities are far more likely to be sexually assaulted, attacked by inmates, beaten by staff, perceive unfair treatment, and commit suicide.[29] Other corrections research indicates that younger inmates, who typically lack the experience needed to deal with the prison environment, are at the greatest risk for physical and sexual assault and exhibit the greatest fear and vulnerability. Further studies show that correctional administrators have serious concerns regarding the placement of juveniles in adult facilities and about what the adult system does and does not offer these youth, because many adult institutions and programs do not provide the specialized services that usually are supplied in the juvenile system. In sum, it is hard to believe that the conditions and culture of the adult correctional system could be an effective way to punish and rehabilitate most serious and violent juvenile offenders.

General and Specific Deterrence

A great deal of evidence suggests that effective treatment and rehabilitation can be provided to serious and violent youthful offenders and that the juvenile system generally provides a better chance for positive behavioral change. Another important question pertains to the deterrent effects of formal sanctions provided through expanded waiver policies and practices. Supporters of this practice contend that, in adult court, a message can be sent to the offenders that the lenient treatment of the juvenile system is no longer an option. Instead, harsh criminal court sanctions will be imposed, which will increase public safety and reduce individual motivations to commit future crimes. Overall, then, adult court is believed to provide greater deterrence through stronger punishment.

Throughout the past 250 years, scholars (and, more recently, empirical researchers) have distinguished between two types of deterrence: general deterrence and specific deterrence. General deterrence refers to the effect of possible punishments on potential offenders in the greater community. The situations in which sanctions are imposed on one person demonstrate to everyone else the expected costs of crime, thereby discouraging criminal behavior among the general population. Specific deterrence pertains to the effect of punishment on the behavior of the individual who is sanctioned. In other words, when someone is deterred in the future through the previous experience of punishment, this constitutes specific deterrence.

A large body of literature has shown that, in terms of general deterrence, the perceived certainty of punishment for illegal acts tends to be more important than the perceived severity of punishment. Policies and programs that focus on increasing the certainty of punishment (e.g., directed police patrols of crime "hot spots") have been found to produce the greatest crime reduction effects.[30] Furthermore, studies focused on the specific deterrent effects of formal sanctions, including many that have examined juvenile offenders, have produced mixed results at best. In fact, many of these studies have found that while controlling for other explanatory factors, harsher sanctions are associated with greater future offending among those who are punished.

Concerning the general deterrent effect of juvenile transfer itself, the weight of the available scientific evidence suggests that expanding waiver laws has little or no impact on aggregate adolescent crime rates.[31] These findings probably are not surprising, because the abovementioned research supports the general deterrent effect of the perceived certainty of punishment over its severity, and juvenile transfer laws (and their proponents) tend to focus on punishment severity. Limited evidence does suggest that some juvenile offenders cease or reduce their offending as a consequence of reaching the official age of adulthood, but before this time, many adolescents may not be aware of, or fully understand, existing or expanded transfer laws and the associated possibility of being prosecuted in adult court.[32] Without this knowledge or a strong belief that transfer to adult court and enhanced punishment will occur, general deterrence from juvenile waiver really is not possible.

In terms of specific deterrence, a number of studies consistently have shown that as compared with similar youths retained in juvenile court, adolescent offenders waived to the adult system exhibit greater, more serious, and faster recidivism.[33] These findings hold particularly true for juveniles charged with a violent crime. The issue of selection bias is inherent in this research, whereby the "worst" offenders (or those most at risk for recidivism) are more likely to be sent to adult court. The reliable findings on this topic, however, refute the argument that treating juvenile defendants as adults will produce greater specific deterrence.

Juvenile transfer is an extreme response to youthful offending, with potentially severe consequences. Adolescents who are treated as adults often are subjected to a lengthy adjudicatory process, sometimes involving an extended stay in jail, a criminal conviction, and a prolonged prison sentence. Regarding the conditions of confinement, youths in adult jails and prisons appear to receive less-than-adequate treatment services and are more likely to be victimized than similar offenders in juvenile correctional facilities. Subjecting young offenders to this potentially harsh punishment essentially is viewed as being necessary for enhanced public safety and community protection. Available contemporary evidence on the effectiveness of correctional rehabilitation and the general and specific deterrent effects gained from waiver to adult court indicates, however, that these benefits are not nearly as large as expected. In reality, possible short-term gains achieved through longer incarceration in the adult system are offset by greater recidivism once these youths are released from confinement. Therefore, a much more limited use of juvenile transfer appears warranted.

THE FUTURE OF JUVENILE TRANSFER

Following nearly two centuries of efforts to distinguish juvenile delinquents from adult criminals, in the 1990s, the American public and policy makers voiced strong support for treating greater numbers and types of serious and violent juvenile offenders as adults. By the mid-1990s, in response to a decade-long rise in youth violence and fears about a coming wave of juvenile superpredators, almost all states had revised their laws to facilitate the waiver of juveniles to adult court. Since that time, juvenile arrest rates for serious and violent crimes have dropped to a 20-year low, and youth violence is no longer at the top of the list of public and political concerns. But as concerns about terrorism and an emphasis on homeland security have taken center stage, trends and patterns in juvenile offending also are starting to change.

Many have noted that with diminished support and resources being provided to prevention and intervention programs, declines in serious and violent youthful offending have ended, and increases are again being observed.[34] For example, in Boston, a city well known for its dramatic decreases in youth violence during the latter half of the 1990s, the number of murder victims younger than age 24 nearly doubled during a recent one-year period. This rise followed several years of cuts in federal and state funding that previously supported youth services and programs provided by nonprofit agencies. Nationally, gang violence has reemerged as a disturbing issue. Gang-related homicides dropped from 1,200 in 1995 to fewer than 700 in 1999, but then rose to more than 1,000 by 2003. Furthermore, more than 40 percent of the 2,182 cities responding to the 2002 National Gang Survey reported that gang activity was getting worse (an increase from 27 percent the previous year), and 87 percent of U.S. cities with populations of at least 100,000 reported significant problems with gangs.

These signs of reversing trends in youth violence and gang activity come not only at a time when attention and resources have been shifted elsewhere, but also when the U.S. juvenile population is projected to grow well into the foreseeable future. More juveniles combined with rising rates of youth violence and a lack of adequate funding and resources is a recipe for disaster. Moreover, if recent trends continue, it is quite likely that by the time a growing problem with serious and violent youthful offending is fully recognized, policy makers will react by supporting another crackdown effort that again encourages greater use of transfer to adult court. Studies to date from a variety of researchers suggest that this is the wrong approach on which to rely and that greater use of knowledge about adolescent development and the effectiveness of prevention and early intervention programs is needed.

Adolescent Development and a Comprehensive Strategy

At their root level, juvenile transfer policies assume that adolescents will rationally consider the consequences of their actions; will know about and understand the provisions provided in transfer laws; and, therefore, will choose not to commit serious and violent crime (i.e., they will experience general deterrence). Moreover, if they do decide to commit illegal acts, the experience of being waived to adult court and subsequently punished in a harsh manner will cause them to choose law-abiding behavior upon their return to society (i.e., they will experience specific deterrence). The research evidence previously discussed questions these assumptions, and based on the findings of recent studies on adolescent development, it seems that adolescents simply do not think about and weigh the consequences of their actions in the same manner as adults do.[35]

The teenagers typically targeted by juvenile transfer laws are often psychologically immature and have experienced a variety of negative life circumstances (known as risk factors), which contribute to their impulsive behavior, limited perspective on life, and propensity for engaging in risk-taking to achieve short-term gains while disregarding long-term consequences. This is particularly true for younger youth (such as Abraham), although modern psychological literature suggests that these same characteristics apply to adolescents up to at least the age of 18. In other words, the lack of maturity in judgment displayed in adolescence seems to make the rational assumption of deterrence theory less than applicable to most juveniles. Furthermore, the stigmatization, sense of injustice, victimization, and exposure to criminal norms and values experienced by transferred youth likely go a long way toward explaining their heightened future offending.[36]

Since the mid-1990s, support has been growing for a more comprehensive, collaborative, and integrative approach to dealing with serious and violent juvenile offending.[37] This strategy is based on research regarding the causes and correlates of delinquency, effective prevention and early intervention efforts, and successful treatment and rehabilitation programs. Rather than responding to youth violence after it has escalated to a high level, as juvenile transfer laws seek to do, the evidence suggests that a combination of prevention and early intervention programs with a coordinated system of treatment and graduated sanctions will be more effective in reducing juvenile crime. This strategy has been supported at the national level by the Office of Juvenile Justice and Delinquency Prevention, which from 1994 to 2002 provided more than $1 billion in funding through its Community Prevention Grants Program. The grants help states and communities to implement programs that can reduce risk factors, enhance protective factors, and decrease adolescent problem behaviors.

Although services to children and their families sometimes are described as fragmented, crisis-oriented, and mismanaged, these problems have been overcome when a comprehensive, community-wide strategy is employed and sufficient funding and other resources are provided. In addition, the development of comprehensive prevention, intervention, sanctioning, and treatment strategies corresponded in time with declining rates of serious and violent juvenile offending. It is therefore important to stress that contemporary investments in children and youth should not be lost because of a renewed faith in punishment-oriented practices (such as transfer to adult court), which are politically wise but limited in their societal benefits.

Final Recommendations

Will transferring juveniles to adult court come to an end in the United States? The answer is probably "no." As long as a separate system of justice is in place for dealing with children and youth, which very likely will continue to be the case in the future, there also will be a perceived need and desire to treat some of these young people as adults. Few would argue that there are not certain older, chronic, and violent adolescent offenders who, for the sake of public safety, should be removed from society for long periods of time. Furthermore, waiver to adult court will continue to exist because of its symbolic importance. Society can use this procedure to express both its fear about serious and violent youth crime and its revulsion for the young offenders who commit it. Having this symbolic importance makes juvenile transfer resistant to rational and scientific arguments. Nevertheless, the information and evidence that has been gathered on treating juveniles as adults indicate that extending this approach beyond those who are deemed the "most deserving" is not good public policy. The real issue is not whether young offenders should be waived to adult court, but rather which adolescents should be transferred and how they should be processed and sanctioned once they get there.

Various sources indicate that 75 percent or more of all transferred youth are age 16 or older.[38] These findings, combined with what is known about adolescent development and decision making, suggest that a minimum age of 16 should be the standard for adult court processing and sanctioning, at least for all crimes other than murder. This would ensure that younger offenders receive juvenile correctional services and also avoid the potential negative consequences associated with contacting adult criminals and public labeling in the adult system.

Next, instead of using broad categories of serious and violent offenses to establish transfer eligibility, a focus on firearms seems more justified. Firearm use was a key factor in the surge in youth violence from the mid-1980s to the mid-1990s, particularly with regard to the dramatic increases that occurred in juvenile murder rates and youth homicide victimization. Research suggests that violent juvenile gun users tend to receive the most immediate attention and severe sanctions in adult court and that justice system officials believe waiver laws should target gun offenses.[39]

Still, not all adolescent gun users are equal in terms of their behaviors and future risk to society, and many could be effectively handled in juvenile court. Therefore, a youth's prior offending history is another important factor to consider. Juveniles with more serious and extensive offending backgrounds tend to be given more immediate attention and are punished more severely, particularly in adult court, but these same youths also pose a higher risk for recidivism. This implies that a relatively small number of serious and violent adolescent offenders (less than 10 percent of all delinquents, based on current research) with substantial prior records are the most likely to continue their chronic offending well into adulthood, justifying the need for longer periods of incapacitation to ensure public safety.[40]

If the above information was combined for policy purposes, youth age 16 and older who employ a gun and display a notable delinquent background would be the focus of juvenile waiver laws. To specify the needed prior record, one option would be to require a prior adjudication of delinquency on a violent felony offense. Another would be to develop a prior-record scoring system, common in adult sentencing guidelines, which would consider all prior adjudications. This would require improved juvenile record-keeping systems that would need to be made more accessible, at least to those working in the juvenile and adult justice systems.

Following these recommendations would ensure that juveniles in the adult criminal justice system would be older and more violent and chronic offenders who pose the greatest threat to public safety. This would reduce the likelihood of negative experiences and longer-term adverse consequences for younger and less serious offenders, and it would allow for lengthy incapacitation of the most dangerous youth. This approach contrasts with most modern waiver laws that encompass broad categories of younger, less serious, and lower-risk adolescent offenders. It also suggests greater consideration of how serious and violent young offenders should be processed and sanctioned in both the juvenile and adult systems.

Although there are exceptions, most states use 18 as the age at which criminal courts receive jurisdiction over young offenders.[41] Almost all states also define a maximum age greater than 18 (for example, 21 or even 25) for which the juvenile court can retain custody and supervision beyond the original age of jurisdiction. Rather than waiving increased numbers of juveniles to adult court, an alternative in most states would be to raise the maximum age at which the juvenile court can retain jurisdiction, which would allow for lengthier confinement, treatment, and supervision. This, in turn, would avoid many of the adverse consequences and negative outcomes associated with sending adolescents to the adult system. This approach is compatible with the fact that crime (including violent offending) peaks by the late teenage years and declines thereafter.

It seems logical that juvenile courts should be able to keep control of known offenders into young adulthood, rather than "cutting them loose" at a time when they are most likely to break the law. To fully implement this approach, however, requires a greater investment in the juvenile justice system and a shift in the funding and resources that currently are devoted to dealing with younger offenders in the criminal justice system. Moreover, a relatively small number of older, chronic, and violent adolescent offenders still will need to be prosecuted in adult court and will likely end up in adult jails in prisons, either through standard waiver procedures or blended sentences that entail confinement in juvenile and adult correctional facilities. Minimally, these offenders should be segregated from the rest of the adult inmate population, preferably until the age at which juvenile court jurisdiction would end if these offenders were retained in juvenile court (e.g., at least age 21, but perhaps 24 or 25). A better approach would be to provide smaller and separate facilities and treatment services for these youth, because many will be returned to society and will be expected to be productive and law-abiding community members upon their release.

The key lesson to be learned from more than 100 years of experience with transferring juveniles to adult court is that this practice is not a cure-all for serious and violent youthful offending. As long as we ignore the evidence that is available and emphasize a reactive approach to adolescent problem behavior, cycles of serious and violent youth crime will be met with calls for greater use of juvenile waiver. As informed citizens, however, we could take on the responsibilities of influencing public officials and making a greater investment in children and youth through a more proactive approach to preventing and reducing delinquency and youth violence. We are beginning to more fully understand childhood and adolescent development, as well as what works to guide children toward success in life and correct adolescent problem behaviors. What we choose to do with this information will go a long way in determining how future generations of young people are viewed.

NOTES

1. Snyder & Sickmund, 2006.
2. Snyder & Sickmund, 2006.
3. Bennett, DiIulio, & Walters, 1996; DiIulio, 1995, 1996; Wilson, 1995.
4. Sickmund, Snyder, & Poe-Yamagata, 1997.
5. Myers, 2005.
6. Myers, 2005.
7. Myers, 2005.
8. Myers, 2005.
9. Myers, 2005.
10. Snyder & Sickmund, 2006.
11. Snyder & Sickmund, 2006.
12. Myers, 2005.
13. Snyder & Sickmund, 2006.
14. Myers, 2005.
15. Snyder & Sickmund, 2006.
16. Myers, 2005.
17. Snyder & Sickmund, 2006.
18. Bishop, 2000.
19. Myers, 2005.
20. Cable News Network, 1999, 2000.
21. Moore, 2000.
22. Myers, 2005.
23. Moore, 2000.
24. Myers, 2005.
25. Myers, 2005.
26. Myers, 2005.
27. Myers, 2005.
28. Bishop, 2000.
29. Myers, 2005.
30. Myers, 2005.
31. Myers, 2005.
32. Redding, 2006.
33. Myers, 2005; Redding, 2006.
34. Myers, 2005.
35. Myers, 2005.
36. Redding, 2006.
37. Howell, 1997, 2003; Loeber & Farrington, 1999.
38. Myers, 2005.
39. Myers, 2005.
40. Myers, 2005; Redding, 2006.
41. Snyder & Sickmund, 2006.

REFERENCES

Bennett, W. J., DiIulio, J. J., & Walters, J. P. (1996). *Body count: Moral poverty . . . And how to win America's war against crime and drugs.* New York: Simon & Shuster.

Bishop, D. M. (2000). Juvenile offenders in the adult criminal justice system. In M. Tonry (Ed.), *Crime and justice: A review of research* (Vol. 27, pp. 81–167). Chicago: The University of Chicago Press.

Cable News Network. (1999, October 29). *Prosecutor: Boy, 11, bragged he'd kill, then did.* Retrieved July 25, 2003. http://www.cnn.com/us/9910/29/young.murder.suspect.02/index.html?eref=sitesearch.

Cable News Network. (2000, January 13). *Michigan judge sentences boy killer to juvenile detention.* Retrieved July 25, 2003. http://archives.cnn.com/2000/us/01/13/abraham.sentencing.03/index.html.

DiIulio, J. J. (1995). The coming of the super-predators. *Weekly Standard, 1,* 23–28.

DiIulio, J. J. (1996). They're coming: Florida's youth crime bomb. *Impact,* 25–27.

Howell, J. C. (1997). *Juvenile justice and youth violence.* Thousand Oaks, CA: Sage Publications.

Howell, J. C. (2003). *Preventing and reducing juvenile delinquency: A comprehensive framework.* Thousand Oaks, CA: Sage Publications.

Loeber, R., & Farrington, D. P. (1999). *Serious and violent juvenile offenders: Risk factors and successful interventions.* Thousand Oaks, CA: Sage Publications.

Moore, E. A. (2000). Sentencing opinion: People of the state of *Michigan v. Nathaniel Abraham. Juvenile and Family Court Journal, 51*(2), 1–11.

Myers, D. L. (2005). *Boys among men: Trying and sentencing juveniles as adults.* Westport, CT: Praeger.

Redding, R. E. (2006). Adult punishment for juvenile offenders: Does it reduce crime? In N. E. Dowd, D. G. Singer, & R. F. Wilson (Eds.), *Handbook of children, culture, and violence* (pp. 375–394). Thousand Oaks, CA: Sage Publications.

Sickmund, M., Snyder, H. N., & Poe-Yamagata, E. (1997). *Juvenile offenders and victims: 1997 update on violence.* Washington, D.C.: Office of Juvenile Justice and Delinquency Prevention.

Snyder, H. N., & Sickmund, M. (2006). *Juvenile offenders and victims: 2006 national report.* Washington, D.C.: Office of Juvenile Justice and Delinquency Prevention.

Wilson, J. Q. (1995). Crime and public policy. In J. Q. Wilson & J. Petersilia (Eds.), *Crime* (pp. 489–507). San Francisco: Institute for Contemporary Studies.

CASES CITED

Kent v. United States, 383 U.S. 541 (1966).

CHAPTER 4

Juvenile Specialty Courts

Victoria Simpson Beck, Lawrence F. Travis III, and Robert J. Ramsey

Until late in the nineteenth century, youths accused of committing crimes were lumped together with adults and faced charges and punishments in the adult system of justice. By the start of the twentieth century, reformers had come to believe that most, if not all, juvenile offenders were "redeemable," and that treating children like adults was a mistake. At common law, children under the age of seven were assumed to be incapable of forming criminal intent—knowing right from wrong. Youth between 7 and 14 years of age were presumed to be incapable of forming intent, but the prosecutor could present evidence to prove the youth "knew better."

Throughout the late 1800s, those concerned with child welfare were confronted with the specter of thousands of young people being tried, convicted, and punished as adult criminals. The consensus of opinion was that this treatment turned wayward youth into hardened criminals. A better system, reformers argued, was to divert youth from the criminal courts. To that end, in 1899, the first juvenile court was founded in Chicago. The solution to the problem of youth crime was defined as the development of a specialized court and separate justice system.

The juvenile court was to be therapeutic and concerned with the best interests of the child. The state, through the juvenile court judge and other juvenile justice officials, would act as a concerned and caring parent, providing help and guidance to the delinquent youth in hopes of returning a law-abiding citizen. The juvenile court was not punitive.

In the past 20 years, the specialized juvenile court has been the subject of two related reform movements. On the one hand, juvenile processing of what are called serious juvenile offenders has been criticized as ineffective at protecting the public and too lenient toward these dangerous offenders. In response, the juvenile court has become more punitive in its treatment of juvenile delinquents. On the other hand, there has been a rebirth of interest in a therapeutic approach to the problems of youth who are involved in crime.

Although the juvenile court in many jurisdictions has become more similar to the adult courts in its handling of serious juvenile offenders, the notion of a specialized court has also expanded. Current juvenile diversion practices include, for example, "informal adjustment" strategies that "allow youths to avoid formal court processing and adjudicating and the stigma that typically accompanies formal action."[1] Adjustment strategies involve the informal handling of youths by community agencies and programs and may include counseling, crisis intervention, and mediation. A second approach is to develop special dockets in the juvenile court or separate courts to deal with selected types of youth or delinquency problems.

SPECIALTY COURTS

During the 1980s at the height of the crack cocaine epidemic and the "war on drugs," adult criminal courts in many places were overwhelmed with drug offense cases. Many of the defendants in these cases were low-level offenders with substance abuse problems. Attempts to control the criminal and substance-abusing behavior of these offenders generally were unsuccessful. Drug users crowded jails and prisons and substance-abusing offenders swelled probation caseloads and other community programs.

At the same time, treatment professionals grew frustrated with frequent conflicts between the requirements of therapy and those of the criminal justice process. For example, there is reason to believe that motivation to engage in treatment is highest when the user is in crisis. For most offenders, arrest represented a crisis that spurred them to seek treatment. Unfortunately, these offenders had to wait for the courts to take action before they were convicted and ordered into treatment. Often the moment of crisis had passed before offenders entered treatment. In like fashion, substance abuse treatment is full of setbacks and failures. People under criminal justice supervision who "backslide" found themselves removed from therapy and sentenced to jail or prison. Treatment professionals sought a process in which the criminal sanctions could become part of a system of care.

The first formal drug court was established in Miami in 1989. Drug courts are specialized courts, or dockets within courts, designed to deal solely with substance-abusing offenders. The courts rely on identifying eligible offenders (usually those whose criminal behavior is drug related, but who are nonviolent offenders) and merging the criminal justice and drug treatment systems. Offenders are placed under community supervision (probation or other conditional release) and closely monitored by the court. They are supervised by criminal justice agents and enrolled in specialized treatment programs. The goal of the drug court is to prevent future crime by getting the offender to stop abusing drugs.

A drug court can reduce caseload pressures in the general criminal court by removing many of those cases in which the defendant is known to have a drug problem. Specializing the caseload of the court not only allows judges and other court personnel to develop specific expertise in the handling of drug crimes and drug offenders, but also can streamline the criminal court process in general by removing a large number of cases. At the same time, the drug court emphasizes treatment. To date, evaluations of drug courts indicate that, when well designed and operated, the courts succeed in both reducing court delay in the criminal courts and improving the success of treatment efforts.

The federal government supported the development of drug courts by providing funds to local courts to develop and implement drug courts. Nearly 1,200 drug courts are in operation and hundreds more are in the planning stages.[2] The drug court model set the stage for the development of a variety of specialized courts. These courts, focused as they are on particular types of offenses or offenders, have been called "problem-solving courts."[3] This move toward specialized courts that has struck the adult criminal courts has spread to the juvenile court as well. Originally a specialized court in its own right, over the past two decades, the juvenile court has experienced an accelerated movement toward additional specialization.

The past 20 years have seen the development of separate courts or specialized dockets that focus on drug offenders, domestic violence, offenders suffering mental health problems, people accused of driving while intoxicated, "reentry" courts, and community courts. Huddleston, Freeman-Wilson, and Boone write, "There is no doubt that the expansion of problem solving courts is well underway in every state across America. No longer may drug courts, and other problem solving courts, be described as anything other than an appropriate, effective, and productive way for the justice system to function."[4] Although some people might have reservations about problem-solving courts, it is clear that the expansion of these courts is well under way. A survey of courts in early 2004 identified nearly 1,700 problem-solving courts in operation at that time.

JUVENILE SPECIALTY COURTS

Juvenile specialty courts focus on specific types of delinquency (e.g., minor offenses, drug-related offenses, gun-related offenses) and have been designed to address the special needs of youthful offenders. A variety of juvenile specialty courts have developed to divert youthful offenders away from the more punitive and potentially developmentally threatening aspects of the traditional juvenile court system. All juvenile specialty courts are characterized by their small case loads, frequent hearings, immediate sanctions, family involvement, and treatment services. Juvenile specialty courts offer innovative and integrated treatment approaches reflecting community norms and values, encouraging community involvement in the juvenile justice process, and increasing treatment options for youthful offenders.

The underlying principles of juvenile specialty courts are consistent with those of the traditional juvenile court. Most specialty court programs strive

to promote self-esteem, enable self-improvement, and foster a healthy attitude toward rules and authority. Nonetheless, juvenile specialty courts are
relatively new and much remains to be learned about how practitioners
can most effectively intervene with youthful populations. The remainder
of this section describes existing types of juvenile specialty courts discussed
in the literature, beginning with the juvenile drug court.

Juvenile Drug Courts

Adapted from the popular innovation in adult courts, juvenile drug
courts are special courts that handle substance-abusing youthful offenders
through comprehensive supervision, drug testing, treatment services, and
sanctions. The juvenile drug court provides intensive judicial intervention
and supervision of juveniles and families involved in substance abuse,
although other types of youthful offenders may be referred to the court.
The judge works with an intervention team (composed of individuals from
social service programs, the legal system, and the community) to design
an individualized plan that addresses substance abuse problems and other
related issues.

Development

Modeled after adult drug courts, juvenile drug courts began to appear
in the mid-1990s to address the alarming increase in drug and alcohol use
among high school students. The outbreak of juvenile drug courts has
been extraordinary. As of 2006, there are 406 juvenile, 166 family, and
14 combined (juvenile and family) drug courts in the United States.[5] An
important force behind the drug court movement was the Violent Crime
Control and Law Enforcement Act of 1994, which provided federal support for planning, implementing, and enhancing drug courts for nonviolent drug offenders. Additionally, by lending their support to the drug
court movement, national leaders raised the status of drug courts.[6]

Process

Because juvenile drug courts are implemented at the local level, they
vary by jurisdiction in terms of structure and scope. All share similar goals,
however, as noted in Table 4.1.

The Juvenile Drug Court, operating within Jefferson County Family
Court, in Birmingham, Alabama, provides one example of juvenile drug
court processing. According to the Birmingham Bar Association,[7] a
juvenile offender with a substance abuse problem may be referred to the
Drug Court from their disposition hearing. Once referred, the youth is
ordered into an Adolescent Substance Abuse Program, and then the case
is reviewed to determine whether the program is appropriate for the youth
(Drug Court will not take a client that is not suited and may not respond
well to the less-structured, lighter-sanctioned program). After these initial

Table 4.1.
Goals of the Juvenile Drug Court

Immediate Intervention	Provide immediate intervention, treatment, and structure in the lives of juveniles who use drugs through ongoing, active oversight and monitoring by the drug court judge.
Improve Functioning	Improve juveniles' level of functioning in their environment, address problems that may be contributing to their use of drugs, and develop/ strengthen their ability to lead crime- and drug-free lives.
Skills Training	Provide juveniles with skills that will aid them in leading productive substance-free and crime-free lives—including skills that relate to their educational development, sense of self-worth, and relationships in the community.
Strengthen Families	Strengthen families of drug-involved youth by improving their capability to provide structure and guidance to their children.
Promote Accountability	Promote the accountability of juvenile offenders and those who provide services to them.

Source: Bureau of Justice Assistance, 2003.

steps, there are four phases to the program: (1) participants attend court weekly and drug test weekly; (2) participants attend court biweekly and the frequency of drug tests is individualized; (3) participants attend court monthly and the frequency of drug tests is individualized; and (4) aftercare participants attend court and submit to a drug test only if they received a letter or phone call from the court specialist.

In the drug court model, the judge is both the leader and a member of a team designed to reduce drug and alcohol abuse by youth engaged in delinquency. The juvenile drug court deals with similar issues as does the adult court, but juveniles pose specific problems. Because of their age, use and possession of alcohol is an offense for youth when it might not be for adults. Again, because of their age, many delinquents do not have as serious addiction problems as are found in an adult population. As minors, juvenile delinquents have school attendance requirements, and interventions with youth often require family interventions.

Youth identified as eligible for drug court interventions are enrolled in the program. Eligibility is usually defined as showing evidence of drug or alcohol involvement that is related to the delinquency problem, not having a record of violent behavior, and demonstrating evidence to suggest the youth can be helped by treatment. The drug court team usually includes the judge, prosecutor, defense attorney, probation officer, treatment personnel, police, and any other family or community members who might assist (schools, clergy, and so on). The youth normally is placed into some sort of conditional release to the community (probation or even a residential setting such as a halfway house). Among other things, these conditions usually include drug testing, participation in treatment programs, and frequent reporting. The judge provides supervision and monitoring, sometimes including weekly appearances in court. The team assesses the youth's progress in treatment and decides the best course of action to take.

Effectiveness

There have been many evaluations of drug courts, especially of those serving adult offenders. In general these studies report positive results. Drug courts seem to be effective in selecting and serving offenders with drug problems, retaining these offenders in treatment, and reducing the general caseload of the criminal courts. Drug court programs appear to provide better supervision than traditional probation and to reduce the number of offenders who are sent to jail or prison. Recidivism studies report mixed results, with most evaluations showing that drug court graduates commit fewer new crimes in the short term, at least. Still, the effects of drug court treatment on long-term rates of crime or drug abuse are unknown. For the newer and less numerous juvenile drug courts, as a special subset of all drug courts, the evidence is even less strong.

Concerns

One concern surrounding drug courts is that they provide an incentive to create an overreliance on arrests as a way to address substance abuse problems. Furthermore, the program may not be well suited for all youth. For example, it is not possible to coerce sobriety, and some youth may not be voluntary participants in assigned substance abuse treatment programs. Additionally, drug courts may hold youth accountable without holding the drug treatment facilities accountable. The threat of "net-widening" exposes youth who would not have been subjected to court oversight to the juvenile justice process so that they can be enrolled in the drug court program. This may be especially relevant because most drug courts exclude more serious offenders and those with any record of violence. This not only denies a possibly effective treatment to some youth, but also may mean that youth who do not need the attention of the drug court are now kept in custody. Finally, expectations of the drug courts may be too high. Is it reasonable to assume that juvenile drug courts can really solve a complicated social problem like substance abuse?

Juvenile Gun Courts

Juvenile gun courts intervene with youth who have committed gun offenses that have not resulted in serious physical injury. Unlike other juvenile specialty courts, gun courts augment rather than replace typical juvenile court procedures. Juvenile gun courts were formed as a juvenile justice system response to high levels of violent juvenile crime and criticism of juvenile courts for not having provided appropriate sanctions and program services.

Development

The first adult gun court was established in Providence, Rhode Island, in 1994. It appears that the first juvenile gun court may have been modeled after this adult court and implemented the following year in Birmingham, Alabama, although the literature is not clear on this point. At last report, there were six juvenile gun court programs, and the federal Office of Juvenile Justice and Delinquency Prevention was taking steps to support further development.

Process

Juvenile gun courts are implemented at the local level, resulting in variation across programs. According to Sheppard and Kelly,[8] however, several key elements are included in a successful juvenile court program (see Table 4.2). In comparison with traditional juvenile court processing, gun courts involve the early screening and referral of youth who can benefit from the program, an expanded role of the judge as educator and case manager, and a wider involvement of community members. Sheppard and Kelly write that gun courts can serve not only those youth charged with gun offenses but also youth charged with other weapons offenses, youth who possessed a firearm but were not charged, or those otherwise "at risk" for gun involvement, including gang members, drug dealers, those whose codefendant was armed, and the like.[9]

Table 4.2.
Key Elements of a Juvenile Gun Court Program

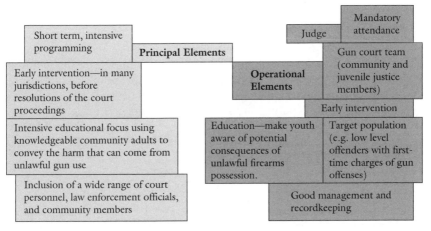

Source: Sheppard & Kelly (2002).

Jefferson County's program, in Birmingham Alabama, provides an example of juvenile gun court processes. The Jefferson County Juvenile Gun Court was established, in 1995, in response to an increase in juvenile deaths the preceding year. The goal of the court is to deliver swift and suitable consequences to juveniles found in possession of a gun. Cases in Jefferson County Gun Court are processed as follows: (1) arrest for a qualifying offense (e.g., a first-time offender charged with a nonviolent offense); (2) court intake, during which youth are retained and there is no discretion to transfer case from formal prosecution to diversion programs; (3) detention hearing, which is held within 72 hours, at which time youth may request a trial or plead true; (4) if a youth requests a trial, then the trial must be held within 10 working days; (5) youth who plead true are sent to an intensive boot camp, focusing on, for example, improving social skills, physical exercise, and academics; (6) parents are required to attend workshops, targeting the underlying issues that led to the offense; and (7) after release from boot camp, youth are placed on probation supervision for a period of one to six months.[10]

Effectiveness

Juvenile gun courts are among the most recently developed specialty courts. Consequently, little is known about their effectiveness. A recent evaluation on program outcomes in the Jefferson County Juvenile Gun Court has indicated that the typical program youth was a 15.5-year-old black male, with 88 percent having been charged with gun possession. Additionally, the study findings indicated that youth processed through the Gun Court had significantly lower rates of recidivism. Finally, in examining overall trends in Birmingham, the analyses indicated that between 1995 and 1999 formal juvenile gun charges decreased by 54 percent and violent crime decreased by 57 percent.[11]

Concerns

Before the implementation of juvenile gun court, typically, youth were not arrested for gun possession; they were released to a parent without the filing of charges.[12] Consequently, net-widening is a particular concern for gun courts. The broad boundaries around the types of youth who might benefit from gun court programs (more than just youth currently involved with guns) raises concerns that these programs could significantly increase the reach of the juvenile justice system. Gun and violent crime rates decreased across the country during the 1990s, and it is not clear how, if at all, gun courts contributed to this decline. Until more reliable data are available, gun courts remain a promising, but unproven, response to some juvenile delinquency.

Teen Courts

Teen courts are programs in which juvenile offenders, having committed minor acts of delinquency (e.g., truancy, petty theft), are questioned, defended, and sentenced by their peers. Youthful offenders voluntarily choose teen court, with parental approval, as an alternative to formal juvenile justice court processing and delinquency adjudication.

Development

Teen court appears to be the pioneer of juvenile specialty courts. Although the exact date of the first teen court has not been established, the literature has noted that in the 1940s a Mansfield, Ohio, youth-operated bicycle court dealt with the minor traffic violations of youth. In 1972, the Odessa, Texas, teen court was implemented, which appears to be the most widely known teen court and regarded as a national model.[13] Teen courts are the fastest-growing specialty court. By 2002, more than 900 teen court programs were operating in 46 states and the District of Columbia.[14]

Process

Diversion to teen court prevents the need for formal juvenile court adjudication and a court record. All teen courts operate within the parameters of state and local law, but most states do not formally endorse teen courts. Rather, most states rely on the discretion of local jurisdictions to fund and operate teen courts.[15] Thus, teen courtroom models and processes may vary considerably across jurisdictions. There are four basic teen courtroom models (see Table 4.3).

The teen court processes vary, but in general the process begins with an arrest or school referral (e.g., truancy, fighting). Once a case has been referred to teen court, an intake agency (e.g., police, court, prosecutor, juvenile justice agency) must confirm eligibility, which is typically determined based on the type of offense and prior record. During the intake process, the charges are reviewed and teen court processes are explained to the offender and the parent to ensure that participation is voluntary. The youth and parents must sign a contract agreeing to diversion to teen court and the youth must accept responsibility for the charges. If the youth

Table 4.3.
Four Models of Teen Courts

	Adult Judge	Youth Judge	Youth Tribunal	Peer Jury
Judge	Adult	Youth	Youth(s)	Adult
Youth attorneys included	Yes	Yes	Yes	No
Role of youth jury	Recommend sentence	Recommend sentence	No jury present	Question defendant, recommend sentence

Source: National Youth Court Center, 2006.

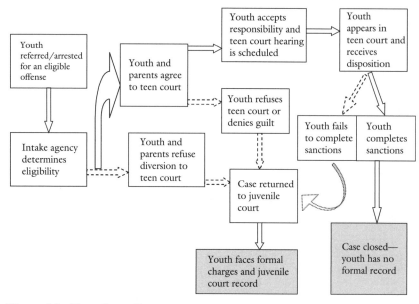

Figure 4.1. Teen Court Process
Source: Butts, Buck, & Coggeshall, 2002.

denies responsibility or the contract is not signed, the case is returned to the juvenile court. If the youth accepts responsibility for the charges and the teen court contract is signed, then the teen court hearing is scheduled.[16] Figure 4.1 depicts this process.

All youth appearing before the teen courts receive some type of informal sanction, which typically requires the youth to repair or repay at least part of the damage caused to the community or specific victim. For example, an offender may be ordered to perform community service, pay restitution, or write a letter of apology. According to a national survey of teen courts, community service is the most common sanction.[17]

Teen courts are structured in one of three basic ways. Some courts are operated by the juvenile courts or juvenile probation agencies. In other places, teen courts are administered by community-based service agencies, including the police and private or nonprofit organizations. Finally, some of these courts are operated in schools. The thinking behind teen courts suggests the programs can be effective in three ways (as shown in Table 4.4).

Effectiveness

Although teen courts have been around longer than the other juvenile specialty courts, relatively little information is available on the effectiveness of these programs. One available study, the Evaluation of Teen Courts (ETC) Project, was conducted by the Urban Institute in 2002. The ETC Project studied teen courts in Alaska, Arizona, Maryland, and Missouri.

Table 4.4.
Methods of Effectiveness

Effect	Process
Peer Justice	Just as association with deviant or delinquent peers is commonly associated with the onset of delinquent behavior, peer pressure from prosocial peers may propel youth toward law-abiding behavior.
Law-related Education	Youth avoid illegal behavior as they develop citizenship skills and procitizenship knowledge, including a belief in the value of democracy and pluralism, dedication to the ideal of justice, respect of human dignity, and an understanding of the role of law in the legitimate resolution of conflicts.
Skill Building	Youth avoid illegal behavior as they develop effective like skills, including conflict resolution, interpersonal communication, public speaking, and group problem solving.

Researchers measured the postcourt recidivism of 500 youths referred to teen court. Based on a six-month follow-up period, the ETC Project found that, in general, programs in all four study sites had low rates of reoffending. More specifically, they found teen court youth were significantly less likely to reoffend than were the comparison group youth in two of the four study sites. In one site, teen court youth were less likely to reoffend, but the difference was not significant; in the fourth site, the findings slightly favored the comparison group, but the difference again was not significant. Furthermore, study findings indicated that there was no statistical difference in reoffending across courtroom models.[18] Officials in many jurisdictions report that the teen court process leads to increased respect for the law and the juvenile justice system by holding youth accountable for their first, minor offenses. These officials also argue that the teen court can respond more quickly and more efficiently to youthful offenders than the formal juvenile court.

Concerns

One particular concern with teen courts is that they provide youth with the ability to determine the punishment of an offender. The peer "jury" in a teen court determines penalties. Use of peer judges may contribute to the labeling of offenders who must admit guilt before their peers. In addition, perhaps even more than with other courts, teen courts have substantial potential for net-widening. Indeed, one of the reported strengths of teen courts is that they involve youth who otherwise may very well have been diverted from the juvenile justice process entirely.

Mental Health Courts

One problem facing courts in the entire criminal justice system has to do with the handling of mentally ill offenders. Developments in patient rights, the closing or downsizing of mental health hospitals, and the development of drug treatments for many mental conditions have all combined to increase the number of mentally ill individuals residing in our communities. Often these individuals experience legal problems and come to the attention of the courts. Approximately 40 percent of adults suffering from a serious mental illness come in contact with the criminal justice system, and 20 percent of youths in the juvenile justice system have serious mental health problems.[19] Ron Honberg, the legal director for the National Alliance for the Mentally Ill, said, "[O]ur nation's jails and prisons have become de facto psychiatric treatment facilities.... It is frankly unfair—and very poor public policy—to saddle criminal justice systems with responsibility for responding to people with mental illnesses in crisis."[20]

As with drug offenders, mentally ill offenders contribute to court delays and may not be receiving adequate treatment and service in the criminal courts. To respond to this problem, several jurisdictions created special adult "mental health courts" during the 1990s. It was not long before some juvenile courts also created mental health dockets.

Development

The forerunner to mental health courts may well have been screening and diversion practices in the New York criminal courts in the 1960s.[21] Responding to a growing number of criminal defendants with mental illness issues, the New York courts instituted a pretrial screening process that sought to identify offenders suffering mental illness and divert them to mental health treatment outside the court and criminal process. In the 1990s, building on the perceived success of the drug court model, some adult courts began to develop specialized caseloads for the mentally ill.

The first adult mental health court was started in Ft. Lauderdale, Florida, in 1997. Criminal defendants found to be suffering from mental illness are asked to volunteer for the mental health court program. Criminal charges are postponed for those who agree to the program and the judge, working with a variety of criminal justice and treatment staff, manages a mental health treatment regimen that is supported by criminal sanctions. Successful completion of treatment results in the dismissal of charges and avoidance of a criminal record. The program began in response to the large number of defendants exhibiting mental health problems. These individuals posed serious problems in terms of jail crowding and court delay. In addition, it was clear that traditional criminal justice approaches to these individuals resulted in a "revolving door" and did not seem to improve the conditions of defendants or reduce future crime.

Relatively soon the idea spread to some additional adult courts, including those in San Bernardino, California; Seattle, Washington; and Anchorage, Alaska. As with other specialty courts, congressional attention to the promise of effective interventions led to the provision of federal funding to test the mental health court concept in dozens of jurisdictions. By the late 1990s the idea of a specialized mental health docket had been adopted in some juvenile courts as well. The leading examples of juvenile mental health courts include those found in the state of California and Hamilton County in Cincinnati, Ohio.

Process

Although variations exist across different courts, they all share some common characteristics. All of the courts require voluntary participation. In some cases, the defendant must plead guilty, in others the defendant agrees to participate and no action is taken on the criminal charges. All of the courts provide mental health assessments and link participants to treatments that are enforced or supported by the use or threat of criminal sanctions. In all the programs, the court relies on teams of mental health and criminal justice professionals and the court maintains supervision over the case.

The Santa Clara, California, juvenile mental health court is called the Court for the Individualized Treatment of Adolescents (CITA). CITA is reserved for youth who have been diagnosed with a serious mental illness that is related to their criminal involvement or involvement with the juvenile court. All youth are screened for mental illness, and those who seem eligible receive additional testing. The mental health court team includes the prosecution, defense, probation office, and a mental health coordinator. The team selects the youth who are invited to participate.

Serious offenders may be kept in residential placements, but most are placed on electronic monitoring. The program seeks to keep youths in their homes. To remain in the program, youths must agree to any medication, show a willingness to participate in counseling, and generally have a positive attitude. Cases are reviewed in court every one to three months that the youth are on probation. Other California courts include school personnel and community representatives in the mental health court team. The Hamilton County, Ohio, court accepts youth diagnosed with major depression, posttraumatic stress, or bipolar disorders. The program usually involves intensive treatment at home. The program was developed in response to a perceived lack of adequate mental health services for youth in the county.

Effectiveness

Mental health courts are so new that, to date, evaluations of court effects have not been completed. Early reports suggest that the courts are successful at selecting appropriate candidates and that most participants are receiving services that normally would not be available to offenders processed through the courts. It is not clear what, if any, impact these courts will have on recidivism. Many mental health problems are chronic illnesses for which it is difficult to identify "outcome" measures. It is also not clear how to contrast participation in treatment (one measure of "success") with new criminal involvement (one measure of "failure"). It will be some time before conclusions about the impact of mental health courts can be drawn.

Concerns

As with other specialty courts, mental health courts raise concerns about net-widening. Indeed, there is an argument that people whose involvement in crime or the criminal/juvenile courts is the product of mental illness are, by definition, not guilty of criminal behavior and should not be subject to court control. Additionally, although the courts require voluntary participation, it is not clear whether offenders suffering mental illness are competent or capable of volunteering to participate.[22] Other issues include concerns about how to balance the goals of mental health treatment with the goals of criminal processing, a fear that the courts result in forced treatment, and questions about the impact of these courts on the availability of mental health services to individuals not involved in crime.

Miscellaneous Juvenile Specialty Courts

Although we may not hear about them as frequently, throughout the United States at the local level there are probably a variety of locally individualized juvenile specialty courts. For example, since 1958, Hamilton County, Ohio, has had an Unofficial Juvenile Community Courts program. The focus of this program is to divert first-time nonfelony offenders away from official processing to prevent stigmatization and instill "the discipline necessary to remain out of trouble."[23] The juvenile court appoints and trains community volunteers as referees for the 28 diversion courts throughout Hamilton County. Referrals to the diversion program are made by police departments and schools. If the parents and child consent to an unofficial hearing (contested cases are referred to the Juvenile Court), a hearing date is set and the volunteer referee conducts a semiformal hearing focusing attention on the delinquent behavior of the child, reviewing the child's behavior with parents, lecturing the child, and then making a disposition based on parents' prior consent. Dispositions may include, for example, essays, unofficial work details, unofficial probation periods, restitution, and counseling. If no new complaint is filed within a one-year period, the initial report is destroyed and no official juvenile court record is created.

Beck, Travis, and Ramsey[24] conducted an effectiveness evaluation study of the Unofficial Juvenile Community Court, measuring (among other variables) reoffending. Study findings indicated that, of the 393 cases included in the evaluation, only 10.1 percent had reoffended during a one-year follow-up period. Furthermore, 88.7 percent of the parents of children in the study reported that participation in the program was in the best interest of their child, and more than half of the parents expressed gratitude for the program.

This chapter has focused on identified specialty courts serving juvenile delinquents or located within juvenile courts. Hundreds of what are called "community courts" are in operation in the United States. These courts are designed to deal with the crime and disorder problems of communities. They involve court officials and community representatives in efforts to solve problems that result in crime or disorder in communities. Some of these problems might be disputes about parking on the streets of a neighborhood, arguments about property maintenance, trespassing, and similar low-level criminal matters that are actually symptomatic of neighborhood issues. To the extent that these neighborhood problems involve adolescents or younger children, community courts also could become involved as juvenile specialty courts. Data are not available to allow us to estimate what portion of community court caseloads involve juveniles or how effective these courts may be. It is a safe bet, however, that as these courts spread they will increasingly touch the lives of youth.

THE CONTROVERSY SURROUNDING JUVENILE SPECIALTY COURTS

With the exception of juvenile gun court, specialty courts divert youth away from juvenile court processing, thus providing youth with a second chance. Proponents of juvenile diversion programs have argued that the programs "guard against the continuation and exacerbation of delinquency by being less stigmatizing"[25] and result in reductions in recidivism,[26] and that diversion provides services to youth where none existed previously. Opponents have argued, however, that diversion programs extend social control to youth who ordinarily would have been released at the intake or arrest state (an outcome known as net-widening), do not prevent stigmatization,[27] and may increase recidivism.[28] According to opponents, selection for diversion may be arbitrary[29] and participation in juvenile specialty courts requires an admission of guilt, which undermines the principals of due process.

Because of the dearth of research on juvenile specialty courts, it is difficult to determine whether the courts are creating more harm or whether they are taking innovative steps to protect youth. It is clear that the various court programs tend to be competing with each other for the same population of youth. With the possible exception of mental health courts, none of these specialty courts target serious, dangerous offenders. Drug and mental health problems coexist in most offenders, so it is not clear whether a drug court placement or mental health court placement would be best. It may be that the spread of these specialty courts will result in a relatively small percentage of juvenile court cases receiving overwhelming amounts of attention and resources, while the bulk of delinquent youth will be subjected to increasingly punitive treatment.

The juvenile court itself was originally designed as a sort of specialty court that diverted less serious and less dangerous offenders from the adult criminal courts. It is somewhat ironic that this diversionary reform now seems to require new diversionary reforms. In theory, at least, the traditional juvenile court was well suited to provide the kinds of services and problem-solving efforts that are associated with these specialty courts. That the original juvenile court model is now in need of reform raises troubling questions about the future of today's problem-solving courts.

Many of the specialty courts began as local initiatives aimed at solving local problems, but all of these courts soon attracted national attention and federal support. It is not clear how much the current popularity of problem-solving courts owes to the availability of federal support or to the pressing problem of court delay. Many of these courts, although aimed at particular crime problems or difficulties of delinquents, were motivated by concerns about court delay, jail crowding, or the availability of federal funding. Even if successful at solving the drug or mental health problems of youth, would these courts continue if federal support dried up or if the court caseload was otherwise reduced?

CONCLUSION

Francis Allen's writings on the criminal justice system during the 1950s and 1960s were collected in a volume entitled *The Borderland of Criminal Justice*.[30] One of his primary concerns had to do with the use of the criminal process to provide treatment services. Allen argued that the criminal system, and we can add the juvenile court to this, is not well suited to the provision of mental health assistance. Using the essentially punitive justice process to identify treatment needs and deliver treatment services, he says, is most likely to result in ineffective treatment and a corruption of the justice process. Is it really best to subject a youth involved in a fight at school to a "teen court" hearing in front of his or her peers? Is a jail time sanction the best therapeutic response to a mentally ill person who misses a counseling appointment, as could happen with mental health court cases? Are those who engage in treatment programs to avoid jail, as may happen with drug court clients, really motivated to change their behavior?

The problems addressed by specialty courts are real and important, and the goals of court personnel are praiseworthy. Time will tell whether these courts serve to improve the conditions of our communities and whether they provide needed help to the youth who pass through them. We can only hope that continued monitoring and assessment of the operations and impact of specialty courts will provide us with the guidance needed to improve court practices and effectiveness.

NOTES

1. Regoli & Hewitt, 2000, p. 400.
2. Huddleston, Freeman-Wilson, & Boone, 2004.
3. Casey & Rottman, 2003.
4. Huddleston et al., 2004, p. 6.
5. National Criminal Justice Reference Service, hereafter NCJRS, 2006a.

6. NCJRS, 2006b.
7. Birmingham Bar Association, 2006.
8. Sheppard & Kelly, 2002.
9. Sheppard & Kelly, 2002, p. 2.
10. Birmingham Bar Association, 2006.
11. Sheppard & Kelly, 2002.
12. Sheppard & Kelly, 2002.
13. Herman, 2002.
14. Herman, 2002.
15. Butts, Buck, & Coggeshall, 2002.
16. Butts et al., 2002.
17. Butts & Buck, 2000.
18. Butts et al., 2002.
19. Berg, 2005.
20. Quoted in Berg, 2005, p. 16.
21. Goldkamp & Irons-Guynn, 2000.
22. Harris & Seltzer, 2004.
23. Lipps & Hendon, 2004, p. 1
24. Beck, Travis, & Ramsey, 2006.
25. Krammer & Minor, 1997, p. 51.
26. Shelden, 1999.
27. Krammer & Minor, 1997.
28. Shelden, 1999.
29. Regoli & Hewitt, 2000.
30. Allen, 1964.

REFERENCES

Allen, F. (1964). *The borderland of criminal justice*. Chicago: University of Chicago Press.

Beck, V. S., Ramsey, R. J., Lipps, T. R., & Travis, III, L. F. (2006). Juvenile diversion: An outcome study of the Hamilton County Ohio unofficial juvenile court. *Juvenile and Family Court Journal, 57*(2), 1–10.

Berg, M. (2005). Mental health courts: A new solution to an old problem. *Behavioral Health Management, 25*(4), 16–21.

Birmingham Bar Association. (2006). Jefferson Family Court Programs Web site. Retrieved May 5, 2006, from www.birminghambar.org/jefferson_family_programs.cfm.

Bureau of Justice Assistance. (2003). *Juvenile drug courts: Strategies in practice*. Washington, D.C.: Office of Justice Programs, U.S. Department of Justice (NCJ 197866).

Butts, J. A., & Buck, J. (2000). Teen courts: A focus on research. *Juvenile Justice Bulletin*. Washington, D.C.: Office of Juvenile Justice and Delinquency Prevention, U.S. Department of Justice (NCJ 183472).

Butts, J., Buck, J., & Coggeshall, M. B. (2002, April). *The impact of teen courts on young offenders*. Washington, D.C.: Urban Institute Justice Policy Center Research Report.

Casey, P., & Rottman, D. (2003). *Problem-solving courts: Models and trends*. Washington, D.C.: National Center for State Courts.

Goldkamp, J., & Irons-Guynn, C. (2000). *Emerging judicial strategies for the mentally ill in the criminal caseload: Mental health courts—In Ft. Lauderdale,*

Seattle, San Bernardino, and Anchorage. Washington, D.C.: U.S. Department of Justice.

Harris, E., & Seltzer, T. (2004). *The role of specialty mental health courts in meeting the needs of juvenile offenders.* Washington, D.C.: Judge David L. Bazelon Center for Mental Health Law.

Herman, M. (2002). *Juvenile justice trends in 2002: Teen courts—A juvenile justice diversion program.* Washington, D.C.: National Center for State Courts.

Huddleston, C. W., Freeman-Wilson, K., & Boone, D. L. (2004). *Painting the current picture: A national report card on drug courts and other problem solving court programs in the United States.* Alexandria, VA: National Drug Court Institute.

Krammer, J. J., & Minor, K. I. (1997). An outcome study of the diversion plus program for juvenile offenders. *Federal Probation, 61*(2), 51–56.

Lipps, T. R., & Hendon, S. S. (2004). *Hamilton County Juvenile Court volunteer referee program manual.* Hamilton County, OH: Juvenile Court.

National Criminal Justice Reference Service. (2006a). In the Spotlight—*Drug courts—facts and figures.* Retrieved May 5, 2006, from http://ncjrs.gov/spotlight/drug_courts/facts.htm.

National Criminal Justice Reference Service. (2006b). In the Spotlight—*Drug courts.* Retrieved May 5, 2006, from http://ncjrs.gov/spotlight/drug_courts/Summary.htm.

Regoli, R. M., & Hewitt, J. D. (2000). *Delinquency in society* (4th ed.). Boston: McGraw-Hill.

Shelden, R. G. (1999). Detention diversion advocacy: An evaluation. *Juvenile Justice Bulletin.* Washington, D.C.: Office of Juvenile Justice and Delinquency Prevention, U.S. Department of Justice.

Sheppard, D., & Kelly, P. (2002). *Juvenile gun courts: Promoting accountability and providing treatment.* Washington, D.C.: Office of Juvenile Justice and Delinquency Prevention.

CHAPTER 5

Restorative Justice and Victim Awareness

Alida V. Merlo and Peter J. Benekos

The original philosophy of the juvenile court focused on the offender and the treatment of the offender's problems. However, substantive changes occurred in the last 25 years that have redefined the purpose of the juvenile court, the important role of the victim, and the need for accountability. In this evolution, the court moved from a strictly rehabilitative model to a more punitive and retributive model. Rather than concentrating solely on the offender or on punishment, restorative justice is an alternative approach that actively engages the offender, the victim, and the community. It requires the offender to resolve the conflict between the individuals, that is, the primary victim, and the state, and to repair the damage that his or her behavior has caused.[1] Unlike the traditional and retributive models, restorative justice has three clients or customers of the system: the offender, the victim, and the community.[2] Restorative justice operates on an underlying assumption that rehabilitation, sanctioning of deviant behavior, and public safety cannot be accomplished without the participation and involvement of the victims and the community.[3]

The future of the juvenile justice system became a topic of debate in the early 1990s. Traditional juvenile court advocates contended that the court should continue as it had been originally envisioned. They proposed that the court should reaffirm its commitment to the original goals and continue to redirect or reform children through rehabilitation. Conversely, proponents of a punitive model advocated more adult-like handling of youth with stricter sanctions, including adult prison terms.[4] Simultaneously, society's perceptions of youth were also shifting radically. Adolescent behaviors were not viewed as youthful transgressions, but rather as crimes.

Generally, the public's perception was that the perpetrators deserve punishment. Little thought was given to the youths' needs or the risks that they are exposed to in society.[5] Overall, there was a sense that the victim, the offender, and the community were not being well served by the current system, and that a paradigm shift to a fully punitive model was not the solution. It is with this backdrop that restorative justice, an alternative model, emerged in the juvenile justice system.

EVOLUTION OF RESTORATIVE JUSTICE

Restorative justice can be traced to practices and ideas that existed before the Middle Ages. Before the development of systems of law, victims and their families played a significant part in determining the punishment for the offender. Once formal justice systems were instituted, however, the victim's role was reduced and the state assumed the role of the victim.[6] Contemporary interest in restorative justice was preceded by a number of developments in the 1970s and 1980s. Restitution, victim-offender mediation, the victims' movement, the emergence of informal neighborhood justice and dispute resolution techniques, new approaches to human relationships and equity affected by the women's movement, and the peace and social justice movements all affected the reemergence of restorative justice.[7] Restorative justice has also been influenced by the balanced approach that Maloney, Romig, and Armstrong advocated.[8] Instead of dealing only with the offender, the balanced approach acknowledges and includes all three clients in the juvenile justice system: the offender, the victim, and the community.[9]

In addition, the restorative justice movement has been affected by Braithwaite's theory of "reintegrative shaming."[10] Braithwaite discusses the ideas of crime, shame, and reintegration. According to Braithwaite, loving families demonstrate this behavior regularly. These families are highly effective agents of social control in most societies that can impose punishment while maintaining respect for each other.[11] In this model, the community informally condemns the wrongful acts or behavior of the offender, but also provides opportunities to reintegrate the offender into the community.[12]

Shaming and reintegration, however, occur sequentially as opposed to simultaneously. Unlike stigmatization in which there is no attempt to reconnect the offender with the community, reintegrative shaming is a finite period of time that ends with forgiveness. In the process, efforts are made to support bonds of love and respect throughout the shaming period.[13] In his pioneering work, Braithwaite advocates principles of justice that are consistent with restorative justice. The inclusion of the victim in the restorative justice model was a result of deliberate actions and a federal commitment to recognize the role of victims in the system.

The Victim Movement

During his first term of office, President Clinton prioritized victims' rights as part of his public policy agenda and advocated an amendment to the Constitution guaranteeing their rights.[14] Victim and witness programs had been established in the 1970s, and a victims' bill of rights was part of legislation that many states adopted beginning in the 1980s. Victims' rights groups mobilized and lobbied their state governments demanding a voice in the process. In many states, legislators amended the state constitution and drafted new language and victims' rights amendments that guarantee victim participation in the criminal justice process.[15] The important role of the victim has even been recognized by the courts that have upheld the right of victims to make impact statements at sentencing hearings.[16]

The emergence of the victim as an active participant in the juvenile justice and adult systems has transcended victim impact statements at sentencing or dispositional hearings and evolved into a more active role in victim-offender conferences and mediation. In some states, these changes have occurred through legislation that mandates juvenile courts to involve victims in the process in the same ways that they are involved in the adult system.[17] In the restorative justice model, crime or delinquency is perceived as harmful behavior, and "justice" is a way to reduce the harm that the crime caused. This idea of repair necessitates significant involvement of the individuals who were harmed by the offense in the justice system.[18]

Characteristics of Restorative Justice

Restorative justice is concerned with three specific concepts: offender accountability, competency development, and community protection. In this model, the offender, the victim, and the community are equally important. Restorative justice places certain obligations on all the relevant parties. Furthermore, there is an implicit understanding that rehabilitation cannot succeed until the offender recognizes the harm that he or she has caused victims and communities and tries to make amends or compensate for those wrongdoings.[19] In addition, those who were injured by the harm have to be fully engaged in the criminal justice processes.[20] With offender accountability, the offender is required to either repay or restore losses to the individual victim and to the community These actions can take many forms. For example, the offender may write letters of apology, pay monetary compensation, or engage in volunteer work for the victim or the community.

In conjunction with accountability, youth who enter the juvenile justice system are expected to leave the system better equipped to succeed as productive and responsible citizens. Restorative justice operates on the belief that the youth will undergo some competency development during his or her involvement in the juvenile justice system. Services for youth may include education, drug and alcohol treatment, and vocational and counseling programs.

The third dimension focuses on community protection, and it necessitates that attention be equally directed toward public safety and security. It is the responsibility of the juvenile justice system to protect the public from juveniles who have been referred to the court and to maintain an environment in which conflicts can be addressed peacefully.[21] In this way, the community is an active participant in preventing and addressing delinquent behavior. When a youth has successfully completed the restorative justice process, other rituals may signify his or her reintegration in the community. For example, some jurisdictions formally participate in reengagement activity by inviting a youth who has successfully completed a restorative justice program to be a member of a teen court jury in the future.[22]

Restorative justice differs from both the original juvenile court orientation and the more contemporary punitive orientation. It represents a significant departure from the traditional juvenile court philosophy. The first juvenile court was based on an individual treatment model. In this model, a youth was perceived as "sick" and in need of "treatment." Routinely, that treatment required juveniles to participate in some type of counseling program, remedial services, or recreational programs.[23] The majority of the youths were placed on probation, but some were sent to institutions designed to offer treatment and restraint. Theoretically, each disposition was made in the "best interests" of the juvenile.[24] By contrast, restorative justice does not exclusively focus on the juvenile offender. Its principles support parity: offender, victim, and the community are equals.

Restorative justice differs from the retributive or punitive model that characterized juvenile justice in the 1990s. Retributive justice is often associated with a "get-tough" philosophy for juvenile offenders, and it is consistent with the Classical School of criminology, which views offenders as needing swift, sure punishment.[25] For example, retributive justice typically focuses on deciding whether the offender is guilty and then applying the punishment through an adversarial process. By contrast, restorative justice focuses on a problem-solving approach and attempts to determine what should occur through a dialogue between the offender and the victim, while following a negotiation model. It is through the relationships among offender, victim, and the community that the conflict can be resolved.[26] Retributive justice views crime or delinquency as an instance of law violation or a violation of the authority of the government. Restorative justice views criminal behavior in terms of its injury to victims, communities, and offenders.[27] In that sense, restorative justice is more concrete; crime is against a person or a community.[28]

In short, proponents of restorative justice contend that it is a departure from both the individual treatment model and the retributive punitive model, which they characterize as insular and one-dimensional. According to Bazemore and Day, their insularity is demonstrated by their focus on only the offender, and their one-dimensionality is manifested in their failure to deal with the community's different interests.[29] Furthermore, advocates of restorative justice perceive it as a way to preserve the juvenile court. With critics advocating the abolition of the juvenile court, restorative justice offers an alternative to redesign the existing court in which "juvenile justice reflects community justice."[30]

Before we examine some examples of restorative justice programs for juveniles, it is helpful to review the events that transpired in juvenile justice.

Models of Juvenile Justice

During the 1980s and early 1990s, juvenile crime and juvenile arrest rates were steadily increasing. In response, legislators throughout the United States reacted with a series of get-tough laws that targeted youth for severe sanctions. This included lowering the age for transfer of youth to criminal court, increasing the number of offenses that qualified youth for transfer, limiting juvenile court judges' discretion, granting more power and authority to prosecutors, and incarcerating youth in adult institutions. These reactive, punitive policies threatened the original intent of the juvenile justice system and changed attitudes toward youth.[31] The ideals of rehabilitation and treatment were eclipsed by retribution and punishment, and the best interests of the child were replaced with the best interests of society and concern for public safety.

At the same time that these reactive policies were polarizing the views and ideologies on juvenile justice (e. g., rehabilitation versus retribution), emergent efforts were seeking to balance treatment and punishment.[32] Some policy makers recognized that the juvenile court's mission to intervene in the lives of youth and to help them overcome delinquency could be consistent with goals of restoring the community and responding to the victims of crime. The concept of restorative justice offered elements for a new model of juvenile justice.

In their study of juvenile justice reform, Bazemore and Schiff found that "restorative justice by the mid-1990s had become surprisingly popular with administrators and policymakers in a number of jurisdictions."[33] They also noted,

> The restorative justice focus on the extent to which harm is repaired, and the extent to which communities increase their capacity to respond to crime and conflict, seemed to offer a broader framework that challenges the role of punishment and treatment as the primary currencies of intervention.[34]

This model recognizes three primary "stakeholders" in the restorative process—victim, offender, and community—and emphasizes strategies that repair the harm to victims and communities, while holding youthful offenders accountable to both and also intervening to improve the youths' skills and competencies.[35] The idea is that all three parties to the harm receive balanced attention. The restorative concept sees crime as a harm to victim, community, and offender that needs to be repaired rather than a violation of law that needs to be punished.

The BARJ Project

As early as 1977, the Office of Juvenile Justice and Delinquency Prevention (OJJDP) recognized that juvenile restitution was a promising intervention that held youth accountable while reducing recidivism and, therefore, as a strategy, warranted further development.[36] In 1992, with a grant to Florida Atlantic University, OJJDP charged a "consortium of national juvenile justice experts" to develop a comprehensive plan that would incorporate the goals and elements of restitution into a systemwide approach to juvenile justice.[37] This initiative focused on community-based programs that incorporated principles of the restorative justice philosophy and balanced community safety, youth accountability, and opportunities for competency development for juveniles.[38] The initiative is known as the Balanced and Restorative Justice Project (BARJ).[39]

Contrary to the view that BARJ was a "repackaging" of the traditional treatment model, the BARJ approach required "new performance objectives; new priorities for intervention; and a new view of the role of offenders, victims, and the community."[40] The BARJ Project identified a new philosophy, principles, values, and mission for juvenile justice and underscored the importance of shifting the juvenile justice system away from the debate between rehabilitation and retribution and toward a restorative model. By the mid-1990s, 24 states "had adopted or were examining ... the balanced approach or restorative justice model."[41] By 2004, "virtually every state (was) implementing some aspect of the restorative justice principles."[42]

Pennsylvania BARJ

Pennsylvania was one of the states that initially recognized the principles of restorative justice in its "purpose clause" for the juvenile justice system and adopted the BARJ model.[43] In the mid-1990s, three demonstration sites were selected by the BARJ Project to receive "technical assistance" in "implementing major systemic change in accordance with the BARJ model": Dakota County, Minnesota; West Palm Beach County, Florida; and Allegheny County, Pennsylvania.[44]

In 1995, Pennsylvania amended its Juvenile Act to "envision new roles" for court and probation staff as well as for victims, offenders, and the community.[45] In 2000, and again in 2002, surveys were conducted to determine the extent of implementation and the outcomes of BARJ initiatives. The most prevalent programs that were established in the state included the following: community service, victim notification, competency development, victim-impact statements, and restitution projects.[46] In addition, 61 of 67 counties had established new positions (e. g., Community Justice Officers) or redefined old ones to integrate restorative principles in department policies and operations.

By identifying a commitment to "balanced attention" and accountability, the Pennsylvania approach defined a juvenile crime as incurring "an obligation to the victim and community."[47] This includes the opportunity for victims to have an active role in all stages of the proceedings and it requires the juvenile justice system "to develop community service options that are valued by communities and crime victims."[48]

While acknowledging initial staff resistance to BARJ implementation in Allegheny County, Pennsylvania (which includes Pittsburgh), Seyko concluded that probation officers have learned new skills, formed "new partnerships with community organizations," established specialized programs, and instituted "innovative projects."[49] In her study of Pennsylvania probation departments, Blackburn concluded that implementation has not yet been fully achieved, but the goals and principles of BARJ have been recognized and are being integrated into daily operations.[50]

BARJ in Other States

As described for Pennsylvania, many states revised their legislation to adopt restorative justice principles and incorporate BARJ components into their juvenile justice systems. Similar to Pennsylvania, in Idaho, the Juvenile Corrections Act of 1995 established a balanced approach in responding to juvenile offenders:

> The legislative intent ... states that the "court shall impose a sentence that will protect the community, hold the juvenile accountable for his actions and assist the juvenile in developing skills to become a contributing member of a diverse community.[51]

The Idaho model includes a continuum of juvenile programs that emphasizes community involvement in prevention and early intervention. Restorative principles are evident in the philosophy and goals of the Department of Juvenile Corrections, which is defined as a "participatory" rather than a regulatory agency.[52]

In 1999, the General Assembly of Colorado amended its legislation to "improve the public safety by creating a system of juvenile justice that will appropriately sanction juveniles who violate the law and ... provide the opportunity to bring together affected victims, the community, and juvenile offenders for restorative purposes."[53] Although this legislation recognizes the importance of public safety, the state's legislators reemphasized that the juvenile justice system was still committed to the "best interests of the juvenile" and viewed this approach as an effective strategy for reducing the rate of juvenile recidivism.

In Illinois, where the first juvenile court was established in Cook County in 1899, the Illinois BARJ initiative was enacted in 1999. In describing the Illinois experience, Covey identified the importance of "inclusion" in developing programs and implementing the BARJ principles. By engaging community stakeholders and developing quality relationships, Illinois has focused on the sustainability of successful initiatives in reforming its juvenile justice system.[54] As in other states, Illinois has recognized the challenges of changing organizational culture and establishing new rules and roles that ensure that the elements of restorative justice are incorporated in the delivery of services to victims, community, and offenders.

The state of Maine has also faced these challenges in implementing restorative principles in its justice systems, but it has demonstrated a commitment to restorative justice by opening a Restorative Justice Center in Hallowell.[55] The Center brings a more visible profile to the restorative process and provides education and training, technical assistance, and evaluation of restorative approaches. When it was opened in 2004, the Center was "believed to be the first Center in the United States outside a university setting dedicated exclusively to promoting restorative justice."[56]

Police and Restorative Initiatives

Implementation of restorative justice is generally identified with state legislation, juvenile courts, and juvenile probation departments, but law enforcement agencies also recognize the value of restorative practices in responding to young offenders. In Woodbury, Minnesota (a suburb of St. Paul), police have implemented a community restorative justice strategy that includes victim-offender mediation and conferencing circles as components of a diversion program.[57]

The Woodbury program has developed a partnership between police and community volunteers who facilitate face-to-face meetings between victims and community members and the juvenile offenders to decide "how to repair the harm done and prevent future incidents."[58] Youth qualify on an individual basis and offenses range from felony assaults, school incidents, and drug cases. The most frequent types of offenses include alcohol, theft, and assault. Although the offense and attitude of the juvenile are important, Hines reports that "victim wishes and needs are the most significant factor in deciding how a case will be handled."[59]

In demonstrating that community restorative justice works, an evaluation of 600 cases determined that 85 percent of the "conference cases are successfully completed" and more than 90 percent of agreements are completed. In addition, 97 percent of restitution payments are paid in full and recidivism rates are 33 percent compared with 72 percent before the programs were implemented.[60] Over the nine years that the programs have been implemented, 90 percent of the victims report "satisfaction" with the process and outcomes; 86 percent of the youthful offenders and 91 percent of the parents report satisfaction with the Woodbury program.[61]

Restorative justice policing was also studied in New Zealand by Winfree, who identified elements of "reintegrative shaming" as a goal of specially trained police officers called youth aid officers (YAOs).[62] In describing the philosophical basis for the New Zealand police model of restorative justice, Winfree discussed the role of shaming and mutuality of obligation in intervening with youthful offenders and in using family group conferencing as a method of dispute resolution and sanctioning.[63] In 1989, the Children, Young Persons and Their Families Act formalized family group conferencing (FGC) as "the main decision-making body" in dealing with child welfare and criminal justice for youth.[64] FGC does not begin until after a youth admits to the offense or guilt has been determined. The YAOs are involved early in the process and "play an essential gatekeeping role in RJ [restorative justice] programs"[65] and "is also one of the key participants in the FGC."[66] As Winfree notes, the restorative justice process "involves formal policing structures" and reflects a nationwide commitment to the principles and practice of restorative justice and reintegrative sanctions.[67]

Conferencing determines the harm to victims and the reparations that need to be made. Some of the values and qualities of conferencing include effective communication, building relationships, assessment and analysis, managing and facilitating the conferencing process, self-awareness, and teamwork.[68] In their review of outcomes of dialogue-based restorative justice programs such as FGC, Umbreit, Vos, and Coates found "fairly high satisfaction responses from participants."[69] The opportunity to talk with the offender and explain the impact of the crime was identified as a very helpful component of conferencing. Similarly, McCold and Wachtel found that parents who participated in conferencing were more satisfied and reported a higher sense of fairness than parents of youth who were formally adjudicated.[70]

CONCLUSION

As this brief review indicates, restorative juvenile justice has been widely adapted and includes various practices that reflect the principles of reintegrative shaming, balanced attention, accountability, community protection, and competency development. As summarized by Bonta, "Restorative Justice invites the victims of crime and the community to participate in a process of dealing with offenders and repairing the harm caused by the offender."[71]

The U.S. Department of Justice has identified nine "promising practices" of restorative justice:

- Victim-Impact Statements (VIS)
- Restitution
- Sentencing Circles
- Community Service
- Family Group Conferencing
- Victim Offender Mediation (VOM)
- Victim Impact Panels
- Victim Impact Class
- Community Restorative Boards[72]

Research on the impact of participation in such programs and the outcomes of restorative justice practices indicates that victims, offenders, parents, and police officers express high levels of satisfaction.[73] In addition, Cullen and his colleagues have found that the public supports early intervention programs for youth and generally recognizes the value of prevention and intervention rather than incarceration: "the public supports early intervention strongly and prefers it to incarceration as a strategy to reduce offending."[74]

Restorative juvenile justice and elements of promising practices have been widely recognized and adopted; however, unrealistic expectations and system cooptation of restorative justice principles could diminish the effectiveness of the restorative justice model. Levrant, Cullen, Fulton, and Wozniak, for example, caution that even with good intentions, restorative justice programs can be "corrupted to serve less admirable goals and inter-est."[75] They discuss "unintended consequences" of restorative justice, including programs that are more symbolic than substantive and that serve only as a means to get tougher on offenders: "although restorative justice policies are being advocated as a benevolent means of addressing the crime problem, they may increase the punitiveness of the social control imposed on offenders."[76] Winfree also noted the concern that the progressive phi-losophy of restorative justice could be "co-opted by persons with non-progressive goals."[77]

Another issue that has been raised addresses the offender's participa-tion, which may not be entirely voluntary. For example, it is possible that participants must commit to the restorative justice conference and other protocols or return to the court where they face a more severe sanction. In this view, the juveniles may comply because of fear rather than any real desire to engage in a restorative justice program.[78] Like other kinds of diversion programs, restorative justice programs in Vermont mandate that offenders accept some responsibility before they attend a conference or meeting.[79] Programs in other states may require that the offenders admit their guilt before participating in victim-offender mediation.[80]

McShane and Williams describe another problem—that is, extended vic-timization. Restorative justice conferences potentially can result in the labeling of the offender's family because of the youth's delinquent act. The family may be perceived as equally criminal as, if not more criminal than, the youth who was involved in the delinquency. The result is even closer scrutiny of family members and less likelihood that the reintegrative processes will succeed.[81]

Victim involvement in the juvenile court process appears to be related to juvenile court judges' perceptions of the system. There is evidence of judicial support for restorative justice, particularly in the programs dis-cussed previously, but also there is concern that judges may be reluctant to embrace restorative justice because of their perceived conflict between victim and offender needs. Bazemore and Leip surveyed juvenile court judges and then conducted focus groups in four states with these courts. They found that judges who indicate a strong commitment to the rehabili-tative focus of juvenile court view this philosophy as incompatible with the goal of victim involvement in the system.[82] Because restorative justice is not technically a part of the courts themselves, judges exercise discretion in choosing to use it as a diversion alternative or in making dispositions that facilitate the referral of youths to restorative justice programs.[83] If the perception exists that such programs do not serve the needs of the of-fender, judges may refrain from actively implementing the restorative jus-tice model in their courts.[84]

In spite of these concerns, the principles and practices of restorative ju-venile justice present a viable paradigm for the juvenile justice system. By including stakeholders, developing comprehensive strategies, and balancing the interests and needs of victims, offenders, and community, the ideals and objectives of the BARJ Project offer a model that appeals to both con-servatives and progressives. This model transcends the rehabilitation or retribution debate and uses language and approaches that suggest more holistic, healing considerations. Restorative justice sanctions have the potential to connect accountability and positive social action. The goal is to restore the youthful offender as a responsible member of the community. The research on the effectiveness of restorative juvenile justice is promising, and the outcomes of adopting the BARJ mission are encouraging.

NOTES

1. Umbreit, 1995, p. 32.
2. Office of Juvenile Justice and Delinquency Prevention, hereafter OJJDP, 1997, p. 11.
3. OJJDP, 1997, p. 18.
4. OJJDP, 1997, p. 1.
5. OJJDP, 1997, p. 5.
6. McShane & Williams, 1992, p. 260.
7. Bazemore & Umbreit, 1995, pp. 301–302; OJJDP, 1997.
8. Maloney, Romig, & Armstrong, 1988.
9. Umbreit, 1995, p. 27.
10. Braithwaite. 1989.
11. Braithwaite, 1989, p. 56.
12. Braithwaite, 1989.
13. Braithwaite, 1989, p. 101.
14. Orvis, 2003, p. 1.
15. Orvis, 2003, pp. 2–3.
16. Orvis, 2003, p. 4.
17. Bazemore & Leip, 2000, p. 200.
18. Bazemore & Leip, 2000, p. 200.
19. OJJDP, 1997, p. 18.
20. Van Ness & Strong, 1997.
21. Bazemore & Leip, 2000, p. 200; OJJDP, 1997, pp. 13–14, 16.
22. Kirby-Forgays & DeMilio, 2005, p. 109.
23. Bazemore & Day, 1996, p. 4.
24. OJJDP, 1997, p. 5.
25. Arrigo & Schehr, 1998, p. 636.
26. Bazemore & Umbreit, 1995, p. 302; Umbreit, 1995, pp. 32–33.
27. Bazemore & Umbreit, 1995, p. 302.
28. Kirby-Forgays & DeMilio, 2005, p. 109.
29. Bazemore & Day, 1996, p. 4.
30. Bazemore & Day, 1996, p. 13.
31. Benekos & Merlo, 2000.
32. Merlo & Benekos, 2003.
33. Bazemore & Schiff, 2005, p. 10.
34. Bazemore & Schiff, 2005, p. 10.
35. Bradshaw & Roseborough, 2005.
36. Freivalds, 1996.
37. Bazemore & Umbreit, 1994, p. 1.
38. Bazemore & Umbreit, 1994; Freivalds, 1996.
39. See www.barjproject.org for details.
40. Bazemore & Umbreit, 1994, p. 2.

41. Freivalds, 1996, p. 1.
42. *Kaleidoscope of Justice*, 2004a, p. 6.
43. Seyko, 2001.
44. Freivalds, 1996, p. 1.
45. Blackburn, 2004, p. 2.
46. Blackburn, 2004, p. 4.
47. Juvenile Court Judges' Commission, 1997, p. 5.
48. Juvenile Court Judges' Commission, 1997, p. 10.
49. Seyko, 2001, p. 204.
50. Blackburn, 2004, p. 4.
51. Olsen & Callicut, 2004, p. 60.
52. Olsen & Callicut, 2004, p. 63.
53. House Bill 99–1156, 1999, p. 1.
54. Covey, 2004, p. 2.
55. *Kaleidoscope of Justice*, 2004b.
56. *Kaleidoscope of Justice*, 2004b, p. 6.
57. Hines, 2004.
58. Hines, 2004, p. 12.
59. Hines, 2004, p. 12.
60. Hines, 2004, p. 13.
61. Hines, 2004, p. 13.
62. Winfree, 2004, p. 190.
63. Winfree, 2004, p. 192.
64. Winfree, 2004, p. 197.
65. Winfree, 2004, p. 193.
66. Winfree, 2004, p. 197.
67. Winfree, 2004, p. 195.
68. Winfree, 2004, pp. 201–202.
69. Umbreit, Vos, & Coates, 2006, p. 4.
70. McCold & Wachtel, 1998.
71. Bonta, 1998, p. 1.
72. U.S. Department of Justice, n.d.
73. McGarrell, 2001; Rowe, 2002; Umbreit, Vos, & Coates, 2006.
74. Cullen et al., 1998, p. 187.
75. Levrant, Cullen, Fulton, & Wozniak, 1999, p. 6.
76. Levrant et al., 1999, p. 9.
77. Winfree, 2004, p. 208.
78. Karp, Sweet, Kirshenbaum, & Bazemore, 2004, p. 200.
79. Karp et al., 2004, p. 214.
80. Arrigo & Schehr, 1998, p. 637.
81. McShane & Williams, 1992, p. 268.
82. Bazemore & Leip, 2000, p. 219.
83. Bazemore & Leip, 2000, p. 217.
84. Bazemore & Leip, 2000, p. 200.

REFERENCES

Arrigo, B. A., & Schehr, R. C. (1998). Restoring justice for juveniles: A critical analysis of victim-offender mediation. *Justice Quarterly, 15*(4), 629–666.

Bazemore, G., & Day, S. E. (1996). Restoring the balance: Juvenile and community justice. *Juvenile Justice, III*(1), 3–14.

Bazemore, G., & Leip, L. (2000). Victim participation in the new juvenile court: Tracking judicial attitudes toward restorative justice reforms. *Justice System Journal*, 21(2), 199–206.

Bazemore, G., & Schiff, M. (2005). *Juvenile justice reform and restorative justice: Building theory and policy from practice.* Portland, OR: Willan Publishing.

Bazemore, G., & Umbreit, M. S. (1994). *Balanced and restorative justice.* Washington, D.C.: U.S. Department of Justice, Office of Juvenile Justice and Delinquency Prevention.

Bazemore, G., & Umbreit, M. S. (1995). Rethinking the sanctioning function in juvenile court: Retributive or restorative responses to youth crime. *Crime & Delinquency*, 41(3), 296–316.

Benekos, P. J., & Merlo, A. V. (Eds.). (2000). *Controversies in juvenile justice and delinquency.* Cincinnati, OH: LexisNexis/Anderson.

Blackburn, S. (2004). Spotlight on Pennsylvania: Balanced and restorative justice implementation making significant progress. *Kaleidoscope of Justice*, 4(1/2), 2–4.

Bonta, J. (1998). Restorative justice: An alternative to traditional criminal justice. *Research Summary*, 3(6). Ottawa, Ontario, Canada: Solicitor General. Retrieved August 1, 2006, from ww2.psepc-sppcc.gc.ca/publications/corrections/199811_e.asp.

Bradshaw, W., & Roseborough, D. (2005, December). Restorative justice dialogue: The impact of mediation and conferencing on juvenile recidivism. *Federal Probation*, 69(2), 15–21.

Braithwaite, J. (1989). *Crime, shame and reintegration.* Cambridge, England: Cambridge University Press.

Covey, S. (2004). The future of BARJ reform for Illinois: A vision for the future. *Kaleidoscope of Justice*, 4(3), 2–3.

Cullen, F. T., Wright, J. P., Brown, S., Moon, M. M., Blankenship, M. B., & Applegate, B. K. (1998). Public support for early intervention programs: Implications for a progressive policy agenda. *Crime & Delinquency*, 44(2), 187–204.

Freivalds, P. (1996). *Balanced and restorative justice project (BARJ).* Washington, D.C.: U.S. Department of Justice, Office of Juvenile Justice and Delinquency Prevention.

Hines, D. (2004). Conferencing and law enforcement: Woodbury community justice program. *Kaleidoscope of Justice*, 4(1/2), 12–14.

House Bill 99–1156. (1999). *Concerning a restorative justice program in the juvenile justice system.* Denver, CO: General Assembly of the State of Colorado.

Juvenile Court Judges' Commission. (1997). *Balanced and restorative justice in Pennsylvania: A new mission and changing roles within the juvenile justice system.* Harrisburg, PA: Pennsylvania Juvenile Court Judges' Commission, Commonwealth of Pennsylvania.

Kaleidoscope of Justice. (2004a). Balanced and restorative justice policy and practice in the United States. *Kaleidoscope of Justice*, 4(1/2), 6–10.

Kaleidoscope of Justice. (2004b). Restorative justice center opens in Maine. *Kaleidoscope of Justice*, 4(3), 6.

Karp, D. R., Sweet, M., Kirshenbaum, A., & Bazemore, G. (2004). Reluctant participants in restorative justice? Youthful offenders and their parents. *Contemporary Justice Review*, 7(2), 199–216.

Kirby-Forgays, D., & DeMilio, L. (2005). Is teen court effective for repeat offenders: A test of the restorative justice approach. *International Journal of Offender Therapy and Comparative Criminology*, 49(1), 107–118.

Levrant, S., Cullen, F. T., Fulton, B., & Wozniak, J. F. (1999). Reconsidering re-storative justice: The corruption of benevolence revisited? *Crime & Delin-quency, 45*(1), 3–27.

Maloney, D., Romig, D., & Armstrong, T. (1988). Juvenile probation: The bal-anced approach. *Juvenile and Family Court Journal, 39*(3), 1–57.

McCold, P., & Wachtel, T. (1998). *Restorative policing experiment: The Bethlehem Pennsylvania police family group conferencing project.* Pipersville, PA: Com-munity Service Foundation.

McGarrell, E. F. (2001). *Restorative justice conferences as an early response to young offenders.* Washington, D.C.: U.S. Department of Justice, Office of Juvenile Justice and Delinquency Prevention.

McShane, M. D., & Williams, F. P., III. (1992). Radical victimology: A critique of the concept of victim in traditional victimology. *Crime and Delinquency, 38*(2), 258–271.

Merlo, A. V., & Benekos, P. J. (2003). Defining juvenile justice in the 21st cen-tury. *Youth Violence and Juvenile Justice, 1*(3), 276–288.

Office of Juvenile Justice and Delinquency Prevention. (1997). *Balanced and re-storative justice for juveniles: A framework for juvenile justice in the 21st cen-tury.* Washington, D.C.: U.S. Department of Justice.

Olsen, M., & Callicutt, L. W. (2004, February). Juvenile justice collaboration in Idaho. *Corrections Today, 66*(1), 60–63.

Orvis, G. P. (2003). Balancing criminal victims' rights and criminal defendant rights. In L. J. Moriarty (Ed.), *Controversies in victimology* (pp. 1–14). Cin-cinnati, OH: LexisNexis/Anderson.

Seyko, R. J. (2001). Balanced approach and restorative justice efforts in Allegheny County, Pennsylvania. *The Prison Journal, 81*(2), 187–205.

Umbreit, M. S. (1995). Holding juvenile offenders accountable: A restorative jus-tice perspective. *Juvenile and Family Court Journal, 46*(2), 31–42.

Umbreit, M. S., Vos, B., & Coates, R. B. (2006). *Restorative justice dialogue: Evi-dence-based practice.* Center for Restorative Justice and Peacemaking. Retrieved August 1, 2006, from www.rjp.umn.edu.

U.S. Department of Justice. (n.d.). Restorative Justice On-Line Notebook. Retrieved January 15, 2007, from www.ojp.usdoj.gov/nij/rest-just/index.htm.

Van Ness, D, W., & Strong, K. H. (1997). *Restoring justice.* Cincinnati, OH: Anderson.

Winfree, L. T., Jr. (2004). New Zealand police and restorative justice philosophy. *Crime and Delinquency, 50*(2), 189–213.

CHAPTER 6

Juvenile Probation: Supervision or Babysitting?

Wesley A. Krause

For almost 80 years, juvenile courts have relied on probation to provide the mixture of supervision and sanction that will hopefully deter youth from greater involvement in delinquency. With almost half a million young offenders under supervision today, probation has become the cornerstone of those who advocate both rehabilitation and accountability. In fact, 4 out of every 10 delinquency cases ultimately end up in probation. Although some youth volunteer to serve a term of probation as part of a diversionary process that will eventually erase their record of wrongdoing, most are adjudicated by the court and enter into a formal contract of conditions overseen by a probation officer. And, although the number of young females serving probation has increased over the years, the profile of an average juvenile probationer at the turn of the century was a white or Hispanic male, 14 to 16 years of age who was adjudicated for a property offense.[1]

The decision to place a youth on probation is often difficult and the juvenile justice system must constantly assess its performance in terms of risks and consequences when someone in the community reoffends. After a delinquency hearing, when the judge is determining an appropriate disposition, he or she relies on the presentence report prepared by the probation department. The presentence report typically examines not only individual risk factors, such as mental health or a history of drug use or child abuse, but also protective factors that may insulate or support youths in their attempts to remain law abiding. This may include positive role models or involvement in sports and civic activities. In addition, judges will weigh the youth's offense history, school performance, record of violence, relationships with peers and family members, and participation in community organizations.

Realistically, the court may be swayed by external circumstances, such as the availability of beds in more secure facilities, access to treatment programs, and service in the community, as well as any interactions and personal experiences the reporting officer may have had with the offender or family members in the investigative process. Runaways, for example, are less likely to be put on probation than other status offenders and, ironically, those labeled "ungovernable" are more likely to be granted community supervision.

Once placed on supervision, the conditions of probation are not without controversy. Some people think that young offenders are coddled, while others see the tight control as invasive and counterintuitive to the nature of youth, as well as potentially oppressive to nonoffending family members. Conditions often include adherence to curfews and restitution, participation in community service, and attendance at victim-impact, drug treatment, or anger management programs. Some conditions have been challenged in terms of their constitutionality, including those that infringe on places where a youth might seek work, restrict the freedoms of family members (i.e., searches within the homes), and attempt to regulate clothing, music, associations, and language.

THE CHANGING MODELS OF JUVENILE PROBATION

Specific guidelines used in probation may have evolved over time, but there have always been attempts to develop models that reflect the spirit of the community and its concern for the well-being of children. Probation models in the state of California will be explored as an example of the various facets and turns taken by juvenile probation over the past 30 years.

The California Subsidy Program

In the late 1960s, the state of California faced a dilemma concerning its youthful offenders. The population of its juvenile institutions operated by the California Youth Authority was burgeoning. Youth crime was on the rise and the number of commitments to the Youth Authority reflected the increase in juvenile crime. However, the criminal histories of many of the youthful offenders sent to the Youth Authority by the juvenile courts throughout the state did not seem appropriate for the state training schools. The California Youth Authority was designed to accommodate youthful offenders deemed too delinquent, because of the serious nature of their offenses and criminal history, to be supervised by probation officers or housed in local county institutions.

Additionally, state legislators were impressed with the promise of recently developed concepts for supervision and treatment in the community.[2] The state conjectured that the lack of resources in most counties resulted in youth who might benefit from local correctional programs being sent to the state institutions. If the counties could improve the options available to the juvenile courts, the courts might be inclined to keep these youth in local programs. Then, the county probation departments would be able to offer enhanced local services and effective supervision for offenders entrusted to their care and control. Thus, California began a program of subsidizing county probation departments.

Counties received a subsidy amount based on their reduction in state commitments. The primary focus of the effort was (1) to reduce the ratio of juveniles to probation officer in caseloads and (2) to develop a wide range of innovative and hopefully effective interventions with high-risk, Youth-Authority-bound juveniles. The state would offer training and support to the counties in developing new approaches to supervision and treatment but would leave it to the individual counties to determine what approaches might be most effective in reducing commitments.

Caseload Ratios

Many counties adopted a caseload ratio of juvenile to probation officer of 30 to 1 in subsidized assignments. This ratio had become the accepted ideal caseload by most practitioners.[3] No research supported the effectiveness of supervision when caseloads were kept at this level, and few time and motion studies had been made of probation officers activities. Such studies would have suggested how much and what kind of work probation officers do and how long it takes to do it. No definitive studies indicated that a caseload of 30 would ensure lower recidivism rates, but the standard seemed to have consensus among practitioners in the field.

Treatment Programs

The state of California made no specific demands for treatment programs to be offered by probation officers working in these subsidized caseloads. Nor was the assignment of youth to the subsidized caseloads to follow any established procedure or standard. The youths were simply to be high-risk offenders who, absent this option, were in imminent danger of being sent to the Youth Authority. It did not mean that the juvenile court would have committed the youth on his or her most recent appearance before the court, but rather that the youth was on the path to a commitment because of a serious crime or a series of incidents that brought the youth to the attention of the juvenile court. The bottom line was that if counties did a good job of selecting youth for the program and developing innovative strategies, the commitment rate would be reduced and the state subsidy maximized.

The probation subsidy program operated successfully in California for more than a decade. Overall, the goal of significant reduction in institutional commitments was achieved. However, many believe that it was a combination of social, political, and economic factors that produced the reduction, not the effectiveness of the subsidized interventions. Probation departments faced many challenges to reducing commitment rates. The diversity of options for innovative supervision and treatment allowed great flexibility and creativity. However, little research was available to guide administrators in the selection of effective interventions.

Many treatment modalities from the world of popular psychology found their way into probation interventions. Therapeutic techniques from marriage and family counseling, such as Reality Therapy and Transactional Analysis, were adapted to probation programs. Simplified personality tests, such as the Firo-B and Luscher Color Test, were also adopted. They were used to match a probation officer to a set of juveniles with complementary personalities to facilitate rapport and the effectiveness of counseling. Administered by probation officers rather than licensed therapists, these tools were often poorly understood and improperly applied. The array of treatment options was diverse and innovative, but the effectiveness of these many new approaches received little study.

Status Offenders

The broad jurisdiction of the juvenile law also presented challenges. California, like most other states, has a juvenile court that has jurisdiction over youth who committed not only violations of laws but also violations of ordinances designed to control youthful behaviors deemed unacceptable by current social standards. These "status offenses" included such behaviors as truancy, curfew violations, running away from home, and general incorrigibility. In the late 1970s, major changes in the juvenile court law restricted the courts' authority over status offenders. But during the subsidy program, these offenders represented a large portion of the juvenile court cases and probation caseloads and as much as 60 percent of the juvenile hall population.[4] These cases often represented the most difficult cases for probation officer.

As might be expected from the incorrigible behavior that brought them to the attention of the juvenile justice system, these juveniles defied parents, educators, probation officers, and juvenile court judges. They were uncooperative with treatment efforts and frequently ran away from their homes and residential programs. The status offender was seen as the "incipient delinquent." It is believed that status offenses and criminal delinquency are strongly related. For many juveniles, incorrigibility and other status offenses are among many delinquent behaviors that will be exhibited throughout adolescence.[5] Failure to redirect the behavior of a status offender ultimately results in escalating delinquency and serious crime.

During these years, much of the available resources of juvenile probation agencies were devoted to addressing the issue of incorrigibility. As the subsidized caseloads reached their maximum, filled in large part by these difficult-to-manage juveniles rather that highly criminal youth, the resources available to supervise juveniles who had committed serious offenses were significantly diminished.

Intensive Supervision

The more intensively a youth was supervised, the more likely that the probation officer would discover minor violations. Some action on these minor violations was expected. After all, these juvenile were deemed high risk and placed on these special caseloads to control significant delinquent behaviors, protect the community, and protect the juvenile from him or herself. As often as not, the action taken for a violation of probation was detention in a juvenile facility, return to court for a modification of the courts orders, and, ultimately, commitment to the California Youth Authority. The result would be a tendency for intensive supervision probation (ISP) to increase commitments to the Youth Authority. This phenomenon associated with reduced caseloads and intensive supervision would be explored and better understood in research conducted by Petersillia and Turner nearly a decade later when ISP was implemented as a strategy in the control of probation caseloads that had become predominately populated with high risk felons.[6]

The End of Treatment

California abandoned the subsidy program following rising crime rates, political conservatism, and the implementation of determinate sentencing in 1977. It remains a controversial program. Although some maintain that it was successful in reducing state commitments, others question the effectiveness of the community corrections programs that were developed. The demise of the innovative treatment programs was hastened by Martinson's famous 1974 article, "What Works?" Martinson is attributed with the sound bite "nothing works" in corrections. In reality, what he said was "the represent array of correctional treatments has no appreciable effect—positive or negative—on rates of recidivism of convicted offenders."[7] In subsequent publications, Martinson modified his position finding that some correctional treatments did have an appreciable effect. The political wind was blowing in a more conservative direction, however, and the "nothing works" sound bite worked for the new public policies emphasizing incarceration, just desserts, and abandonment of the concepts of correctional treatment and rehabilitation.[8]

Lessons of the Subsidy Program

The California Subsidy Program is offered as an example of a departure from traditional supervision in community corrections. It demonstrates many of the problems that lead to disappointment if not total failure in the implementation of innovative supervision practices. Some of the lessons from subsidy probation follow:

- Probation treatment and supervision are broad, poorly defined concepts among its practitioners. The lack of uniformity reduces confidence in the community corrections by the public and other criminal justice practitioners. The implementation of probation services varies over time and geography, constantly changes with administrative philosophies, and increases and decreases in funding, regional priorities, and political influences.

- Quantity of contact alone may increase the discovery of minor misbe-
  haviors and occasionally uncover criminal activities but by itself will not
  significantly deter undesirable behaviors.
- The use of new and innovative programs not built on a theoretical foundation appropriate to the corrections environment and tested with evaluation research is unlikely to provide positive results.
- There is no "ideal" caseload size. Some offenders do better with minimal contact and, in fact, may be influenced negatively by interventions
  intended to reduce criminality. At the other extreme, some habitual and
  serious offenders require intensive interventions to ensure a meaningful
  level of community protection. Between the two extremes, when the
  intervention is appropriate to the offender's needs and the individual
  has motivation to change, it works. The size of the caseload is a matter
  of determining what interventions are to be offered and to how many,
  and how much time it will take an officer to deliver the required
  services.
- A phenomenon known as "net-widening" is likely to occur when an
  enhanced supervision program is implemented. Absent an effective controlling policy and effective practices to make the policy work, many of
  the individuals selected for an enhanced supervision program will likely
  be those who did not need it in the first place. Traditional sanctions,
  such as incarceration, will continue to be applied to many of the individuals for whom the program was designed.

SURVEILLANCE AND JUVENILE PROBATION

Can surveillance alone deter delinquent behavior? Let's "do the math"
on intensive supervision probation. Taking the old ideal standard of 30
cases, what portion of a juvenile's life is affected by the probation officer's
supervision? A probation office probably works a standard 40-hour week,
but after subtracting off-task hours (including vacation, sick days, meetings, coffee breaks, and so on), the average probation officer has less than
30 hours of on-task time. This leaves one hour per week for each juvenile.
And this time would include the time to travel to the juvenile's home or
school, assuming not all of the interactions between officer and offender
occur in the probation office. That hour, amounts to less that 1 percent of
the juvenile's waking hours, leaving 99 percent of the youth's life to be
influenced by parents, school, friends, and even the media or other enter-
tainment options (like video games). Some of the juvenile's activities that
occur in that 99 percent may be reported to the officer by parents or
school officials. Parents and other positive adults in the juvenile's life may
reinforce some of the directives and treatment programs provided by the
probation officer. Much time is left, however, for the undeterred influence
of delinquent peers and for negative behaviors that likely will go undetected. Deterrence is more about the probability of getting caught than
the severity of consequences. For most juveniles, even those under

intensive supervision programs, the opportunity to do something and get away undetected is much greater than the probability of getting caught and suffering a consequence. Delinquency is associated with risk-taking and, here, the risk is minimal.

Setting a New Supervision Standard—The Wisconsin Model

In the late 1970s, the Wisconsin Department of Probation and Parole was seeking funding to support the magic 30 caseload ideal. Their legislature questioned the basis for this caseload standard and set the department on a task of defending requests for staffing of probation and parole services. The research and program development that followed would create such a defendable and logical model of probation services that it would be adopted by the National Institute of Corrections as a model for all probation and parole services across the country.[9]

The model first attacked the question of who should receive intensive probation supervision. Using actuarial models, much like an insurance company would employ to determine automobile insurance premiums for different drivers, the Wisconsin team developed an offender classification system that differentiated between probationers unlikely to succeed while on probation and those who were very likely to succeed. By analyzing variables believed to be correlated with criminal behavior and other problematic behaviors associated with probation violations, the researchers developed a classification instrument that predicted which offenders within the total probation population were most likely to fail.

These individuals were designated as being at high risk of further criminal behavior and in high need of interventions to change conditions in their lives. They were assigned to "maximum" supervision caseloads for which officers would supervise a relatively small number of offenders. Those with a lower probability of recidivism, but still more likely than not to have some problems, would receive "regular" supervision on caseloads for which officers would supervise a much larger number of juveniles and have much less contact with them. A third category included probationers whose risk and need assessment predicted a very low probability of recidivism. These individuals would be assigned to "minimum" supervision caseloads for which a single probation officer might supervise well over a hundred cases and have little contact with the any of the juveniles.

The Wisconsin team recognized that supervision was not only about the quantity of supervision and the frequency of contacts, but also about the quality of those contacts. If probation was to be effective, different offenders who presented different problems would require variations in the approach to supervision. Some high-risk offenders, who were committed to a criminal lifestyle, did not suffer from a mental deficiency or handicap, and drug habituation was not a significant factor in their offending. For these offenders, treatment was unlikely to be effective. Setting limits and providing surveillance and control was necessary to reduce the recidivism in this group and to protect the community from their criminal behavior. Other offenders did suffer from mental illness or handicap and yet others suffered from drug addiction. For both of these groups, addressing their problems through effective treatment options could reduce recidivism. A third group represented the largest portion of the probation population. These were situational offenders, that is, individuals who usually were not inclined to associate with delinquent peers or to commit delinquent acts. Because of a set of influences or circumstances in their lives, however, they did commit a crime. For these individuals, intensive supervision and most treatment programs were unnecessary. With minimal contact and little treatment, this group could fulfill their obligations to the court and successfully complete probation.

The question remained, how large would these different caseloads be? The Wisconsin team analyzed the amount of time a probation officer actually had to supervise offenders. As discussed before, this amounted to substantially less than a 40-hour workweek. The Wisconsin researchers looked at how much time it took for a probation officer to complete various tasks, such as home contact, verification of school attendance, interviews with parents, dispositional reports, and so on. By developing a caseload plan for each offender that was based on the assessment of risks and needs and the classification of treatment needs, the probation officer could determine what kind of activities would be required to effectively supervise an individual. From the analysis of the time it took to complete these various tasks, it would be possible to determine the amount of time that a case would require. When this process was applied over the whole range of cases, the number of officers required to effectively supervise all of the probationers under the department's control could be determined.

The Orange County "Discovery"

Orange County, California, was one of the first counties to fully embrace the Wisconsin model. During the 1990s, this department embarked on a thorough exploration of the recidivism rates of its juvenile probationers. Based on the findings of preceding cohort studies, the Orange County researchers believed that only a small portion of juveniles who come to the attention of the Juvenile Justice System went on to become habitual offenders. Furthermore, they believed that these high-risk repeat offenders consumed the majority of the department's resources and committed a large portion or all juvenile crimes.

Their findings became known as the "Eight Percent Problem."[10] The research team discovered that approximately 8 percent of all juveniles entering the juvenile justice system over a given time would go on to become serious habitual delinquents. One-quarter would have more than one or two additional arrests, but their delinquent careers would fade away. Two-thirds of the juveniles arrested and referred to the probation department would never be arrested for another offense. As had been found in Wisconsin (and in other similar studies), the majority of "juvenile delinquents" were adolescents who, because of a set of circumstances, made poor choices over a relatively brief period of time and then would move on to make better decisions.

DOES SUPERVISION MAKE A DIFFERENCE?

If the majority of juvenile offenders referred to probation departments are unlikely to commit further offenses, is this a glowing endorsement of the effectiveness of probation supervision? In an informal and unpublished survey of juvenile shoplifters arrested for the first time, the choice of official response appeared to have little or no impact on recidivism rates. In the late 1980s, a supervising probation officer in a southern California county probation department responsible for diversion programs conducted a survey of dispositions and recidivism rates among first-offense juvenile shoplifters. The dispositions of the cases were the result of individual officer judgment and discretion among 15 probation officers. Some cases were submitted to the juvenile court for formal adjudication, some were given a program of informal supervision without going to court, and some were counseled and released or assigned to community service. A large group was sent through an educational program designed to raise awareness of the impact of shoplifting on victims and the community. The supervising officer also selected a sampling of cases and simply set them aside without further contact or intervention. After a year, a search was done for subsequent offenses committed by each of these juveniles. Across the board, only 5 percent of the juveniles had been arrested on a new offense. Is it possible that for most juvenile offenders, supervision serves no purpose?

Diversion Programs

In the early 1990s, this same department (and supervising probation officer) developed a community diversion program for first-time juvenile offenders. The program called Youth Accountability Boards allowed a panel of community volunteers to meet with offenders and their parents and resolve minor offenses completely outside of the juvenile justice system. What consequences and supervision came from these boards were administered completely by community volunteers, not the probation department. The program was highly successful with these first-offense youth. More than 90 percent completed their contract with their community board, and recidivism studies revealed that fewer than 10 percent were rearrested over a one-year follow-up period.[11]

Labeling Youth

These informal studies certainly can't be cited as proof that probation supervision has no effect on many young offenders. But, it is pause for thought. If, as found in the Orange County, California study, two-thirds of youth referred to the juvenile justice system do not reoffend, then perhaps their success has little or nothing to do with the intervention they received regardless of whether that intervention is minimal or intensive. In fact, it is possible that there may be a reverse effect. Some theories of delinquency, notably "labeling" theory, suggest that exposure of low-risk

youth to the intensive interventions of the juvenile justice system may stig-
matize the juvenile and increase the probability of further delinquent
behavior.[12]

A study prepared by Lowenkamp and Latessa for the National Institute
of Corrections in 2004 discouraged the practice of exposing low-risk
youth to intensive interventions and punitive sanctions. Their meta-
analysis strongly suggests that such practices would likely increase recidivism in this group. Placing nondelinquent youth in an environment in
which they will associate with delinquent individuals is not a good idea.
Nor is it a good idea to place them in a highly structured, restrictive
program that would "disrupt the factors that make them low-risk."[13]

In the world of criminal justice (especially with today's crime control
mandate), it is difficult if not impossible to study the effect of doing nothing. The emphasis in community corrections today is concerned with protecting the public and holding offenders accountable.[14] However, if it is
true that, for the majority of juvenile offenders, probation supervision has
no positive effect on their future delinquency (and for many may be negative), then probation interventions are little more than babysitting. It is a
waste of probation resources that could be better used for that one-third
of juvenile offenders who likely will commit one, two, three, or many
more crimes.

Diversion programs are still a viable option for many low-risk offenders.
Diversion may be described as any processing of minor juvenile offenses
that does not involve the juvenile court and may, as described with the
Youth Accountability Boards, entirely remove the processing of the
offender from the juvenile justice system. Such programs avoid the stigma
of delinquency adjudication, may involve the victim and community members, and save time and money by reducing the burden on the court
system. In the long run, they are an exercise of "wise restraint."[15]

EFFECTIVE INTERVENTION

An important question to ask is how can we tell, from his or her first
encounter with the juvenile justice system, whether a juvenile is likely to
become a serious or habitual delinquent. If we could identify this high-risk
group, what is the efficacy of probation services for those juveniles who
pose such a serious threat to their communities? Are effective interventions
available or is this just more expensive babysitting?

The "Scarce Resource" Approach

In 1995, the Office of Juvenile Justice and Delinquency Prevention
(OJJDP) published a guide for juvenile justice practitioners outlining a
comprehensive strategy for serious, violent, and chronic juvenile offenders.
The guide recognizes that "scarce resources are often wasted on non-
career juvenile delinquents who are unlikely to commit further offenses
because they are at the end of their short offending span."[16] The guide

concentrates on that small group of juveniles, representing perhaps 10 percent of the total cohort of youthful offenders entering the juvenile justice system each year, who will become serious, habitual delinquents.

Prevention Programs

In addition to the wasted resources mentioned above, other obstacles to effective intervention and tactics to develop effective programs are cited. First, most violent offending is not brought to the attention of juvenile justice authorities. Second, when it is brought to their attention it is often toward the end of the offending career. For the vast majority of these youth, the first arrest for a serious or violent crime occurred "years after their initiation into this type of behavior."[17] Although prevention programs are more desirable than interventions, to be effective, they must attempt to reduce risk factors that over time lead to delinquency. Intervention programs must target career offenders early. They must be comprehensive in nature, addressing multiple risk factors. Effective intervention must be long-term to overcome the negative interactions of multiple risk factors. Finally, some violent and chronic offenders are simply too dangerous and represent too great a threat to their communities to be treated in the juvenile justice system. These individuals are better handled in the criminal justice system.[18]

A Comprehensive Strategy

The Comprehensive Strategy recommended a seven-part approach beginning with prevention and moving through a series of graduated sanction. The full spectrum of interventions would include the following:

- Programs for all youth
- Programs for youth at greatest risk
- Intermediate interventions
- Intermediate sanctions
- Community confinement
- Training schools
- Aftercare[19]

According to the OJJDP, juvenile corrections is responsible for providing "treatment services that will rehabilitate the juvenile and minimize the chances for reoffending." To accomplish this, a continuum of effective services must be offered. But, are there effective interventions within the correctional inventory available to juvenile probation agencies?

Echoing previous findings and policies established by many probation agencies across the country, OJJDP urged differentiated interventions with juvenile offenders recognizing that "all juvenile offenders arrested by police do not need to be detained; all those placed on probation do no need intensive supervision; and all those committed to the custody of a

State correctional agency do not require secure care placement."[20] To differentiate between juvenile offenders and determine the level of supervision or type of placement, OJJDP supported the use of risk assessment instruments (which have grown significantly in accuracy and sophistication since the work of the researchers in Wisconsin two decades earlier). Additionally, they supported need assessment tools to help identify the specific type of interventions to be delivered.

Evidence-based Decision Making

In the shadow of Martinson's "nothing works" declaration, the new offering of interventions must be empirically studied and found to be effective for the specific types of offenders they would impact. In 2002, the National Center for Juvenile Justice (operating under a grant from OJJDP) enlisted contributions from the National Council of Juvenile and Family Court Judges, the American Probation and Parole Association, and the National Juvenile Court Services Association to develop the *Desktop Guide to Good Juvenile Probation Practices*. The guide begins with a rethinking of juvenile probation. The professional consensus recognizes a "more active, collaborative, results-oriented juvenile probation practice."[21]

The current philosophy of juvenile probation practices incorporates a large measure of public protection and juvenile accountability. It holds the probation agency accountable, stressing mission-driven practices and performance-based, outcome-focused programs.[22] The new probation practices address Martinson's allegations by applying the large body of research in juvenile interventions that was accumulated in the 1980s and 1990s (primarily as a result of funding for such research by OJJDP). Research into adolescence and development of delinquency supports the appreciation for the challenges of adolescence with its extraordinary physical, intellectual, emotional, and social growth.[23] Most individuals, however, survive the challenges of adolescence without serious behavioral issues. Again it is stressed that "a very small subsets of youth embark on serious delinquent careers."[24]

Research has enlightened practitioners with an understanding of risk factors that are associated with increased risk of delinquency. These factors are associated with individual attributes and traits and also with peers, family, school, and the community. Practitioners seek to develop programs that are effective in protecting the individual from these risk factors. The identification of protective factors and the effective delivery of them is a key to prevention. Effective deployment of protective programs involves the participation of many individuals and institutions affecting the lives of youth.

Effective parenting is of great importance. Supervision of a juvenile's activities and involvement in their activities along with love, caring, and family stability provide a protective environment and resistance to delinquency. Juvenile corrections has always included work with the family. The need for improving parenting skills and bolstering the positive influence of parents suggest that working with parents of juveniles on probation is as critical as working with the youth.

Schools are also important in the development of protective factors. Clear rules and consistent enforcement are important but so is reinforcement of positive behaviors. Teaching stress management, problem-solving, and self-control is important to the prevention of delinquency.[25] School-based probation programs can influence the kinds of programs delivered by educators and provide more contact and better monitoring of juveniles on probation.

Additionally, the community can provide protective factors. Positive opportunities, mentoring programs, and afterschool activities promote positive behavior and association with prosocial peers.[26] Probation agencies can work closely with community leaders to encourage the development of protective programs. In some cases, they may directly offer the services through such programs as day reporting centers where juveniles and their families may receive a variety of educational and family services not offered elsewhere by the schools or community.

A BALANCED APPROACH

The focus of probation today must not ignore offender accountability, victim restoration, or community service, but it is a balanced approach that concentrates on the oldest mission of probation—that is, helping people to change. This approach will involve interventions that address three primary areas of corrections work:

- Skill building: improving living, social, academic, and vocational skills
- Cognitive interventions: making fundamental changes in the way individuals think, solve problems, and make decisions
- Treatment: interventions for serious problems such as drug abuse or mental illness[27]

Cognitive Interventions

The first and third areas of work (skill building and treatment) are not new to corrections practitioners, although the strategies and programs to achieve those goals have evolved and broadened. But the concept of changing the way an individual thinks, solves problems, and makes decisions is something new and different. Past efforts to change behavior may have involved counseling, positive reinforcements, or punishments. Cognitive skill-building interventions and cognitive restructuring are based on the premise that thinking controls overt actions. The interventions target the thinking process to promote behavioral changes.[28] Unlike past interventions designed to change offender behavior—which were based on techniques practiced in other fields of work or based on beliefs rather than empirical evidence—a substantial research foundation supports the positive outcomes of such interventions when delivered by corrections practitioners to delinquent juvenile populations. Gornik describes the two-pronged approach for the National Institute of Corrections:

> There are two main types of cognitive programs: cognitive skills, and cognitive restructuring.
> **1. Cognitive skills training** is based on the premise that offenders have never learned the "thinking skills" required to function productively and responsibly in society. This skill deficit is remedied by systematic training in skills, such as problem solving, negotiation, assertiveness, anger control, and social skills focused on specific social situations, like making a complaint or asking for help.
> **2. Cognitive restructuring** is based on the premise that offenders have learned destructive attitudes and thinking habits that point them to criminal behavior. Cognitive restructuring consists of identifying the specific attitudes and ways of thinking that point to criminality and systematically replacing them with new attitudes and ways of thinking.[29]

The cognitive restructuring and cognitive skills approaches are complementary and can be combined in a single program. When practiced in a community model, resocialization can be enhanced and accelerated. Both cognitive strategies take an objective and systematic approach to change. Change is not coerced; offenders are taught how to think for themselves and to make their own decisions.

Cognitive corrections programs regard offenders as fully responsible for their behavior. Thinking is viewed as a type of learned behavior. Dishonesty and irresponsibility are the primary targets for change. Limit setting and accountability for behavior do not conflict with the cognitive approach to offender change—they support it.

Reinventing Probation

In the summer of 2000, the American Probation and Parole Association published a report urging all probation agencies to "reinvent probation" before critics of community corrections could capitalize on the general lack of faith in corrections service and hasten its demise. The report presented the "Broken Windows" model of probation. Based on the model that spawned the development of community policing, it called for a number of changes to make community corrections more accountable and responsive to public concerns. The report cited the failure of probation to protect the public. It criticized probation officers for ignoring violations of court orders and for hiding in their offices rather than working in their communities. The report noted a general lack of partnerships with law enforcement, treatment service providers, community organizations, schools, and victims.[30]

The Reinventing Probation Council focused primarily on accountability for both offenders and probation agencies, but they did not ignore the need for balance in probation casework. Specifically, they noted that the public wants from corrections not only safety from violent predators, accountability for offenses, and repair for damage done, but also education and treatment.[31]

Today, probation practitioners, both in juvenile and adult community corrections, are focused on the delivery of evidence-based practices. The Summer 2006 edition of *Perspectives*, the quarterly publication of the American Probation and Parole Association, was dedicated to evidence-based practices (EBP). Empirically tested programs are intended to answer the question posed by Martinson three decades ago: "What Works?" It is no longer acceptable to borrow techniques from other disciplines that seem intuitively suited to the practice of community corrections and report on their success with only anecdotal evidence. More difficult for probation practitioners, but necessary to stay on course with effective interventions, will be a movement away from programs that lack empirical evidence of effectiveness but are "politically correct" and therefore easily funded. Various versions of the Scared Straight Program and boot camps will have to pass out of corrections repertoire.

A New Generation of Treatment

The new generation of treatment options delivered in conjunction with the necessary control and surveillance aspects of supervision are guided by three principles. The first two already have been discussed: *risk* and *criminogenic need*. The risk principle requires matching levels of intensity of surveillance and treatment with the probability of continued criminal behavior. Risk assessment instruments have evolved in sophistication to assist practitioners in better identifying high-risk offenders. The criminogenic need assessment is somewhat different from past assessments in that it primarily addresses factors that, if changed, could reduce the probability of recidivism. Noncriminogenic needs may be changeable and could improve the offender's quality of life, but because they are not related to criminal behavior, they are not the primary concerns of corrections practitioners.

The third principle previously has not been a component of assessments, at least not in a formalized fashion. It is the *responsivity* principle. Responsivity refers to the delivery of treatment in a manner consistent with the ability and learning style of the offender.[32] It is an effort to match offenders and treatment much as educators would match teaching methods with the learning style of students. The recognition that offenders must be matched to an intervention is challenging. It requires corrections agencies to develop a full spectrum of programs designed to address low-risk to high-risk offenders and, additionally, to tailor the delivery of these programs to the receptivity and learning style of offenders. The reward for meeting this challenge is programs that work. And programs that work result in better public protection because juvenile offenders develop effective life skills, positive decision-making skills, and prosocial values.

CONCLUSION

To change juvenile probation from babysitting to meaningful supervision and intervention requires community corrections to grow and evolve from a field dominated by practices founded on belief and intuition and driven by political winds to one built on sound theoretical foundations and empirical evaluation. The growth process has been, and likely will continue to be, painful. Probation has for several decades suffered from inadequate funding. But, it has often lamented this handicap, wallowed in self-pity, and allowed fiscal and political obstacles to erode professionalism. As a result, probation has suffered, deservedly, from a lack of public confidence. The road to restoring the value of community corrections will require adherence to high professional standards of its programs and the practitioners who deliver those interventions.

NOTES

1. Puzzanchera, 2003.
2. Greene & Pranis, 2006.
3. Reinventing Probation Council, hereafter RPC, 2000.
4. San Bernardino County Probation, n.d.
5. Elrod & Ryder, 2005, pp. 396–401.
6. Petersillia & Turner, 1993.
7. Martinson, 1974.
8. Lipton, Martinson, & Wilks, 1975.
9. Baird, Heinz, & Bemus, 1979.
10. Kurtz & Moore, 1994.
11. Krause, 1994.
12. Lemert, 1967.
13. Lowenkamp & Latessa, 2004.
14. Griffin & Torbet, 2002.
15. Griffin & Torbet, 2002, p. 49.
16. Griffin & Torbet, 2002, p. 5.
17. Griffin & Torbet, 2002, p. 3.
18. Griffin & Torbet, 2002, pp. 5–6.
19. Griffin & Torbet, 2002, p. 8.
20. Griffin & Torbet, 2002.
21. Griffin & Torbet, 2002, p. 1.
22. Griffin & Torbet, 2002, p. 2.
23. Griffin & Torbet, 2002, p. 21.
24. Griffin & Torbet, 2002, p. 23.
25. Griffin & Torbet, 2002, p. 28.
26. Griffin & Torbet, 2002, p. 29.
27. Griffin & Torbet, 2002, p. 94.
28. Taymans & Jurich, 2000.
29. Gornik, 2003.
30. RPC, 2000.
31. RPC, 2000.
32. Gornik, 2003.

REFERENCES

Baird, S. C., Heinz, R. C., & Bemus, B. J. (1979). *Case classification/staff deployment project: A two year follow-up*. Madison, WI: Wisconsin Division of Corrections.

Elrod, P., & Ryder, D. (2005). *Juvenile justice: A social, historical, and legal perspective.* Boston MA: Jones and Bartlett.

Gornik, M. (2003). *Moving from correctional program to correctional strategy: Using proven practices to change criminal behavior.* Boulder, CO: National Institute of Corrections.

Greene, J., & Pranis, K. (2006). *Treatment instead of prison: A roadmap for sentencing and correctional policy reform in Wisconsin. Justice strategies.* Washington, D.C.: Drug Policy Alliance.

Griffin, P., & Torbet, P. (Eds.). (2002). *Desktop guide to good juvenile probation practices.* Pittsburgh, PA: National Center for Juvenile Justice.

Krause, W. (1994). *Memo to Chief Probation Officer.* San Bernardino, CA: San Bernardino County Probation.

Kurtz, G., & Moore, L. (1994). *8% problem study findings: Exploratory Research Findings and Implications for Problem Solutions.* Anaheim, CA: Orange County Probation Department.

Lemert, E. (1967). *Human deviance, social problems and social control.* Englewood Cliffs, NJ: Prentice Hall.

Lipton, D., Martinson, R., & Wilks, J. (1975). *The effectiveness of correctional treatment: A survey of treatment evaluation studies.* New York: Praeger.

Lowenkamp, C., & Latessa, E. (2004). *Understanding the risk principle: How and why correctional interventions can harm low-risk offenders. Topics in community corrections.* Boulder, CO: National Institute of Corrections.

Martinson, R. (1974). What works? Questions and answers about prison reform. *The Public Interest, 35*(Spring), 22–54.

Petersillia, J., & Turner, S. (1993). *Evaluating intensive supervised probation/parole: Results of a nationwide experiment.* Washington, D.C.: National Institute of Justice. (NCJ 141637)

Puzzanchera, C. M. (2003). *Juvenile delinquency probation caseload 1990–1999.* Washington, D.C.: Office of Juvenile Justice and Delinquency Prevention.

Reinventing Probation Council. (2000). *Transforming probation through leadership: The "broken windows" model.* New York: Center for Civic Innovation.

San Bernardino County Probation. (n.d.). *Annual reports 1970–77.* San Bernardino, CA: San Bernardino County Probation Department.

Taymans, J., & Jurich, S. (2000). Overview of cognitive-behavioral programs and their applications to correctional settings. *Perspectives,* Fall, 48–53.

CHAPTER 7

"You Can't Go Home Again": Disproportionate Confinement of African American Delinquents

John K. Mooradian

If you want to start an argument, all you have to do is solicit opinions about abortion, affirmative action, or American involvement in any war since 1945. Each of these issues has the power to polarize opinions and fire passionate debates. In the field of juvenile justice, the same goal can be accomplished by raising the topic of Disproportionate Minority Confinement (DMC).

DMC refers to the overrepresentation of minority youth in the juvenile justice system and implies that it is a problem. DMC is a controversial issue because it forces community members and juvenile justice professionals to consider issues of punishment and protection, under the deep shadow of race.

The National District Attorney's Association recognizes that prejudice, denial, fear, or a simple lack of information often lead to visceral responses when people are confronted with the issue of DMC.[1] Although the existence of disproportionate racial composition in juvenile justice settings has been empirically established, discussions of its causes, impacts, and resolution often stimulate steamy responses.

In recognition of the controversy surrounding DMC, this chapter attempts to combat prejudice, break denial, calm fears, and provide information that allows movement beyond a visceral response, to one that is more useful. This chapter focuses on African American youth in restrictive placements within the juvenile justice system. It outlines the breadth and depth of the problem, describes its human and systemic effects, charts what is currently known about its causes, and offers suggestions for reducing the imbalance.

RECOGNITION OF DISPROPORTIONATE MINORITY CONFINEMENT

DMC has been defined as a condition that exists when a racial or ethnic group's representation in confinement exceeds their representation in the general population.[2] DMC was officially recognized by the federal government in the 1988 amendments to the Juvenile Justice and Delinquency Prevention Act of 1974 (Public Law 93-415, 42 U.S.C. 5601 *et seq*).[3] Along with recognizing the problem, the federal government instituted a policy that required the states participating in the Title II, Part B, Formula Grants Program to reduce disproportionate confinement of African Americans, American Indians, Asians, Pacific Islanders, and Hispanics in any jurisdiction where it was found.[4]

In 2003, 59,000 minority youth were in residential placements across the United States, and they accounted for 61 percent of the incarcerated population.[5] The national aggregate data break down to show proportions of confined minority youth on a state-by-state basis. Table 7.1 shows that for every state with calculable data, except Hawaii, the ratio of detained minority youth to detained Caucasian youth exceeds 1.0. According to guidelines established by the Office of Juvenile Justice and Delinquency Prevention (OJJDP), a ratio greater than 1.0 indicates the presence of DMC.[6]

The predominant racial or ethnic minority group in juvenile justice settings is African American males. In fact, they made up 38 percent of the total of youth confined in 2003.[7] The Juvenile Justice and Delinquency Prevention Act of 2002 extended the concept of DMC to include minority *contact* with representatives of the juvenile justice system, rather than *confinement* alone.[8]

A review of official statistics from the the U.S. Census Bureau census, OJJDP, and the Federal Bureau of Investigation (FBI) indicates that African American youth are more likely than the general population to be arrested and processed by juvenile courts and to experience dispositions that involve out-of-home placement. These statistics are summarized in Figure 7.1.

African American youth account for 15 percent of the U.S. population between the ages of 10 and 17, but make up 25 percent of all juvenile arrests. Although they represent only 25 percent of the arrests, they make up 36 percent of the cases adjudicated by juvenile courts. They are responsible for 39 percent of the violent crimes reported by victims, but 49 percent of the juvenile arrests for violent crimes. The discrepancies continue to grow as the youth move through the system. The 36 percent of adjudications rises to 43 percent of out-of-home placements, 46 percent of public long-term placements, and 52 percent of the cases waived to criminal courts by juvenile courts. It has been estimated that one in seven African American males will be confined before his 18th birthday, while the estimate for European American youth is only 1 in 25.[9]

These statistics illustrate that African American male delinquents are more likely to be placed out of the home than their European American counterparts, and more likely to be escalated to more restrictive

Table 7.1.
State-by-State DMC, Ratio of Minority to White Rates of Youth Detained, 2003 (overall U.S. ratio 3:1)

State	Ratio	State	Ratio
Alabama	3.1	Montana	3.7
Alaska	5.2	Nebraska	5.5
Arizona	1.3	Nevada	1.7
Arkansas	2.5	New Hampshire	2.3
California	2.2	New Jersey	8.0
Colorado	2.5	New Mexico	1.6
Connecticut	6.9	New York	3.7
Delaware	7.4	North Carolina	3.6
Florida	1.6	North Dakota	5.5
Georgia	2.8	Ohio	3.9
Hawaii	0.6	Oklahoma	2.2
Idaho	2.1	Oregon	2.0
Illinois	4.3	Pennsylvania	5.9
Indiana	3.3	Rhode Island	–
Iowa	3.8	South Carolina	2.5
Kansas	4.0	South Dakota	7.9
Kentucky	5.0	Tennessee	4.0
Louisiana	2.4	Texas	2.3
Maine	1.6	Utah	3.9
Maryland	3.2	Vermont	2.7
Massachusetts	5.6	Virginia	4.4
Michigan	4.4	Washington	1.6
Minnesota	6.9	West Virginia	4.5
Mississippi	3.0	Wisconsin	10.3
Missouri	6.4	Wyoming	2.9

Source: Snyder & Sickmund, 2006.

placements for relatively less serious offenses. Once a youth is placed out of the home, there is a higher likelihood that he will be confined again and again.[10]

Undoubtedly, different readers will react to these facts in different ways. One may be tempted to respond with anger over clear injustice. Another may feel comforted by the effort of the juvenile justice system to protect public safety. Someone else may secretly accept this as an example of what happens in inner-city communities, or as evidence that black youth are more dangerous than their white counterparts.

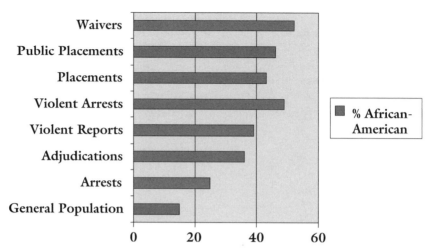

Figure 7.1. Overrepresentation of African Americans in Juvenile Justice
Source: Snyder & Poe-Yamagata, 1995.

Regardless of your reaction, or your concern for social justice, you might recognize that reducing DMC would bring practical benefits. The number of detained youth in the United States increased by 72 percent from 1985 to 1995, and 80 percent of this increase consisted of minority youth.[11] Because the greatest percentage of youth making up this increase were minorities, it is clear that reducing the number of minority youth in secure placements will significantly reduce the public costs associated with expensive confinements.

UNDERSTANDING DMC

The problem of DMC is complex and historical. DMC is complex because it draws attention to criminal behavior perpetrated by youthful offenders who happen to be black. It is historical because differential disposition of juvenile cases involving European American and African American youth has been identified as a long-standing problem of significant proportion,[12] and it extends historical trends in juvenile justice into the present.

The Role of Racism

Discussing DMC without considering the larger issue of racism would be like attempting to ignore the proverbial elephant in the living room. Racism has been described as an ideology that operates at the metalevel of social systems and pervades the American social ecology.[13] Racism consists of a belief that people of a different race are inherently inferior to one's own race, and it uses power structures to systematically disenfranchise, degrade, or divert resources from the subject group. For purposes of this chapter, racism may be thought of as taking two primary forms. Overt racism entails direct racial discrimination that is personally offensive, discriminatory, bigoted, and openly oppressive. It is evident in explicit statements, personal contacts, and stereotyped descriptors. Few observers imply that overt racism governs juvenile justice decisions or results in DMC,[14] but its total elimination as a relevant factor is in doubt.[15] Covert racism, which is akin to "institutional racism," is exceedingly oppressive in its effect because it is pervasive and much harder to detect, as well as restrain. Although covert racism can be deliberate, it often operates beneath the awareness of its perpetrators. In that sense, covert racism is doubly hidden. Covert racism is embedded in resource allocation, "benign" segregation, and imposition of dominant culture values. Observers of the juvenile justice system are more inclined to redefine this set of attitudes and behaviors as "unintentional discrimination,"[16] but clearly implicate it in discussions of DMC.

The complexity of DMC is connected to the issue of social class, which may crosscut racist attitudes or structures. The primary features of low socioeconomic status are poverty, deteriorating urban environments, limited family cohesion, and ineffective parental control. Perhaps unsurprisingly, these factors are correlates of delinquent and violent behavior.

Historical Roots of DMC

The roots of DMC reach back to what Platt called "the invention of delinquency."[17] Before the early nineteenth century, there was no systematic separation of juveniles from other criminals. When the rise of industrialization drew families to urban centers, children began to congregate in peer groups and become a greater social nuisance. Even if young people did not commit felonies, their troublesome behavior seemed to require external controls. To bolster parental and school authority, the new social status known as "juvenile" was constructed. Parents retained primary responsibility for controlling their children, but the doctrine of *parens patriae* was used to legitimate intercession by the state *in loco parentis* when the parents were seen as failures.[18] Once the state assumed authority over the lives of children, decisions could be made to remove minors from their family homes for purposes of individual rehabilitation and community protection.

This application of government power was motivated by concern for social treatment and social control. On one hand, there was a genuine interest in rehabilitating the wayward child.[19] These "child-savers" viewed the child as the helpless victim of society.[20] On the other hand, citizens had a right to feel safe and expected criminal behavior to be controlled. Then, as now, proponents of social treatment for the child, and proponents of social control for the protection of society, take sides on these issues. Instead of seeing them in opposition, however, it may be more useful to visualize an inextricable link (see Figure 7.2) that governs decisions about the placement of juveniles.[21]

It appears that a disparity in confinement rates across cultural groups has always existed. In the nineteenth century, the urban underclass was

Social Control

Social Treatment

Figure 7.2. Link of Social Treatment and Social Control
Source: Mooradian, 2003.

primarily composed of European immigrants who were seen as the "dangerous classes," and it was their children who were predominantly placed outside their family homes.[22] In twenty-first-century America, European Americans no longer occupy this social position, but African Americans and Latinos often do.

IMPACT OF DMC

DMC holds profound implications for individual juveniles and their families, as well as for service providers and the general public. The OJJDP administrator stated that an effective juvenile justice system should treat every offender as an individual and provide needed services to all.[23] He also noted that a persistent inequity in disposition of cases, especially when associated with race, masks individual difference, brings significant human consequences, and counters the goal of equal justice.

The Human Dimension

Statistical presentations and systemic descriptions certainly have their place in understanding DMC, but it might also be useful to consider the life of an individual juvenile named "Daron." He represents the typical African American youth in placement. His story emerged from an empirical investigation of DMC and clinical intervention with delinquents and their families.[24]

Daron is 15½ years old. For the past year, he's been in a campus-based residential facility, but he grew up in a large city about 50 miles away. His mother and grandmother visit him about once a month. His father is in prison and has been, on and off, since Daron was about three. His family is poor. They've experienced a lot of other stressors, including the shooting death of his cousin, his grandmother's hypertension and heart problems, arguments between Daron and his mother and his uncle, fights between Daron and his mother's boyfriend, and his mother's stress over trying to balance being a single parent and working part time in a small factory. Daron was adjudicated for his third felony, which was aggravated assault on another young man who made negative comments about Daron's deaf brother. The other two offenses on his record are auto theft (he took his mother's boyfriend's car after arguing with him) and assault and battery involving a fight at school. He went to detention for four weeks for the car theft, and spent nine months in a residential facility following the assault. Now that he's in his third placement, and almost two years of his life have been spent away from his family, he faces the strong possibility that he will be placed in a transitional program.

Pathways to Placement

In a study of 171 African American males like Daron, pathways emerged that explain multiple out-of-home placements.[25] This study took place in a large multisite private agency that operated court-ordered restrictive programs for state government.

Figure 7.3 shows the observed pathways to placement as a connection of variables that are significantly correlated, in appropriate temporal order across the columns.[26]

To interpret the diagram, look at the direction of the arrows and the valence $(+/-)$ of the connections. For example, the double-headed arrow between *Age at Intake* and *Single-Parent Family Type* shows that they exist in the same time frame and that they mutually affect each other. They are also negatively correlated, so youth from single-parent families are likely to be younger at intake into the juvenile justice system than youth from two-parent families. The arrow from *Age at Intake* to *Felony Offenses*, with its plus sign, shows that older youth are more likely to commit multiple felonies.

Some aspects of the model aren't surprising at all. Being locked up longer in the current placement and going home when confinement is finished, necessarily limit the total number of placements. Other aspects are a bit harder to grasp. Why, for example, does living in an urban environment show a directly negative effect on obtaining a successful release, while entering placement from home has a positive effect on program completion? And why doesn't the number of felony offenses increase the length of stay in the current placement or lead to more total placements? These results are surprising because they show that placement decisions aren't necessarily based on the culpability of the youth. Environmental and juvenile justice system factors come into play as well. Another puzzling finding is that youth with more prior placements actually have more highly functioning families. This may be the case because intervention actually helps stabilize these families by averting crises. Intervention can take many forms, however, and incarceration may not be the only way to help families manage their children.

Other aspects of the model are not as surprising as they are disturbing. Coming from a single-parent family directly increases the likelihood that a youth will accumulate multiple out-of-home placements. The experience of family tensions also has a direct negative effect on the child's chances of being returned home after placement. Perhaps support for families, especially single-parent households, would improve the chances that a youth can be retained rather than detained.

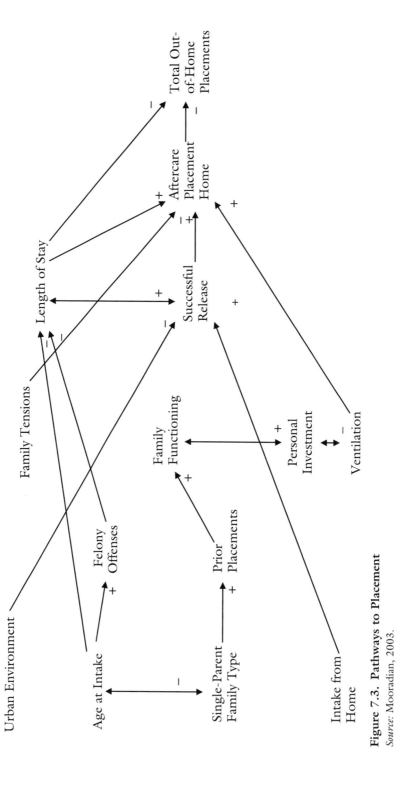

Figure 7.3. Pathways to Placement
Source: Mooradian, 2003.

In summary, there are notable pathways to multiple out-of-home placements for African American male delinquents. These include coming from poor, urban, single-parent families that experience multiple unresolved stressors. Although external intervention seems to stabilize these families while simultaneously controlling criminal opportunities and increasing the confidence of decision makers in the youth's ability to "go straight," options for intervention other than confinement should be tested. In the meantime, for Daron and his brethren, the life story seems to be ominously titled, "You can't go home again."

Causes of DMC

Several causes of DMC have been identified.[27] Among them are differential offending patterns, differential handling of minority youth, indirect effects of race, differential opportunities for prevention and treatment, and unintentionally discriminatory procedural rules.

Some studies indicate that minority youth are more likely to be involved in drug-related offenses,[28] become active in gangs,[29] and commit violent crimes.[30] Patterns of offending also vary by race. For example, white youth are more likely to commit sexual assault and arson, while black youth are likely to commit robberies and drug trafficking.[31]

Without critical thinking, incidence of crime may explain the problem. After all, "if you do the crime," you ought to "do the time," but it's important to remember that delinquency and confinement are two different things. In fact, at least one study found that there was no significant correlation between offense history—including number of felony offenses—and multiple placements for a sample of African American youth.[32] So, although African American involvement in crime may help explain initial contact with law enforcement, it doesn't necessarily explain confinement.

Evidence suggests that African American youth are treated differently at each stage of the juvenile justice process. Both state and aggregate national data show that disparities among races increase at every stage of contact.[33] The causes discussed below may be contributors to this differential treatment.

What has been called the "indirect effects of race" is important to consider. Poverty and exposure to violent communities tend to be associated with race.[34] Therefore, when researchers try to study race effects, they may really be looking at poor, single-parent families, with low academic achievement and exposure to violence, and may not really be studying race itself.[35]

Exposure to violence, in particular, is an inescapable experience for many African American youth in urban environments. The National Centers for Disease Control indicate that homicide is the leading cause of death for African Americans between the ages of 10 and 24.[36] In this context of community violence, including random shootings, drug- and gang-related murders, and the constant threat of physical attacks, many young people learn to use violent solutions themselves. Such learning may be antisocial, but adaptive nonetheless, given their environmental conditions.

Violence can induce trauma. Studies have shown a strong link between exposure to violence and adjustment problems, such as depression, anxiety, and antisocial behavior, as well as post-traumatic stress disorder.[37] Somehow, a future orientation and acceptance of prosocial norms may be adversely affected when a child lives under violent conditions.

Just because these young people are not living in some far-away land ripped apart by military action, their witness of interpersonal violence should not be discounted. One young man in placement told about the time he was sitting next to his uncle, on the couch in the living room of his home, when a bullet pierced the front window and lodged in his uncle's forehead. On a home visit, another teenager located the spot where his niece was wounded by a "stray bullet" in his aunt's front yard.

An additional example of indirect race effects centers on race-related crime and punishment patterns. Alexander and Gyamerah report that possession of three grams of crack cocaine is considered a third-degree felony in Minnesota, punishable by up to 20 years in prison. By contrast, 10 grams of powdered cocaine is considered a fifth-degree felony, punishable by up to five years. This may not seem to be related to incarceration patterns among the races, until you consider that 97 percent of the people arrested for crack possession were African Americans and 80 percent of the arrests for cocaine powder were Caucasian during the period studied.[38]

Recent studies that incorporate improved methodology have begun to establish the indirect effect of race in juvenile justice decision making. Bridges and Steen illustrated the effects of subjective assessments of youth by court workers. In this study, probation officers were more likely to attribute delinquent behavior among African American youth to internal factors such as "lack of responsibility," while they used external factors such as "poverty" to explain delinquency by white youth. Such subjective processes may be seen as covert racism.[39]

Although covert racism is a delicately handled topic because of its potentially inflammatory and divisive nature, it must also be considered as a cause of DMC. A unique experiment conducted by Graham and Lowery investigated the effect of "priming unconscious racial stereotypes" about juvenile offenders among police officers. Two ethnically diverse groups of police officers were formed by random assignment. Before reading hypothetical case descriptions of a racially unspecified youth who committed shoplifting and one who committed an assault on a peer, one group was provided with race-neutral stimuli and the other was subliminally "primed" with words related to the category "black." Officers in the racially primed condition reported more negative ratings of the offenders and judgments of greater culpability, expected recidivism, and the need for harsher punishment. Investigators were careful to assess self-reported racial attitudes of the participants and found no relationship to the outcome. This finding emphasizes the role of unconscious processes. In this study, stereotypes are usefully characterized as "unconscious beliefs" that affect "conscious behavior."[40]

Clear procedural rules for decision making and case disposition have been proposed as solutions to the problem of DMC.[41] Although such reforms can be credited with reducing intentional racial bias, they may not be very effective in other ways. In fact, they may unintentionally draw more African American youth into the juvenile justice system. For example, so called "zero-tolerance" rules used to deter drug possession in public schools are prevalent in minority school districts and have been shown to result in unintentionally harsher treatment of minority youth.[42] A similar effect is possible when risk indexes that are based on seemingly neutral factors are used to determine disposition. Factors such as the number of prior police contacts or arrests can lead to placement escalation, but may simply be artifacts of increased police scrutiny.[43] Some jurisdictions use a decision-making rule that requires detention when two parents or a biological parent are unavailable.[44] Given the composition of many urban poor families, this requirement may be unintentionally discriminatory. Its negative impact may be further extended because of the kinship and non-blood-related structure that exists in some African American families.[45]

To illustrate the effect of this type of rule, let's assume that you are a juvenile court worker attempting to decide which juveniles go into detention. (Let's further assume that you are not a bigot!) One child has two employed, nicely dressed parents in attendance at your meeting, who promise to do their best to control him and who have transportation and telephones to maintain contact with you. The youth has no prior record of offenses. Another child has a status offense and a misdemeanor on his record and is brought to your office by his grandmother who has just been released from the hospital. She tells you that they were a bit late for your meeting because the bus didn't make their stop on time. When you ask about her availability for phone contact, she sheepishly tells you, "The phone's been cut off." In which case would you expect a higher likelihood that the child would show up for a court date and stay out of additional trouble until then? If you chose the first case, you're not alone, and you would be making a decision that's consistent with many protocols based on statistical risk.[46] Now, recognize that the first youth is white and the second is black. Given the prevalence of these family and socioeconomic factors in Caucasian and African American families, you would also be engaging in unintentional discrimination.

WHAT CAN BE DONE ABOUT DMC

The good news is that everyone who works in the juvenile justice system has an opportunity to reduce the number of minority youth in placement without unduly jeopardizing public safety. Perhaps what would be most productive would be to simply focus attention on the issue and try to consider it in decisions that are made at each stage of the juvenile justice process. Knowledge and attitude go a long way toward solving the problem. The specific suggestions for reducing DMC listed below are drawn from successful innovations conducted in various states, as well as general research.

The first thing that can be done to reduce DMC is to encourage involvement and creativity by building cooperative networks that include representatives from law enforcement, the juvenile court, the intervention system, and the community. These people have direct knowledge that can be tapped into for solutions.[47] Most states have already complied with federal requirements to create boards responsible for investigating and reducing DMC, but their results are varied.[48] By 2002, only Colorado, Pennsylvania, and Washington had completed the initial identification and assessment phases required by law and were actively involved in implementing and monitoring reduction strategies; and only 44 states provided usable information about their progress to the OJJDP. South Dakota and Wyoming were exempt from the procedure because they did not accept Formula Grant funds.

By building reliable information systems and ensuring accurate record-keeping, several minority youth might receive an intervention other than confinement. Amazingly, inaccurate record-keeping can result in a low-risk offender being confined for weeks.[49] For example, relatively insignificant police "contacts" are often inaccurately recorded or miscounted as highly significant "arrests," and then used to make charging, disposition, or placement decisions.

With accurate record-keeping, DMC could be more accurately monitored. Recently, relevant data from the city of Detroit were removed from official statistics by the FBI; the removal was due to widespread inaccuracies and irregularities. Because of the high concentration of African Americans within the city limits, this loss of data was catastrophic for those attempting to measure DMC in Michigan. Several other problems with current data collection and management have been exposed, including limited funding for counties and localities to support data management; use of paper records rather than electronic files that make retrieval difficult; unstandardized race and ethnicity categories; and missing data caused by voluntary reporting, time pressures, and irregular responsibilities.[50]

It may also be useful to address covert racism by using educational and experiential learning activities to increase the awareness of decision makers and the general public. For example, the "stereotype priming" experiment described above could be adapted to form an experiential learning module for police officers, court workers, treatment providers, and judges.

Expanded training in cultural awareness might also make inroads on DMC. It has been suggested that learning the language and the behavior patterns of minority youth might prevent misperceptions of the danger they present or the level of motivation they possess to cooperate with representatives of the juvenile justice system.[51] Without requisite knowledge, for example, a court worker may conclude that a 16-year-old African American youth who wears a hood over his head, slumps in his chair, and refuses to make eye contact is disinterested in receiving the help that is being offered. Understanding the value of extended family and non-blood-related relationships in African American families may open placement alternatives that are not immediately recognized by members of the dominant culture. It has also been suggested that representatives of the youth's culture operate as indigenous liaisons between juvenile justice professionals and offenders and their families in the community.[52]

Because minority youth are likely to live in highly patrolled precincts, they are also more likely to come to the attention of the police. Because their high visibility "through the windshield" of the police cruiser, they are more likely to experience police contact. Community policing has been recognized as a means of reducing this type of unintentional bias and simultaneously protecting the community. It may also be a useful response to environmental violence. Community policing is characterized by a partnership of law enforcement professionals and community members. Officers who know their neighborhood and its residents are more likely to take low-level offenders home or to a relative or neighbor rather than make an arrest that results in detention.[53]

Reviewing community risk assessment inventories (standardized protocols) upon which charging, disposition, and placement decisions are predicated could reduce intentional and unintentional bias. In a technical investigation of various risk assessment strategies, Gottfredson and Snyder recognize that race is a *correlate* of recidivism, but emphasize that it is not a *cause*. They identify predictive causal factors as poverty, school failure, unsupervised time, community disruption, and the amount of police surveillance in the community. They suggest that risk-scale developers use a race variable in the early stages of instrument construction, but remove it from the final instrument as a means of reducing racial bias in the application of the instrument.[54]

Specific steps that have resulted from risk assessment reviews include statutory changes like those enacted in California that restricted the criteria for detention, and other states' decisions to open more options for acceptable placement, including family members and neighbors.[55] Another example is provided by Cook County in Chicago, Illinois, where even moderate-risk offenders may be placed in nonsecure placements, based on use of an approved decision-making tree.[56]

Increased availability of legal counsel would help ensure equal protection by providing a knowledgeable advocate for the youthful offender. Obtaining qualified legal counsel could help combat the effects of economic injustice.

Implementation of evidence-based programming as alternatives to detention would be extremely useful in reducing DMC. A meta-analysis of 305 published studies indicates that mainstream treatment programs are just as effective with African American and other minority youth as they are with dominant culture youth.[57] Although culturally specific intervention may be even more effective, simply making sure minority youth and families have access to regular nonrestrictive programs would be a helpful first step.

Several empirically supported interventions have been reported in the treatment literature. Useful prevention approaches include mentoring programs such as Big Brothers/Big Sisters, Across Ages, and the Gang Resistance Education and Training Program.[58] Juvenile court diversion programs have demonstrated success for several years.[59] The recent use of "balanced and restorative justice" conferences, wherein offenders make amends with their victims, also holds promise for intervention with low-level offenders.[60] Family-centered delinquency treatments that have reported impressive efficacy with serious offenders include Functional Family Therapy[61] and Multisystemic Treatment.[62] The Family

Empowerment Intervention has also reported significant success.[63] Many of these evidence-based approaches incorporate the seminal interventions developed in Structural Family Therapy.[64]

Improvement of the measurement of minority contact at each stage of the juvenile justice process would also be useful. To that end, the OJJDP recently encouraged a change in the method used to measure DMC.[65] The old procedure was known as the Disproportionate Representation Index (DRI) and was calculated by simply constructing a ratio of the percentage of confined youth of minority status to the percentage of minority youth in the general population. The new procedure is called the Relative Rate Index (RRI) and uses a rate-based estimator that may be computed at any stage of contact in the juvenile justice process. The computational formula, which appears on the OJJDP Web site, is a bit complicated.[66] It appears that both indexes may underestimate DMC in areas with small minority populations, but the DRI is still most widely reported index of the two.[67]

An additional step would be to conduct further targeted research to learn more about DMC. Pope, Lovell, and Hsia offer specific suggestions for research focused on law enforcement policies and practices, state and local efforts to reduce DMC, and alternatives to confinement.[68] In addition, Nellis suggests that researchers focus attention on identifying factors that contribute to DMC at various stages of contact.[69] It may prove valuable to assess implicit attitudes of decision makers that affect disposition and placement decisions.

CONCLUSION

DMC is a real and complex social justice issue. The complexity of the issue can be daunting, but the issue itself cannot be ignored. The responsibility that comes with living in a free society requires an ongoing examination of any abridgment of liberty. When identifiable groups of citizens are systematically incarcerated, whether by intention or ignorance, justice is limited and freedom is lost in the society as a whole. It would be useful to remember Martin Luther King's words, "Injustice anywhere is a threat to justice everywhere."[70] From today's perspective, the incarceration during World War II of hundreds of American citizens of Japanese descent seems unconscionable. Somehow, people who didn't look European presented more of a threat than German Americans or Italian Americans. In the same regard, we should consider disproportionate confinement of minority youth as equally unconscionable.

The need to protect the community and the need to provide effective intervention in the life of the offender can no longer be seen as exclusive or competing. True protection of society is only possible when freedom for all citizens is valued as highly as security. When juvenile justice professionals and community members strive to overcome the barriers presented by prejudice, denial, fear, and limited information, much can be accomplished, and social justice can be advanced.

NOTES

1. American Prosecutors Research Institute, hereafter APRI, 2001.
2. Devine, Coolbaugh, & Jenkins, 1998.
3. Hsia, Bridges, & McHale, 2004; Pope, Lovell, & Hsia, 2002.
4. Pope et al., 2002.
5. Snyder & Sickmund, 2006.
6. Feyerherm & Butts, 2002.
7. Snyder & Sickmund, 2006.
8. Nellis, 2005.
9. Hsia & Hamparian, 1998.
10. Snyder, 1999.
11. Justice Policy Institute, hereafter JPI, 2002.
12. Hsia & Hamparian, 1998.
13. Goldberg & Hodes, 1992.
14. APRI, 2001.
15. Hsia et al., 2004.
16. APRI, 2001.
17. Platt, 1977.
18. Ferdinand, 1991.
19. Pumphrey & Pumphrey, 1961.
20. Bruno, 1957.
21. Mooradian, 2003.
22. Montgomery, 1909.
23. Bilchik, 1998.
24. Mooradian, 2003.
25. Mooradian, 2003.
26. If you're statistically minded, note that this is not a true path model because it is not fully specified. The model, however, was constructed from a large pool of reliably and validly measured independent variables.
27. Nellis, 2005.
28. Blumstein, 1995.
29. Farrington, Loeber, Stouthamer-Loeber, Van Kammen, & Schmidt, 1996.
30. Hawkins, Laub, & Lauritson, 1998.
31. Snyder & Sickmund, 2006.
32. Mooradian, 2003.
33. JPI, 2002.
34. Nellis, 2005.
35. U.S. Department of Health and Human Services, 2001.
36. National Centers for Disease Control, n.d.
37. McGee, 2003.
38. Alexander & Gyamerah, 1997.
39. Bridges & Steen, 1998.
40. Graham & Lowery, 2004.
41. Hsia et al., 2004; JPI, 2002.
42. Nellis, 2005.
43. Leiber, 2003.
44. APRI, 2001.
45. Boyd-Franklin, 1989.
46. Farrington et al., 1996; Gottfredson & Snyder, 2005.
47. APRI, 2001.
48. Hsia et al., 2004.

49. APRI, 2001.
50. Post, Hagstrom, Heraux, Christensen, & Joshi, 2005.
51. APRI, 2001.
52. APRI, 2001.
53. APRI, 2001.
54. Gottfredson & Snyder, 2005.
55. APRI, 2001.
56. APRI, 2001.
57. Wilson, Lipsey, & Soydan, 2003.
58. Nellis, 2005.
59. Davidson, Redner, Blakely, Mitchell & Emshoff, 1987.
60. McGarrell, 2001.
61. Sexton & Alexander, 2000.
62. Bourdin, 1995; Henggeler, Melton, & Smith, 1991; Sutphen, Thyer, & Kurtz, 1995.
63. Dembo et al., 2001.
64. Minuchin, Montalvo, Guerney, Rosman, & Schumer, 1967.
65. Feyerherm & Butts, 2002.
66. Office of Juvenile Justice and Delinquency Prevention, n.d.
67. Post et al., 2005.
68. Pope et al., 2002.
69. Nellis, 2005.
70. King, 1963.

REFERENCES

Alexander, R., & Gyamerah, J. (1997). Differential punishing of African-Americans and whites who possess drugs: A just policy or a continuation of the past? *Journal of Black Studies, 28*(1), 97–111.

American Prosecutors Research Institute. (2001). *Disproportionate minority confinement: Practical solutions for juvenile justice professionals.* Alexandria, VA: American Prosecutors Research Institute.

Bilchik, S. (1998). A juvenile justice system for the 21st century. *Crime and Delinquency, 44*(1), 89–101.

Blumstein, A. (1995). Youth violence, guns, and the illicit-drug industry. *Journal of Criminal Law and Criminology, 86*(1), 10–36.

Bourdin, C. M. (1995). Multisystemic treatment of serious juvenile offenders: Long-term prevention of criminality and violence. *Journal of Consulting and Clinical Psychology, 63*(4), 569–578.

Boyd-Franklin, N. (1989). *Black families in therapy: A multisystems approach.* New York: Guilford Press.

Bridges, G., & Steen, S. (1998). Racial disparities in official assessments of juvenile offenders: Attributional stereotypes as mediating mechanisms. *American Sociological Review, 63,* 554–570.

Bruno, F. (1957). *Trends in social work 1874–1956: A history based on the proceedings of the national conference on charities and corrections.* New York: Columbia University Press.

Davidson, W. S., Redner, R., Blakely, C. H., Mitchell, C. M., & Emshoff, J. G. (1987). Diversion of juvenile offenders: An experimental comparison. *Journal of Consulting and Clinical Psychology, 55*(1), 68–75.

Dembo, R., Ramirez-Garnica, G., Schmeidler, J., Rollie, M., Livingston, S., Harts-field, A. (2001). Long term impact of a family empowerment intervention on juvenile offender recidivism. *Journal of Offender Rehabilitation, 33*(1), 33–58.

Devine, P., Coolbaugh, K., & Jenkins, S. (1998, December). Disproportionate minority confinement: Lessons learned from five states. *Juvenile Justice Bulletin*. Washington, D.C.: Department of Justice, Office of Justice Programs, Office of Juvenile Justice and Delinquency Prevention.

Farrington, D., Loeber, R., Stouthamer-Loeber, M., Van Kammen, W., & Schmidt, L. (1996). Self-reported delinquency and a combined delinquency seriousness scale based on boys, mothers, and teachers: Concurrent and predictive validity for African-Americans and Caucasians. *Criminology, 34*, 493–458.

Ferdinand, T. N. (1991). History overtakes the juvenile justice system. *Crime and Delinquency, 37*(2), 204–224.

Feyerherm, W., & Butts, J. (2002). Recommended methods for measuring disproportionate minority contact (DMC). Presentation as part of Office of Juvenile Justice and Delinquency Prevention training sessions for Juvenile Justice Specialists and DMC Coordinators, 2002. Retrieved, July 20, 2006, from http://ojjdp.ncjrs.org/dmc/pdf/dmc2003.pps.

Goldberg, D., & Hodes, M. (1992). The poison of racism and the self-poisoning of adolescents. *Journal of Family Therapy, 14*, 51–67.

Gottfredson, D. M., & Snyder, H. (2005). *The mathematics of risk classification: Changing data into valid instruments for juvenile courts*. Washington, D.C.: National Center for Juvenile Justice, Office of Juvenile Justice and Delinquency Prevention.

Graham, S., & Lowery, B. S. (2004). Priming unconscious racial stereotypes about adolescent offenders. *Law and Human Behavior, 28*(5), 483–504.

Hawkins, D. F., Laub, J. H., & Lauritson, J. L. (1998). Race, ethnicity, and serious juvenile offending. In R. Loeber & D. Farrington (Eds.), *Serious violent juvenile offenders: Risk factors and successful interventions* (pp. 30–46). Beverly Hills, CA: Sage Publications.

Henggeler, S. W., Melton, G. B., & Smith, L. A. (1992). Family preservation using multisystemic treatment: An effective alternative to incarcerating serious juvenile offenders. *Journal of Consulting and Clinical Psychology, 60*(6), 953–961.

Hsia, H. M., Bridges, G. S., & McHale, R. (2004). *Disproportionate minority confinement: 2002 update*. Washington, D.C.: Department of Justice, Office of Justice Programs, Office of Juvenile Justice and Delinquency Prevention.

Hsia, H. M., & Hamparian, D. (1998, September). Disproportionate minority confinement: 1997 update. *Juvenile Justice Bulletin*. Washington, D.C.: Department of Justice, Office of Juvenile Justice Programs, Office of Juvenile Justice and Delinquency Prevention.

Justice Policy Institute. (2002). *Reducing disproportionate minority confinement: The Multnomah County, Oregon success story and its implications*. Washington, D.C.: Justice Policy Institute.

King, M. L. (1963, June 12). Letter from Birmingham Jail. *The Christian Century.*

Leiber, M. J. (2003). *The contexts of juvenile justice decision-making*. Albany, NY: State University of New York Press.

McGarrell, E. F. (2001, August). Restorative justice conferences as an early response to young offenders. *Juvenile Justice Bulletin*. Washington, D.C.:

Department of Justice, Office of Justice Programs, Office of Juvenile Justice and Delinquency Prevention.

McGee, Z. T. (2003). Community violence and adolescent development. *Journal of Contemporary Criminal Justice, 19*(3), 293–314.

Minuchin, S., Montalvo, B., Guerney, B. G., Rosman, B. L., & Schumer, F. (1967). *Families of the slums: An exploration of their structure and treatment*. New York: Basic Books.

Montgomery, J. B. (1909, January). Proceedings of the conference on the care of dependent children held at Washington, D.C. Washington, D.C.: Government Printing Office.

Mooradian, J. K. (2003). *Disproportionate confinement of African-American juvenile delinquents*. New York: LFB Scholarly Publications.

National Centers for Disease Control. (n.d.). *Youth violence* (Fact sheet). Atlanta, GA: National Centers for Disease Control. Retrieved July 18, 2006, from www.cdc.gov/ncipc/factsheets/yvfacts.htm.

Nellis, A. M. (2005). *Seven steps to develop and evaluate strategies to reduce disproportionate minority contact*. Washington, D.C.: Juvenile Justice Evaluation Center Justice Research and Statistics Association.

Office of Juvenile Justice and Delinquency Prevention. (n.d.). *Implementing the relative rate index calculation: A step-by-step approach to identifying disproportionate minority contact with the juvenile justice system*. Washington, D.C.: Office of Juvenile Justice and Delinquency Prevention. Retrieved July 18, 2006, from http://ojjdp.ncjrs.org/dmc/pdf/StepsinCalculatingthe RelativeRateIndex.pdf.

Platt, A. (1977). *The child-savers: The invention of delinquency.* Chicago, IL: University of Chicago Press.

Pope, C. E., Lovell, R., & Hsia, H. (2002). Disproportionate minority confinement: A review of the research literature from 1989 through 2001. *Juvenile Justice Bulletin.* Washington, D.C.: Department of Justice, Office of Justice Programs, Office of Juvenile Justice and Delinquency Prevention.

Post, L. A., Hagstrom, J. A., Heraux, C., Christensen, R. E., & Joshi, V. (2005). *Assessing DMC in Michigan: Youth contact with the justice system 2003–2004 report*. DMC Assessment Project, Michigan State University. East Lansing, MI: Michigan State University.

Pumphrey, R., & Pumphrey, M. (1961). *The heritage of American social work*. New York: Columbia University Press.

Sexton, T. L, & Alexander, J. F. (2000, December). Functional family therapy. *Juvenile Justice Bulletin.* Washington, D.C.: Department of Justice, Office of Justice Programs, Office of Juvenile Justice and Delinquency Prevention.

Snyder, H. N. (1999). *Minorities in the juvenile justice system*. Washington, D.C.: Department of Justice, Office of Justice Programs, Office of Juvenile Justice and Delinquency Prevention.

Snyder, H. N., & Sickmund, M. (2006). *Juvenile offenders and victims: 2006 national report*. Washington, D.C.: Department of Justice, Office of Justice Programs, Office of Juvenile Justice and Delinquency Prevention.

Sutphen, R. D., Thyer, B. A., & Kurtz, D. P. (1995). Multisystemic treatment for high-risk juvenile offenders. *International Journal of Offender Therapy and Comparative Criminology, 39*(4), 327–334.

U.S. Department of Health and Human Services. (2001). *Youth violence: A report of the Surgeon General*. Rockville, MD: Department of Health and Human Services, Centers for Disease Control and Prevention, National Center for

Injury Prevention and Control, Substance Abuse and Mental Health Services, and National Institute of Mental Health.

Wilson, S. J., Lipsey, M. W., & Soydan, H. (2003). Are mainstream programs for juvenile delinquency less effective with minority youth? A meta-analysis of outcomes research. *Research on Social Work Practice, 13*(1), 3–26.

CHAPTER 8

Law and the Treatment of Mentally Ill Youth

Jon R. Farrar

The U.S. Surgeon General has stated that mental illness "refers collectively to all diagnosable mental disorders."[1] The National Mental Health Association reports that as many as 60 to 75 percent of incarcerated youth have mental health disorders and 20 percent have severe disorders. Such disorders include substance abuse, conduct disorder, depression, attention deficit/hyperactivity disorder, learning disabilities, post-traumatic stress disorder, and developmental disabilities.[2] The courts in this country, however, rarely look at these disorders when dealing with the children before them. Consideration of a child's mental health is normally limited to the issue of whether he is mentally ill in the context of commitment or delinquency and criminal proceedings.

THE HISTORY OF MENTALLY ILL YOUTH IN THE COURT SYSTEM

The courts' handling of mentally ill youth is a product of the development of the juvenile court system. Up until the late 1800s, children who committed crimes were brought before the same courts that handled crimes committed by adults. Children below the age of 7 were presumed incapable of criminal responsibility, although a rebuttal presumed that children between the ages of 7 and 14 lacked capacity. Children were not exempt from the type of punishment imposed on adults for criminal behavior, including execution.

The Juvenile Court

In 1899, the Illinois legislature established the first juvenile court in Cook County. Juvenile courts were quickly established throughout the country. By 1925, all but two states had juvenile courts. Juvenile courts were rooted in social welfare policy and were designed to handle the punishment and rehabilitation of juveniles. Advocates of the juvenile court system saw a need for a nonpunitive *parens patriae* alternative to the criminal justice offenders. The objectives were to provide a measure of guidance and rehabilitation and protection for society, not to fix criminal responsibility, guilt, and punishment. Reliance was placed on social workers, probation officers, psychologists, psychiatrists, and physicians to provide information to the juvenile court for assessing and treating the needs of an individual child. Cases were handled informally, as opposed to having an adversarial system. Most states prohibited the prosecution of juveniles for crimes, except when permission was granted by juvenile courts.

The Beginnings of Change—1960s and 1970s

The Supreme Court began scrutinizing the treatment of juveniles in court proceedings beginning in the 1960s. The three most significant cases were *Kent v. United States* (1966), *In re Gault* (1967) and *In re Winship* (1970). These cases established the principles that had to be employed in court proceedings involving juveniles, including cases in which mental illness was an issue. These cases eroded the notion that juvenile court proceedings would be informal and without the traditional due process rules.

The *Kent* case concerned the practices of juvenile courts in the District of Columbia. Morris Kent was placed on probation by a juvenile court when he was 14 years old. In 1961, an intruder entered a woman's apartment and raped her. The police found fingerprints belonging to Morris Kent, who was then 16 years old. Kent was taken into custody and interrogated by police. He was detained for almost a week without an arraignment or a judicial determination of probable cause. His mother retained an attorney, who contacted the Social Services Director of the Juvenile Court. Counsel hired two psychiatrists and a psychologist, who determined that Kent was a "victim of severe psychopathology" and was in need of psychiatric care. Counsel made known his opposition to the juvenile court waiving jurisdiction. However, the psychological needs of Kent were ignored. The juvenile court waived jurisdiction without a hearing or explanation. The juvenile court never conferred with Kent or his parents. Kent was tried in criminal court and convicted on six counts with a range of punishment between 30 and 90 years in prison. Counsel challenged the juvenile court's waiver of jurisdiction in this case, along with the failure to accord Kent basic constitutional rights that adults were entitled to receive. The Supreme Court did not address the issue of Kent's constitutional rights; the case was remanded, however, because the Supreme Court found that the juvenile court's waiver of jurisdiction was invalid. The

Supreme Court found that Kent was entitled to due process and entitled to a statement of reasons for the juvenile court's decision.

The Supreme Court's next important decision regarding juveniles came out the following year in *In re Gault*. A juvenile court found that Gault had engaged in delinquent conduct by making a telephone call to a neighbor and making lewd and indecent remarks. Gault was picked up by the police while both parents were at work. No notice was left that he was taken into custody. A policeman filed a formal petition on the following day and a hearing was conducted. Gault's parents did not receive a copy of the petition until more than two months later. It made no reference to any factual basis for the judicial action. It merely said that "said minor is under the age of eighteen years, and in the need of the protection of this Honorable Court; (and that) said minor is a delinquent minor." The hearing was conducted before a juvenile judge. Neither Gault's parents nor the complainant were there. No one was sworn at the hearing. No transcript nor recording was made. No memorandum or record was prepared. The Supreme Court noted that the information it had about the hearing came solely from the testimony of the juvenile judge. There was conflicting testimony, and Gault purportedly admitted making one of the lewd statements. Gault was kept in a detention facility while the juvenile judge decided to "think about it."

A second hearing was conducted a week after Gault's arrest. The parents, another juvenile and his father, and two officers were present. The complainant was not present. The arresting officer agreed that Gault never admitted making a lewd comment, although the juvenile judge recalled at the habeas corpus hearing that Gault made "some admission." At the conclusion of the hearing, Gault was committed to the State Industrial School. No appeal was permitted under Arizona law, thus the parents filed a petition for a writ of habeas corpus. The Arizona Supreme Court affirmed the denial of relief, concluding that the Arizona Juvenile Code "impliedly" implements due process and the commitment did not violate due process.

The U.S. Supreme Court disagreed. The Supreme Court noted that neither the Due Process Clause of the Fourteenth Amendment nor the Bill of Rights is for adults alone. The Court also noted that the rights of the state, as *parens patriae*, in dealing with juveniles were the product of the highest motives and most enlightened impulses to correct the appalling procedures and penalties employed in adult criminal courts. The Court held, however, that the constitutional and theoretical basis for the juvenile system was debatable and that the results had not been entirely satisfactory. The Court further noted that the "condition of being a boy does not justify a kangaroo court." The Supreme Court limited its decision to the procedures discussed by the Arizona Supreme Court and concluded that, contrary to the decision by the Arizona Supreme Court, a juvenile has a right to notice of charges, to counsel, to confrontation and cross-examination of witnesses, and to the privilege against self-incrimination.

The Supreme Court's third significant case involving juveniles was decided three years later in *In re Winship*. The Court was concerned with

the standard to employ in determining whether a juvenile was a delinquent. New York law defined a juvenile delinquent as a person over 7 and
less than 16 years of age who commits any act that, if done by an adult,
would constitute a crime. New York law also provided that any determination at the conclusion of a hearing that a juvenile did an act or acts must
be based on the preponderance of the evidence. Samuel Winship, a 12-
year-old boy, was found to have entered a locker and stolen $112 from a
woman's pocketbook. He was placed in a training school, and, under New
York law, he could be kept there until his 18th birthday. The case focused
on the issue of whether a finding of delinquency had to be based on the
preponderance of the evidence or beyond a reasonable doubt. Justice
Brennan, writing for the majority, noted that the Due Process Clause of
the Fourteenth Amendment requires that the "essentials of due process
and fair treatment" must be employed during the adjudicatory stage when
a juvenile is charged with an act that would constitute a crime if committed by an adult. He also noted that the higher standard of "beyond a reasonable doubt" had been used throughout the history of this country.
The Court rejected the argument that to afford juveniles the protection of
that standard would risk destruction of beneficial aspects of the juvenile
process. The Court held that when a child is charged with stealing, which
could render him or her liable in confinement for as long as six years, then
due process requires that the case against him must be provided beyond a
reasonable doubt.

The Supreme Court has extended most of the constitutional rights of
defendants in adult criminal proceedings to children in juvenile proceedings. In *McKeiver v. Pennsylvania* (1971), however, the Supreme Court
did not extend the right to trial by jury to juvenile proceedings. The justices noted that the juvenile court concept still had high promise and that
they were not yet willing to give up on its rehabilitative goals.

Continuity in the Court

The principles developed in *Kent, Gault,* and *Winship* were important
as the backdrop for three Supreme Court decisions issued in 1979 concerning the commitment of children to mental hospitals. The first decision
was *Addington v. Texas.* Addington's mother filed a petition for him to be
committed indefinitely in a state mental hospital. He had been diagnosed
as suffering from psychotic schizophrenia and had paranoid tendencies. He
caused substantial damage to property during such episodes. As required
by state law, the trial court found that based on "clear, unequivocal and
convincing evidence," Addington was mentally ill and required hospitalization for his own welfare and protection or for the protection of others.
Addington challenged the findings. He conceded that he was mentally ill,
but he argued that there was no substantial basis for concluding that he
was probably dangerous to himself or others. The Supreme Court cited
In re Winship regarding the standards of proof that are required in various
types of hearings and that the beyond-a-reasonable-doubt standard is
reserved for criminal and delinquency proceedings. It was noted that

children and adults have a substantial liberty interest in not being confined unnecessarily and that the state's involvement in the commitment decision constitutes state action. The Supreme Court added, however, that a civil commitment cannot be equated to a criminal prosecution. It was noted that the "subtleties and nuances of psychiatric diagnosis renders certainties virtually beyond reach in most situations."[3] On the other hand, the preponderance standard employed in typical civil cases falls short of the demands of due process in commitment cases, thus the Supreme Court adopted the mid-level burden of "clear and convincing" evidence in commitment cases.

One aspect of the *Addington* case worth emphasizing concerns the basic standard required to involuntarily commit a person. State law required that there must be a showing or burden of proof that the person was mentally ill and that the person was likely to cause serious harm to himself/herself or others. The standard applied to both adults and juveniles, and remains in effect in Texas and many other states today.[4] As a result of *Addington*, the showing or burden of proof must be made by clear and convincing evidence.

Two months later, the Supreme Court decided *Parham v. J.R.*, a class action lawsuit brought by minor Georgia children, who alleged that they were denied due process as a result of their voluntary commitment by a parent or guardian. It was noted that there was some concern that parents could use mental hospitals as a "dumping ground," although no evidence in the record supported this concern. The Supreme Court presumed that parents ordinarily act in the best interest of a child. On the other hand, it was recognized that the state has a significant interest in not unnecessarily confining a patient in a costly mental health care facility. The Court concluded that because of the risk of error inherent in a parental decision to commit a child, some kind of inquiry should be made by a neutral fact finder into whether the statutory criteria for admission was satisfied. Such inquiry should include an examination of the background of the child and include an interview with the child. A formal or quasi-formal hearing was not required; instead, a review by a staff physician was considered sufficient. The decision maker had the authority to refuse admission if a child did not meet medical standards for admission. The Supreme Court further found that the child's continuing need for commitment must be reviewed periodically by a similarly independent procedure.

On the same day, the Supreme Court decided *Secretary of Public Welfare of Pennsylvania v. Institutionalized Juveniles*. The case once again dealt with the voluntary commitment of children into state mental hospitals upon an application of a parent or someone standing in the place of a parent. The Supreme Court cited *Parham* as the standard to use in evaluating the voluntary commitment of children in Pennsylvania. Pennsylvania provided that after an application was filed for a child less than 14 years old, the child was to be examined, provided temporary treatment, and given an individualized treatment plan by a treatment team. Within 72 hours, the treatment team was to determine whether inpatient treatment was necessary and why it was necessary. The hospital was required to inform the child and his or her parents of the necessity for institutionalized treatment and the nature of the proposed treatment. The treatment plan was to be reviewed not less than every 30 days. The child was entitled to object to the treatment plan and obtain a review by a mental health professional who was independent of the treatment team. Any child older than 13 could object to his hospitalization. If the director of the facility felt that hospitalization was still necessary, then he or she had to resort to involuntary commitment proceedings. The Supreme Court concluded that the due process provided in Pennsylvania was sufficient. It was specifically noted that the program was acceptable because of the review by independent mental health professionals whose sole concern under the statute was for a child's needs and whether he or she could benefit from treatment.

The next significant Supreme Court decision concerned the level of care provided to an involuntarily committed patient in *Youngblood v. Romeo* (1982). Nicholas Romeo was involuntarily committed because of profound mental retardation, as opposed to mental illness. He had an intelligence quotient between 8 and 10, could not talk, and lacked the most basic self-care skills. While committed, he was injured numerous times by his own violence and by reactions of other residents to him. At one time, he had to be transferred from his ward to a hospital for treatment for a broken arm. He was physically restrained during portions of the day while in the hospital. His mother filed a lawsuit seeking injunctive relief and arguing that officials at Pennhurst State School and Hospital were not providing appropriate care. The Supreme Court held that people who are involuntarily committed are protected substantively by the Due Process Clause, which includes the right not to be confined in unsafe conditions and the right to freedom from bodily restraint. But these rights are not absolute. In certain occasions, the State may have to restrain the movement of residents to protect them as well as others from violence. Citing *Parham v. J.R.*, the Court concluded that judicial interference with the internal operations of the institution should be kept to a minimum, that a decision by a professional decision maker is presumptively valid, and that liability may be imposed only when there was a substantial departure from accepted professional judgment, practice, or standards. The Court also held that a patient is entitled to minimally adequate training as may be reasonable in light of his or her liberty interest in safety and freedom from unreasonable restraint.

Three of the justices filed a concurring opinion, concluding that Romeo was totally denied treatment and that the majority opinion improperly suggested that he was provided inadequate treatment, as opposed to no treatment whatsoever. They felt that the decision should have further held that Romeo was entitled to minimally adequate training necessary to preserve basic self-care skills, such as the ability to dress himself and care for his personal hygiene as well as training to prevent his preexisting self-care skills from deteriorating because of his commitment. They felt that the issue of degree of training needed further development.

Youngblood v. Romeo focused on the right of patients confined in a state mental hospital to receive treatment. The next inevitable question to be considered concerned the specific treatment a patient is entitled to receive or, alternatively, the type of treatment that may be imposed on him or her. Apart from counseling and psychotropic drugs, most people likely would have no idea about the type of treatment normally provided. The case law covers a wide array of treatment plans. In *Davis v. Balson* (1978), the issue was work. More specifically, forcing mental patients confined in an Ohio State mental hospital to work. Such work included bathing, feeding, changing linens, and mopping floors between four and eight hours a day. The court concluded that mentally ill patients generally could be required to work, although they could not be forced to work when work programs were countertherapeutic. In *Doe v. Public Health Trust of Dade County* (1983), the Eleventh Circuit was confronted with a rule that prohibited communication between a voluntarily committed juvenile and his parents. The court held that the rule could be upheld if it was medically legitimate and therapeutic; in that case, however, there was no medical basis for the rule.

In *Rogers v. Commissioner of the Dept. of Mental Health* (1983), the Massachusetts Supreme Judicial Court held that an involuntarily committed juvenile initially has the right to make treatment decisions, including the refusal to take psychotropic drugs, although a court may find that the patient is incompetent and authorize the forcible use of such drugs. Alternatively, psychotropic drugs could not be forcibly administered until the patient was provided due process, declared incompetent, and substituted consent employed. A similar result occurred in Georgia in *Hightower v. Olmstead* (1996). Patients in a state mental hospital brought a class action lawsuit challenging procedures for the administration of psychotropic drugs. The court noted that Georgia law specified that patients had the right to receive care and treatment that is suited to his or her needs and that is the least restrictive appropriate care and treatment. A patient could consent to the administration of psychotropic drugs;. however, if a patient was incompetent, then substituted consent had to be employed. For juveniles, a parent or guardian could give consent. A court-appointed guardian may be required, in some cases, particularly with adult patients.

A particularly interesting case was *Clevenger v. Oak Ridge School Board* (1984). This case included consideration of the Education for All Handicapped Children Act (20 U.S.C. § 1412). The Act provided for free appropriate public education for all impaired children between 3 and 21 years old. The child in this case suffered a brain injury during birth, was impulsive, aggressive, hostile, and possibly schizophrenic. Specialists believed that the child needed a long-term residential treatment program with locked wards. The local Tennessee school district wanted to place the child in a short-term residential school that provided psychiatric treatment. He had previously been placed there without success. His mother wanted him placed in a more expensive school in Texas that had long-term residential treatment with locked wards. The Sixth Circuit found that the child was entitled to go to the school in Texas where there was a chance of success, as opposed to returning to the local residential school where there was no chance of success at all.

CONTEMPORARY ISSUES

The Eleventh Circuit was forced to contend with today's economic realities in *D.W. v. Rogers* (1997), which examined scarce public resources that resulted in a lack of space for involuntarily committed mentally ill juveniles. An Alabama judge ordered that a schizophrenic teenager, who was a threat to himself and others, be involuntarily committed. The child was placed on a waiting list until space became available. It was noted that children under 12 and adults were immediately admitted when similar orders were issued for them, but space was inadequate for children above 12. The court held that there was no right to treatment until the child was actually committed. In New York, a 2002 class-action lawsuit (*Alexander v. Novello*) focused on a similar problem with juveniles having to wait for months before being admitted to a residential treatment facility for their psychiatric problems. In *Butler v. Evans* (2000), the Seventh Circuit held that parents were not entitled to reimbursement from the State in situations in which they had to temporarily place a child in a private facility until local and state entities were able to arrange placement. These decisions have all too real implications today given that the number of teenagers placed in mental facilities has grown tremendously in recent years and states have not kept up with the need to provide such facilities. This factor has been an important consideration in dealing with mentally ill juveniles who engage in delinquent or criminal behavior. The trend in the juvenile justice system is to simply disregard the mental health considerations of a child in addressing delinquent or criminal behavior and, instead, sentence the child to a juvenile or adult detention facility where the mental health needs of the child may or may not be addressed. This trend will be discussed in more detail later in this chapter.

Mental Illness and Punishment

The previous paragraph raises an important aspect of mental illness concerning how courts consider these illnesses in the context of delinquency or criminal proceedings. The mere presence of mental illness will not excuse a person from punishment for committing a crime. Instead, Anglo-American jurisprudence history has not allowed punishment in cases in which a person cannot be blamed due to insanity. Various tests are used for insanity, but most states use a variation of the M'Naughten Test. The M'Naughten Test specifies that a person who commits a criminal act will be excused from criminal liability if, as a result of a mental disease, the accused did not know the nature or quality of his or her act or did not know that what he or she did was wrong. The distinction between mental illness and insanity for the purposes of criminal proceedings is important.

In *People v. Ricks* (1988), a Michigan court noted that even though a juvenile suffered a paranoia disorder and a schizoid personality disorder, he was able to tell the difference from right and wrong and thus the insanity defense was not viable. While controversial, the insanity defense is actually employed in adult criminal proceedings in less than 1 percent of trials. Interestingly enough, however, the insanity defense is not universally recognized as a defense by all states in juvenile proceedings. The Virginia Supreme Court has noted that the U.S. Supreme Court has held that there is no constitutional right to an insanity defense in adult criminal proceedings, and likewise there is no right to an insanity defense in juvenile proceedings.[5] By comparison, the Supreme Court of Louisiana has held that juveniles do have a fundamental right to plead not guilty by reason of insanity.[6] The procedures for raising an insanity defense in juvenile proceedings vary among the states, assuming such a defense is available. Typically, however, juveniles historically have not been certified to go to adult courts for trial if they were found to be insane.[7]

The rise in crime rates among juveniles in recent years, however, has resulted in a more punitive system that ignores mental illness.[8] The Texas Legislature, for example, significantly moved from a rehabilitative model to a punitive model in enacting changes to the juvenile justice code in 1996.[9] Under the new law, a mentally ill or mentally retarded child who commits a crime will no longer be assigned to the Texas Department of Mental Health and Mental Retardation; instead, the child will be handled as any other juvenile. A typical example is found in *In re J.L.R.* (2000), in which a 13-year-old child with a history of mental illness was sent to the Texas Youth Commission for an indeterminate time after committing various crimes. The court concluded that it was up to the Texas Youth Commission to provide whatever mental health care was deemed necessary.

Incompetency

A concept often confused with the insanity defense is competency to stand trial. Incompetence to stand trial is the idea that a person has a mental illness or defect that makes him or her unable to understand the proceedings against him or her or to assist in his or her own defense. In adult criminal proceedings, a defendant who is found to be incompetent is typically treated in a mental institution until he or she is competent once again, if ever. In *In re Erick B.* (2004), a New York family court found an autistic child with borderline intellectual functioning incompetent to continue proceedings involving four misdemeanors and had him committed. Most states have provisions postponing juvenile delinquency proceedings while the competency of the child is being considered and treatment provided.

What Happens after a Finding of Insanity?

This brings us to the problem of what to do with a person found not guilty by reason of insanity. Typically the person will be committed to a mental facility if he or she is still considered insane and a threat to himself/herself or others. A noteworthy example is John W. Hinckley, who shot President Reagan in 1981. A problem with this approach was evident in *Foucha v. Louisiana* (1992). Foucha was charged with aggravated burglary and illegal discharge of a firearm. He was initially found to be incompetent to stand trial. He was found to be competent to stand trial four months later, although the doctors reported that he was unable to distinguish between right and wrong at the time of the offense. The trial court found that he was insane at the time of the commission of the offense and thus not guilty by reason of insanity. He was committed to a mental health facility, but professionals at the facility found that he no longer had a mental disease or defect. It was noted that he had an antisocial personality, but such a condition was not a mental disease or defect. Under Louisiana law, Foucha could not be released from the mental health facility unless he was able to prove that he was no longer dangerous. Louisiana courts kept him in the mental institution even though he did not have a mental illness. The Supreme Court reversed the Louisiana courts and held that he had been denied due process. He could only be kept confined if he had a mental illness and was a danger to himself or others.

Civil Commitment

Despite the holding in *Foucha*, the Supreme Court has permitted states to civilly confine sexually violent predators even if they have not been convicted of a crime and have not been involuntarily committed because of a mental illness. In *Allen v. Illinois* (1986), the Supreme Court was concerned with an Illinois statute that permitted the state to incapacitate individuals who had a mental disorder that resulted in a propensity to commit sexual offenses. The Supreme Court held that the statute made the proceedings civil in nature, and thus the constitutional safeguards in criminal proceedings were inapplicable. The principle announced in *Allen v. Illinois* has been extended to allow states to commit sexually violent predators upon their release from prison in cases in which the person suffers from a behavioral abnormality that makes him or her more likely to engage in a predatory act of sexual violation.[10] Moreover, the offender can be civilly committed even if incompetent because the right to be competent applies only to criminal proceedings.[11] Seventeen states have passed legislation providing for the civil commitment of sexually violent predators.

This concept of committing individuals after they have completed their sentences has been extended to juveniles. In *United States v. S.A.* (1997), pursuant to the Juvenile Justice and Delinquency Prevention Act, the United States committed a juvenile delinquent upon his release from a juvenile facility. The youth was committed because he suffered from a mental disease or defect and posed a substantial risk of bodily injury to another person or serious damage to property of another. The court found that the juvenile could be hospitalized indefinitely. The statute was designed to protect the public and to ensure that the mentally ill receive proper treatment.

CONCLUSION

This brings us to the issue of what is likely to occur in the future. The public's increasing unwillingness to spend money on social programs makes it unlikely that the lack of facilities for juveniles with mental illnesses will be improved in the near future. Furthermore, the public's attitude of getting tough on crime, including criminal acts by juveniles, makes it more likely that juveniles will be adjudged delinquent or certified as adults and convicted of adult crimes, as opposed to receiving treatment when they suffer from a mental illness. It is also increasingly likely that juveniles will be civilly committed upon the expiration of their sentences if they are still suffering from a mental illness that makes them a danger to themselves or others.

Despite the trend toward getting tough on juveniles and diminishing the role of traditional juvenile courts, alternative approaches have been proposed and implemented in some venues. Interest has been renewed in providing rehabilitation for juveniles, particularly with respect to the creation of therapeutic courts for juveniles with alcohol- and drug-related problems.[12] The first drug treatment court began operation in 1989 in Miami, Florida, and such courts have since proliferated across America.[13] Mental health courts have been established as an alternative to doling out traditional punishment in criminal court. The therapeutic courts have revitalized the concept of rehabilitating juveniles, as opposed to merely placing them in the criminal justice system. The creation of such courts reveals a continuing desire in some venues to handle juveniles with mental needs apart from the criminal courts. The long-term viability of such programs, however, will hinge on financial considerations as well as their ability in the short term to successfully meet societal expectations about youth with mental problems.

NOTES

1. Center for Mental Health Services, 2001.
2. National Mental Health Association, n.d.
3. *Addington v. Texas*, 1979.
4. See, for example, *In re K.S.*, 2004.
5. *Commonwealth v. Chatman*, 2000.
6. *State v. Causey*, 1978.
7. See, for example, *In re K.J.T.*, 2000; *S.D.J. v. State*, 1994; *State v. Simmons*, 2002.
8. Garascia, 1995, p. 489.
9. Johnson, 1998.
10. See, for example, *In re Commitment of Browning*, 2003.
11. *In re Commitment of Fisher*, 2005.
12. Geary, 2005.
13. Geary, 2005, p. 682.

REFERENCES

Center for Mental Health Services, U.S. Department of Health and Human Services. (2001). *Mental health: Culture, race, and ethnicity—a supplement to mental health: A report of the Surgeon General*, 6. Retrieved August 1, 2006, from www.mentalhealth.samhsa.gov/cre/default.asp.

Garascia, J. (1995). The price we are willing to pay for punitive justice in the juvenile detention system: Mentally ill delinquents and their disproportionate share of the burden. *Indiana Law Journal, 80*, 489–515.

Geary, P. (2005). Juvenile mental health courts and therapeutic jurisprudence: Facing the challenges posed by youth with mental disabilities in the juvenile justice system. *Yale Journal of Health Policy, Law & Ethics, 5,* 671–88.

Johnson, M. (1998). Texas revised juvenile justice and education codes: Not all change is good, *Journal of Juvenile Law, 19,* 1–45.

National Mental Health Association. (n.d.). *Prevalence of mental disorders among children in the juvenile justice system.* Retrieved August 1, 2006, from www.nmha.org/children/justjuv/prevalence.cfm.

CASES CITED

Addington v. Texas, 441 U.S. 418, 99 S.Ct. 1804, 60 L.Ed.2d 323 (1979).

Alexander v. Novello, 210 F.R.D. 27 (E.D. N.Y. 2002).

Allen v. Illinois, 478 U.S. 364, 106 S.Ct. 2988, 92 L.Ed.2d 296 (1986).

Butler v. Evans, 225 F.3d 887 (7th Cir. 2000).

Clevenger v. Oak Ridge School Board, 744 F.2d 514 (6th Cir. 1984).

Commonwealth v. Chatman, 538 S.E.2d 304 (Va. 2000).

Davis v. Balson, 461 F.Supp. 842 (N.D. Ohio 1978).

Doe v. Public Health Trust of Dade County, 696 F.2d 901 (11th Cir. 1983).

D.W. v. Rogers, 113 F.3d 1214 (11th Cir. 1997).

Foucha v. Louisiana, 504 U.S. 71, 112 S.Ct. 1780, 118 L.Ed.2d 437 (1992).

Hightower v. Olmstead, 959 F.Supp. 1549 (N.D. Ga. 1996).

In re Commitment of Browning, 113 S.W.3d 851 (Tex. App. – Austin 2003).

In re Commitment of Fisher, 164 S.W.3d 637 (Tex. 2005).

In re Erick B., 777 N.Y.S.2d 253 (N.Y. Fam. Ct. 2004).

In re Gault, 387 U.S. 1, 87 S.Ct. 1428, 18 L.Ed.2d 527 (1967).

In re J.L.R., 2000 WL 424033 (Tex. App. – San Antonio 2000).

In re K.J.T., 542 S.E.2d 514 (Ga. App. 2000).

In re K.S., 2004 WL 254267 (Tex. App. – Ft. Worth 2004).

In re Winship, 397 U.S. 358, 90 S.Ct. 1068, 25 L.Ed.2d 368 (1970).

Kent v. United States, 383 U.S. 541, 86 S.Ct. 1045, 16 L.Ed.2d 84 (1966).

McKeiver v. Pennsylvania, 403 U.S. 528, 91 S.Ct. 1976, 29 L.Ed.2d 647 (1971).

Parham v. J.R., 442 U.S. 584, 99 S.Ct. 2493, 61 L.Ed.2d 101 (1979).

People v. Ricks, 421 N.W.2d 667 (Mich. Ct. App. 1988).

Rogers v. Commissioner of the Dept. of Mental Health, 458 N.E.2d 308 (Mass. 1983).

S.D.J. v. State, 879 S.W.2d 370 (Tex. App. – Eastland 1994).

Secretary of Public Welfare of Pennsylvania v. Institutionalized Juveniles, 442 U.S. 640, 99 S.Ct. 2523, 61 L.Ed.2d 142 (1979).

State v. Causey, 363 S.2d 472 (La. 1978).

State v. Simmons, 108 S.W.3d 881 (Tenn. Crim. App. 2002).

United States v. S.A., 129 F.3d 995 (8th Cir. 1997).

Youngblood v. Romeo, 457 U.S. 307, 102 S.Ct. 2452, 73 L.Ed.2d 28 (1982).

CHAPTER 9

Initiating Faith-based Juvenile Corrections: Exercising without Establishing Religion[1]

Lonn Lanza-Kaduce and Jodi Lane

The Florida Department of Juvenile Justice (DJJ) has instituted a pilot program that incorporates faith-based interventions with secular programming to serve delinquents and the larger community. The secular programming emphasizes evidence-based interventions (largely cognitive behavioral), and the faith-based features include the introduction of chaplains into juvenile facilities, the facilitation of faith-based volunteer activities, and the recruitment of faith-based mentors who will follow the youth from their residential placement into community aftercare. Cognitive behavioral programming has been shown to have some efficacy in behavior change.[2] Research also fairly consistently shows that something about religion relates to lower rates of delinquent and criminal involvement.[3] The hope is that the faith-based and secular components, working independently or in combination, will enhance behavioral reform even while addressing the spiritual needs of young offenders.

Whether faith-based components will affect behavior depends on how well they can be implemented and how well they fit with other interventions. Obstacles to success include (1) failure to implement faith-based components well, (2) constraints on their implementation, and (3) implementation that counteracts or is counteracted by other program features. This paper examines an important set of legal constraints that apply to faith-based correctional programming and that are further complicated because the Florida initiative deals with juveniles.

Three prospects help establish the importance of the legal issues. First, given controversies regarding the separation of church and state and freedom of religion, poor implementation that disregards the law could result in expensive lawsuits and jeopardize the survival of a faith-based program. The administrators in both Florida's DJJ and the federal granting agency are sensitive to that possibility. Second, aggressive religious involvement that exceeds legal strictures may result in lack of coordination between the faith-based components and secular programming—programming selected because of its demonstrated efficacy. The result would be diminished behavior change, and in that sense the faith-based features could do more harm than good. The third prospect is reverse consideration. Defensive, timid implementation of the faith-based components may undercut the efficacy of the program. Timid implementation would make it less likely for resocialization to occur, less likely for prosocial associations to develop, and less likely for personal transcendence.

The purpose of this chapter is not to join a debate about how the law should be applied or what policies should be advanced. Rather it is to show how real tensions develop between legal requirements and the incorporation of faith-based elements into juvenile corrections. Left unaddressed, those tensions threaten the viability and efficacy of faith-based interventions regardless of how well intentioned or promising they might be. The analysis derives from semistructured interviews with key personnel and observations made during various training sessions, site visits, and staff meetings.

THE LEGAL CONSTRAINTS

This overview of legal constraints begins with the First Amendment of the U.S. Constitution: "Congress shall make no law respecting an establishment of religion, or prohibiting the free exercise thereof." The first clause is referred to as the establishment clause; the second as the free exercise clause. These clauses have been infused with more meaning by the courts than first appears. For example, the reach of the amendment goes beyond Congress to prohibit all levels of government from either establishing religion or interfering with the free exercise of religion. Hence, faith-based programming in a state's juvenile corrections is subject to the constraints of the First Amendment.

Free Exercise of Religion

This analysis begins with a review of the free exercise clause, which states that "Judicial interpretation of the ... First Amendment has resulted in a policy that the guarantee of free religious *belief* is absolute, while freedom to *act* in the exercise of religious belief is subject to regulation."[4] At one point, the court announced that the constitutional right to exercise or act on one's religious beliefs could only be regulated if the government could show a compelling reason for the regulation and that no reasonable alternative was available to achieve its compelling interest. In *Sherbert v. Verner* (1963), the court held that a state could not deny unemployment compensation to a Seventh Day Adventist who refused to work on

Saturday, because it unduly burdened her free exercise of religion and the state could protect its interests against fraudulent claims in a less restrictive way.[5]

Once the "hands-off" doctrine for prisons crumbled,[6] it appeared that the same logic might be applied to correctional settings. In *Cruz v. Beto* (1972), a Buddhist prisoner in Texas was not allowed to use the prison chapel, could not correspond with his religious advisor, and was placed in solitary confinement for allowing other inmates to read his religious literature. He challenged the prison on First and Fourteenth Amendment grounds. The Supreme Court, *per curiam*, determined that his lawsuit had to be heard on its merits.

The Supreme Court retreated from the compelling government interest standard in *O'Lone v. Estate of Shabazz* (1987). Muslim inmates claimed that work rules that did not allow them to meet for Friday afternoon prayers infringed on their exercise of religion. The court did not require the state to show a compelling state interest to justify the regulation on security grounds. The court found that

> To ensure that courts afford appropriate deference to prison officials, we have determined that prison regulations alleged to infringe constitutional rights are judged under a "reasonableness" test less restrictive than that ordinarily applied to alleged infringements of fundamental constitutional rights.[7]

The court used a standard announced in *Turner v. Safley* (1987). The court analyzed whether a regulation about inmate correspondence was constitutional by considering four factors: (1) whether the regulation was rationally related to the penal goal, (2) whether there were other ways for inmates to exercise their rights, (3) the degree to which an accommodation would have affected guards, other inmates, and the allocation of resources, and (4) the kind of alternatives to the regulation that were available.

> In general, all First Amendment claims are now determined by applying the *Turner v. Safley*, or "rational-relationship," test. If prison officials can identify a legitimate state interest and show that the rule or regulation in question is rationally related to such interest, they are likely to win against any prisoner challenge.[8]

Federal constitutional restrictions are not the only legal constraints. Both the federal government and the state of Florida have enacted legislation that

> prevents government from placing a "substantial burden" on a person's free exercise of religion unless the burden furthers a "compelling governmental interest" and [i]s the least restrictive means of furthering" that interest.[9]

Congress accomplished this through a narrowly crafted provision in the Religious Land Use and Institutionalized Persons Act of 2000 (RLUIPA).

RLUIPA was used by inmates from "non-mainstream" religions to challenge some Ohio prison regulations. The Supreme Court upheld RLUIPA.[10] Thus, states must show compelling interests to regulate the religious practices of inmates and the correctional regulations must be the least restrictive means of serving those compelling state interests.

The federal and state provisions alter the "due deference" position taken by courts that usually permit correctional authorities to regulate religious exercise primarily on the basis of finding a rational relationship between the regulations and legitimate correctional goals.[11] The statutory provisions call for more activist judicial review of correctional practices that implicate the exercise of religion and alter what is seen as undue establishment by government.

Nonestablishment Considerations

The first part of the First Amendment is known as the establishment clause. Its purpose goes beyond prohibiting an official state religion. It also means that the government should be neutral. The government should not prefer one religion over another (or no religion); it should not favor religious activities over nonreligious ones. Justice Black invoked the words of Thomas Jefferson to insist that "the clause against establishment of religion was intended to erect 'a wall of separation between church and State'."[12]

In 1971, the U.S. Supreme Court set out guidelines for analyzing potential establishment problems (*Lemon v. Krutzman*). According to these guidelines, government activities (1) should have a secular purpose, (2) should neither advance nor inhibit religion, and (3) should not foster excessive entanglement with religion. Subsequent decisions, however, showed the difficulties in sorting out which entanglements were impermissible.[13]

> Beginning in the 1990s the Court began to favor a test that emphasized neutrality, rather than entanglement. In a world of pervasive government benefits and services, the government does not violate the establishment clause [so long as it provides] financial support or other aid to religious entities on the same basis as it does to others.[14]

This position is highlighted in *Rosenberger v. University of Virginia* (1995). Mandatory fees from students at the state university could not be used to fund various student publications without also being available for student religious publications, especially in cases in which funds did not go directly to the religious group itself. The approach to all groups had to be neutral under the establishment clause. Funding did not mean endorsement, so funding religious publications just like other student publications did not endorse or aid religion, but failure to fund religious publications when other student publications were funded was not neutral. The official policy was designed to provide an open forum for diverse viewpoints and disassociated the university from what was published. To be neutral, it could not discriminate against a religious viewpoint by treating religion differently from other viewpoints encouraged in the open forum.[15]

This is the approach that is incorporated into Florida's DJJ chaplaincy guidelines. *"Accommodation efforts should be consistent.* If a substantial effort is made to accommodate one or some faith groups, then similar efforts should be made to accommodate other groups."[16] The planners and administrators in DJJ frequently refer to the open-forum approach as the one that they need to use, particularly in situations in which opportunities are made available so that no group is advantaged over any other group. This means that the initiative must be neutral both among religions and between religious and nonreligious beliefs.

The federal legal constraints may be compounded by state strictures. Florida presents a clear example of this. Its constitutional provision on establishment is more demanding than that of the U.S. Constitution.[17] Article I, section 3, of the Florida Constitution provides that "No revenue of the state or any political subdivision or agency thereof shall ever be taken from the public treasury directly or indirectly in aid of any church, sect, or religious denomination or in aid of any sectarian institution." Florida's chaplaincy guidelines point out that the "no-aid" provision is more restrictive and mandates that Florida's DJJ chaplains refrain from purchasing any religious programming, including paying religious groups or volunteers to support their services (e.g., transportation) unless the service is provided for strictly secular purposes (e.g., taking youth to mental health counseling).

Religious Rights in the Context of Juvenile Corrections

A hallmark of the establishment clause is neutrality—the government must remain neutral regarding its relation to religion. The touchstone of free exercise is whether religious activities or involvements are voluntary. When people's liberties are deprived and they are involuntarily confined, inherent coercion may be involved, requiring special scrutiny to assess how free any religious exercise (or failure to exercise) might be. That assessment is further complicated when dealing with juveniles. Their abilities to make completely voluntary decisions or resist coercion are still developing. To the extent that government actions do not provide an open forum in which all religions (or no religion) are dealt with neutrally, those religious opportunities that are available may unduly sway impressionable youth and affect how they exercise their religious rights.

Champion[18] suggests that another way to appreciate this tension is to look at federal regulations regarding the use of subjects in research. Both "prisoners"[19] and "children"[20] are vulnerable classes for use as subjects, so special legal protections are erected. Because of the prospect of coercion, prisoners must be selected on a fair (e.g., random) basis and their participation must be voluntary. Specific concern is shown for inducements because those living in deprived conditions may be "bought" more easily. Similarly, the use of children is circumscribed. Juvenile involvement not only requires their informed consent but also that of their parents. Because children's wills can be overcome relatively easily, incentives for participating are scrutinized. When research is conducted with juvenile "prisoners," both sets of special considerations are applied. If such oversight is required before children or inmates can be research participants, at least as much scrutiny will attach to their religious rights.

IMPLEMENTATION—MORE THAN A MATTER OF FAITH

Real-life examples of the tensions between faith-based activities and legal constraints can be found in the planning and initial implementation of Florida's Faith and Community Based Delinquency Treatment Initiative (FCBDTI). The examples highlight how the law has practical implications and poses challenges to the incorporation of faith into juvenile corrections. These examples are reviewed in the hopes that others might learn from Florida's experience.

Shifts in Plans—A Dry Hole in Texas and Adjustments in Florida

First Amendment considerations were pivotal from the outset in Florida. According to interviews with DJJ officials, Florida became involved with the federally funded grant only after other states had been approached. The other states were wary of the sticky First Amendment issues.

An Office of Juvenile Justice and Delinquency Prevention (OJJDP) official said, "the states were afraid of the church-state issues that it would raise, and didn't want to get bogged down in that kind of stuff" (Interview 1). The official continued,

> So they [the Office of Juvenile Justice and Delinquency Prevention] put out some feelers, talked to three or four states, ... and everybody was scared to death.
> ... Too explosive.... [But officials in Florida] said, "We are going to do it, get them on the line." (Interview 3)

Florida's original plan was to model a program in a Texas prison, "to replicate the IFI [InnerChange Freedom Initiative] literally" (Interview 6). The "initial idea was to duplicate it with juveniles" (Interview 1). A five-person delegation from DJJ met an official from OJJDP in Texas in November 2003 to learn firsthand about the IFI. One member of the delegation noted the following:

> In 1997, the InnerChange Freedom Initiative (IFI) was given about half the beds of the Texas's Carol Vance prison to operate as a Christian prison ... [sponsored by] the Prison Fellowship Ministries. Prisoners ... must be volunteers for IFI placement ... [and staff] must be practicing Christians.... The concept is to operate a prison as a Christian community.[21]

The IFI program runs for 16 months in-house and 6 months in the community after release. According to another delegate, "[IFI is] a totally Christian-based faith program.... Texas pays for the prison security, food and all that" (Interview 6).

> [IFI offered] a different type of setting, that ... was unabashedly evangelical Christian. The only thing the state of Texas paid for at IFI was the guards on the property. The guards at the entry. Prison Ministries paid for everything else, paid for the programming, paid for the programming staff—of course, the state of Texas paid for their food and their sheets, you know, the basics. (Interview 3)

One of the features of the Texas program that stood out was that it was open to anyone, despite its Christian focus. One delegate explained the following:

> I asked, "What's going on in there?" And he said, "Oh those are the Muslims." I said, "You have Muslims here?" And he said, "Yeah, we don't deny them, and we also have one Jewish guy." But they want to come in, knowing it's Christian, (unintelligible), they can ... participate.... [If] it's a Muslim holy day, or Yom Kippur, they do their thing.... So, they allow anyone in, they don't have to be Christian to get in. (Interview 3)

The Florida delegation immediately discerned some problems with replicating the Texas program for juveniles in Florida. Some of the problems concerned issues of length of stay and of dealing with juveniles rather than adults. One interviewee discussed these problems, "First ... our kids are minors ...; under Florida law, their religious training and orientation is the responsibility of the parents ... The second was that it had to be on a voluntary basis ..." (Interview 1). Another interviewee added, "We realized we didn't have the gift of time that they have in the adult system, our kids may only stay six months. So a lot of what they were doing had to be compressed. We had other things to do as well. Five hours of school each day" (Interview 3). Probably most important, there were potential First Amendment problems. One interviewee explained the following:

> ... [T]hey had replicated IFI in three other locations in the adult system and those three states were all under attack by Americans for Separation of Church and State.... We were in dire need of legal involvement.... At this point they (OJJDP) had decided to get their attorneys involved in Washington. Just like we had. And of course they said the same thing. (Interview 3)

After the trip to Washington, the goal became one of selecting features from IFI (and elsewhere) and adapting them to create something that would work with juveniles in Florida and pass constitutional muster. Those who made the trip knew "we're not going to be able to model this exactly as it was; we had to come up with something ..." (Interview 5).

One of the aspects of the Texas program that impressed the DJJ dele-gation was the use of faith-based mentors who followed the offenders from incarceration into aftercare upon release. One delegate noted the following:

> Essentially, every prisoner was given a mentor … That mentor came from a church. That church had a team that was responsible for pulling together certain things for that inmate: a place to live; supporting the family while they were inside; beginning to work on vocational placement when they got out. Behind this mentor there were a group of people from that church, who were all focused, they were a committee for this inmate. (Interview 3)

Another feature of the Texas program that impressed at least some of the delegation was the coordinated treatment and release plan for inmates. Because most of the Texas inmates were released to the Houston area, some members of the DJJ delegation went to Houston to check out the aftercare component of IFI. The delegates found that:

> … [T]here … was this old house they had bought and restored. And upstairs were computers, for job searches and whatnot; downstairs for meet-ing rooms, like AA was meeting in one room when we were there. There were also counselors from IFI there present for the inmates that had been released. A couple of probation officers came by, some parolees came in while we were there. So it was kind of like a resource center … The amazing thing was that they had the inmate do a plan for their release … by the hour for the first week. (Interview 3)

Florida's faith-based plans had to change, but the Texas lessons were useful in the ultimate structuring of its initiative. To achieve this, the delegation—

> … tried to salvage the basic concepts of having that spiritual support in the facility. Doing that through a provided chaplain…. [W]e recognized we needed … [a coordinator] in each of the facilities…. We needed then some people out in the field to do coordination, just like they did. So we tried to salvage the big pieces. Tempered so that it was more voluntary…. (Interview 3)

The original plan called for government funding of several staff mem-bers, including a program director for the entire initiative, a research as-sistant for the director, and facility program and aftercare coordinators at five juvenile residential facilities.[22] The program director administered the initiative with the help of the assistant—these positions were administra-tive. Each of the five program coordinators were in charge of implement-ing the initiative in one of the respective facilities. They were responsible for supervising the initiative's staff at the facility and for coordinating the initiative's program with the ongoing activities in the institution, including the secular treatment components. Accordingly, their activities were not religious in nature. The aftercare coordinators were tasked with finding mentors for the youth and devising plans for transitions to the community and aftercare that worked with these mentors. The activities of the coordinators were secular in nature. Eventually, a treatment coordinator was added at the sites—with duties that also were secular. The initiative is designed so that the tax dollars for the salaries and support of the staff did not entangle the Florida initiative with religion in ways that violate the First Amendment.

The faith-based component of the Florida initiative derived from *volunteer* mentors and other religious-based voluntary services (e.g., Bible study, worship services). The initiative's staff could recruit volunteers and coordinate such activities with other programming that was provided at the facilities and with the juvenile probation officers during aftercare.

During implementation one further adjustment was made in Florida's initiative to ensure that the state stayed neutral and did not become too entangled with religion. The early implementation concentrated almost exclusively on faith-based mentors—the original operational plan was actually dubbed "The Florida Faith-Based Juvenile Corrections Initiative." Excluding other mentors could have compromised neutrality and left the initiative open to charges of religious entanglements. Inattention to other mentors could also constrain choices and freedom about how religious beliefs could be exercised. Two interviewees explained this solution: "... [T]he Feds [OJJDP] suggested that open forum might be the way to go.... [I]n open forum, you just open the forum and stand back and if faith comes, fine. If Big Sisters/Big Brothers, fine" (Interview 2). "[T]he way we avoided many of the church-state conflict is by making it an open forum ... we can provide a forum for folks to come in, but we do not allow any money spent directly on religious items" (Interview 1).

Under the open-forum principle, the initiative morphed into the FCBDTI and staff were instructed to search out mentors from various nonreligious groups and the larger community in addition to those from faith-based organizations. According to one staff member,

> ... [The program] would be one that they [juveniles and their parents] select from, from a bunch of options.... Now we can have faith mentoring and non-faith mentoring in the same program, as long as it's mentoring. Um, that's more of an open forum kind of style than the voucher [strategy] would be. The ... voucher would be more of a "Oh, here's the faith. There's the non-faith." (Interview 2)

The open forum is not the same as an open door, explains another staff member: an "open forum does not necessarily mean that juvenile facilities are open to all who desire to enter" (Interview 6). For example, a south Florida Kabbalah group wants to get involved in the FCBDTI. The south Florida site, however, has "no kids that are ascribing to that faith and they're not involved with the Kabbalah at all.... We're gonna let people in if we get a kid that needs services" (Interview 6).

The need to have an open forum also emerged when considering how to secure consent. Because of the potential of a faith-based component, participation in the initiative needed to be voluntary to meet First

Amendment standards. Therefore, the juveniles and their parents or guardians had to grant informed consent. Because mentoring offers potential advantages over other DJJ programs, parents and youth could not be placed in the position of being disadvantaged if they wanted a mentor but not a faith-based mentor. Voluntary participation required that they be given a choice.

Voluntary participation provided a reason for broadening the initiative to include community mentors. Truly voluntary participation in religious activities means that participants can withdraw from those activities at any time without penalty or consequence. Youth or parents who, for any reason, decided that they did not want to continue with faith-based mentoring had to have the right to withdraw. That choice, however, would be constrained if withdrawal meant having no mentor at all. Such a limited option would not be neutral. The open-forum solution, the neutral approach, would provide the option of a community mentor or a faith-based one.

None of those instrumental in securing funding and implementing the FCBDTI raised issues about whether or not the faith components were compatible with the secular programming. One interviewee said that the cognitive behavioral programs (e.g., Thinking for a Change, Motivational Interviewing, and Strengthening Families) were all "amenable" to the faith perspective (Interview 1). Another averred that these "are evidence-based programs with demonstrable results ... and they are completely, absolutely compatible and complimentary to all basic Western systems of belief—Judaism, Islam, Christianity ..." (Interview 3). The secular and faith-based components are intended to be complementary.

Chaplain Challenges

Within the correctional context, the establishment and free exercise clauses can converge. In fact the legal rationale for allowing tax dollars to pay for chaplains stems from such a convergence. The logic is like that which extends to military contexts—because of constraints on freedom, chaplains can be hired with tax dollars because affirmative steps help people exercise their religious rights.

> The Free Exercise Clause provides the legal authority for correctional chaplaincy—the reason why the State of Florida can pay a chaplain in a prison or detention facility when it would be quite out of the question to subsidize a priest, minister, imam, or for that matter a chaplain, in almost any other setting.... "If an inmate is locked up, away from his books and his minister, a government practice of 'strict neutrality' ... is not truly neutral. To refuse special treatment for religion in this context is to stifle religious expression and practice...."[23]

According to Florida's *Chaplaincy Guidelines*,

> *Children retain their right to freely exercise their religion when they are detained or incarcerated. Therefore, Florida can hire chaplains when necessary to accommodate the free exercise rights of youth in custody.*[24]

Note that this logic does not require a chaplain; it merely permits it.

Chaplains do not have free rein to do as they wish. They must serve the religious needs of the detained residents as best they can, and they must remain neutral in that process. The *Guidelines* state that "[t]he chaplain's primary obligation is to take all reasonable steps to ensure that youth of whatever religious persuasion who wish to practice are served."[25] So, for example, early in the Florida experience a youth began to ask questions and show interest in Buddhism, the faith of his parents. The chaplain, an evangelical Christian, spoke with our evaluation team about how he had to stretch to find accurate and appropriate sources of information for the youth. It was part of his job.

The challenge to remain neutral is not always so easy. In another instance, there was discussion of a youth who wanted to break from the Jehovah Witness religious preferences of his mother. To the extent that a chaplain for juveniles cannot disregard the parents' wishes in attending to the religious needs of her or his charges, the chaplain is constrained.[26]

Issues also arise regarding confessions and religious rites. The importance of this challenge surfaced at a meeting of the faith-based staff from all the sites. Although confession is an important religious rite in some faiths, chaplains were reluctant to perform the rite because of their dual roles—religious leader and employee within the juvenile justice system. The participants agreed that the "best practice" would be to ask volunteer priests and religious leaders from the community to perform rites and rituals to avoid potential conflicts, especially because the chaplain can only perform rituals within her or his own faith tradition.[27] These limitations on the role of chaplain need to be made clear to the juvenile detainees. The restrictions in the *Chaplaincy Guidelines* are explicit: "*Sacramental, ceremonial or otherwise formal rites of initiation should not be conducted under ordinary circumstances.*"[28]

Neutrality, Inducements, and Faith-based Services and Activities

Faith-based staff and facility administrators have to take care to remain neutral. Consistent with the open forum principle, the chaplain's services cannot favor one religion. Alternative activities are necessary, as explained in the *Guidelines*: "*Presenting a single program may be impermissible establishment.* Chaplains should not make their sole offering a 'one size fits all' version of the majority faith."[29] Moreover, a "reasonable effort should be made to accommodate all faith groups represented in the facility's population."[30]

In strict observance of neutrality, some of the alternative activities offered in the facility should be secular so youth are not pressured into faith activities because nothing else is available. Facilities that offer only faith-based activities from outside volunteers (e.g., Bible study, evening religious services, faith mentors) may need to seek volunteers from other organizations to ensure that they do not breach the wall of separation or constrain free exercise rights. The Florida initiative had to broaden its efforts to secure community mentors in addition to faith mentors.

The issue is compounded when food or rewards are provided for activities. According to the DJJ,

> *Providing inducements may constitute establishment.* When youth are offered special inducements to participate in chaplaincy programming [and by extension other faith-based activities], government may be deemed to have endorsed religion over non-religion.[31]

Certainly, the faith-based staff cannot show preference by treating those in the faith-based program to something not available to other residents. If the volunteers who conduct faith-based activities also provide rewards (e.g., pizza/food, Bibles, or small gifts), the best practice is to make such incentives available to all residents regardless of whether they participate in the faith-based activity. An interviewee explained the approach: "Now if the church brings dinner for the entire crew, ... they can come and do that" (Interview 6). Rewards for only some of the incarcerated residents may compromise the requirement that choices regarding faith are voluntary. Our field notes show frequent discussions of these issues by faith-based staff members.

The neutrality of the faith-based effort can be compromised in other ways. One concern is that the staff may share the same religious orientation and present, whether consciously or not, a kind of orthodoxy that may override, even subconsciously, the choices and preferences of the juveniles. An interview articulated this concern: staff "who come out of a church, they rely on that church ... The kids don't get to see different styles" (Interview 7).

Several situations have emerged that illustrate the problem. The first cropped up in mentor recruitment materials. An early draft featured a form with a response option of Christian versus other (lumping together believers and nonbelievers alike) much to the consternation of DJJ and OJJDP officials.

A second illustrative situation involved faith-based staffing. An interviewee who was involved early on with the initiative was concerned that in one facility, too many of the faith-based staff came from the same church. "It even made colleagues uncomfortable and may have contributed to the turnover of one of the team members" (Interview 4).

A third example presented a form of role conflict. A few members of the budgeted faith-based staff (with roles that require neutrality) also volunteered to conduct Bible study classes. The issue is whether the switch in roles gives at least the appearance of endorsing a religion. Will confined juveniles distinguish between the staff member as neutral implementer of the FBCDTI and the staff member as a volunteer for a particular faith? Is there subtle pressure on a juvenile whose aftercare coordinator in FCBDTI is teaching Bible study so that the juvenile may see some extrinsic benefits[32] to participate in "voluntary" Bible study? One interviewer? found that juveniles do turn to faith: "I've seen enough kids that, they found God in detention" (Interview 5).

Unlike many adult prisons, juvenile facilities have a lot of unscheduled time. It can be difficult to schedule activities around the various treatment programs, educational demands, and work details; there aren't always enough hours in the day. So activities involving people from the outside (including researchers and mentors) can create challenges that have to be balanced in a neutral way. In one facility, where common areas have to be shared by high-risk and moderate-risk units, so much "free" time on nights and weekends is taken up by religious activities that time for other activities (including visitation) is squeezed. Mentors and family members may compete over the same time slots—choices may be constrained.

Because some facilities in the Florida initiative have their beds completely filled with faith-based volunteers, another issue is now emerging. How much pressure does the lack of bed space place on youth to stay in the program? Are youth who are in facilities that are totally faith-based really free to withdraw? Can we determine how voluntary their continued participation is? Clear and colleagues[33] remind us that even for adult inmates some of the reasons for engaging in religious activities are extrinsic: safety considerations, material comforts, access to outsiders, getting along with other inmates, and angling for release. To be sure, these considerations primarily raise questions about the sincerity of the religious beliefs, but in the minds of less mature youth, they may also militate against free exercise of religious choice. And even if juveniles were to assert their rights, the system may be slow to respond. An interviewee explained the problem:

> So ... what about the kid who ... gets in the program and says, "Hey, you know I really don't want to participate with your weekly baptisms and whatever?" ... We're just going to transfer a kid because of faith? Excuse me, no! That's, that's not why we transfer kids out of programs. (Interview 5)

This issue is compounded by some concerns over informed consent. Faith-based staff members tell of instances in which youth and their parents (who all signed informed consents at the time of commitment) really do not understand what will happen until they are in the program. Interviews with youth sometimes pick up on this. Although the informed consent may be "legal" in the technical sense that the program was explained and signatures were obtained, it may be based on less than an optimal understanding. Once enrolled, how difficult is it for detained juveniles to withdraw?

Reining in Proselytizing

Proselytizing, no matter how well intentioned, provides two challenges for the FCBDTI. One is programmatic. Proselytizing interferes with evidence-based treatments and may make them less effective. All the cognitive behavioral programs (e.g., Thinking for a Change, Motivational Interviewing, and Strengthening Families) in the initiative stress the importance of nonjudgmental approaches so that the youth learns to think through issues in different ways. Judgmental views and pronouncements about what is right are explicitly rejected. This position is made clear in the programs' respective manuals and in the training that the evaluation research staff attended. The FCBDTI mentoring training and manual make the same point:

> It is important during your conversations with your youth not to proselytize or give non-solicited spiritual opinions or judgments with the purpose of converting your mentee to your particular religion or denomination.[34]

The position is thought necessary, among other reasons, to foster trust (with the youths and their families) and to facilitate two-way communication so that a long-term mentoring relationship can develop. W. Wilson Goode, former Philadelphia mayor and advisor to President Clinton, forcefully admonished the FCBDTI staff to avoid proselytizing because it does not work. At least that has been his experience with the Amachi organization, a large mentoring program operating to assist the children of inmates.[35]

The second challenge arising from proselytizing is legal. Under the open-forum approach, "the mentoring is going to be content neutral" in that DJJ does not tell the mentors and mentees that "they have to talk about anything in particular" (Interview 2). The *Chaplaincy Guidelines* are blunt: *"Proselytizing must not be permitted."*[36] When DJJ staff members, even the chaplain, engage in proselytizing, they breach the wall of separation between church and state and interfere with the youth's freedom of religious exercise.

By definition, proselytizing is coercive. Proselytizing juveniles under state supervision raises concerns about their freedom to exercise their own religion. Given the doubly vulnerable status of juveniles who are in state custody, faith-based programs that are facilitated by the FCBDTI cannot turn a blind eye to heavy-handed messages of faith volunteers. Arguably, just as the state could adjust affirmatively to the constraints incarceration imposes on the free exercise of religion by funding chaplains, it should also take affirmative steps to ensure that others who the state encourages to work with its wards are not unduly coercive regarding the juveniles' First Amendment rights. Florida's DJJ *Chaplaincy Guidelines* recognize this affirmative obligation: "... the chaplain should ensure that resident youth are not being proselytized. This includes making it clear to chaplaincy volunteers that the nature of their ministry must be pastoral—not missionary."[37] An interviewee explained the rule: "I guess the rule is invite, perhaps even encourage [faith], but not persuade or coerce. So there's, I guess there's, a fine line at some point" (Interview 2).

In practice, the fine line between inviting and proselytizing presents some challenges. A chaplain "can't tell that boy he's going to hell if he doesn't believe in God....[I]f you're having a Bible study, that's different. They [the residents] volunteer to come into it and you're educating and learning about the Bible" (Interview 6).

An interview with one of the DJJ officials who helped launch the FCBDTI raised an interesting prospect. The interviewee took the position that many in the line staff in residential facilities have strong personal faiths and would be "empowered" by the faith-based components—"like to grab a kid and go take him to the chapel" (Interview 3). The official had less clear-cut advice when asked about how to prevent those staff members from proselytizing, and suggested "[f]rank, open discussion with staff and modeling" (Interview 3).

The challenge of educating workers about boundaries and then monitoring them is consequential, especially given the decentralization of service provision (i.e., entire facilities or important services like mental health programs are often "privatized"). The evaluation researchers have observed prominent Christian emblems and heard strong religious sentiments from staffers at various sites. We have seen evidence of some orthodoxy in public testimony about faith and belief in God in facilities and in various meetings. We have observed this in the presence of juveniles. In our role as evaluators, we are not in a position to judge whether or when any of this becomes "coercive" to the incarcerated youth or chips away at the wall of separation. Our evaluation team, however, is in a position to say that questions about proselytizing arise in practice and to wonder whether the decentralization of service provision makes it harder to rein in.

CONCLUSION

The FCBDTI foray to find a way to incorporate faith-based programming in juvenile corrections was necessarily uncharted at the outset. The vagaries of the First Amendment's establishment and free exercise clauses, and the tension between them, left much unknown. Questions about how the legal constraints translate into juvenile corrections only magnified the uncertainties. No wonder several states declined invitations to consider fashioning pilots before Florida accepted the challenge. What emerged from Florida's efforts could be a kind of road map for others if they wish to traverse the terrain and avoid the legal pitfalls.

Because of the special vulnerability of confined juveniles in matters of faith and because of the additional complications of parental authority over religious issues, Florida's choice of the open-forum model seems particularly strategic. It accommodates the religious beliefs and practices of youth and their parents, including those who do not endorse religion. It can avoid viewpoint discrimination in that it is open to different faith and community groups. In that sense, the FCBDTI is content neutral—it facilitates the forum in which youth can develop their beliefs, but it does not pressure them about their beliefs (including rejecting religion). The neutrality is carried over into training—the mentors (faith and community alike) are admonished to avoid proselytizing as are the FCBDTI staff members. This neutrality is consistent with the nonjudgmental approaches of the evidence-based cognitive behavioral secular treatment programming. Thus, pragmatic and programmatic reasons (in addition to legalities) militate toward the neutrality that the open-forum model emphasizes. The

FCBDTI deserves credit for a design that incorporates faith-based components with secular programming within legal strictures and in complementary ways that enhance the prospect of successful outcomes. The design is a necessary first step. At this juncture, it is too early to evaluate whether the design will actually yield the prosocial changes in attitudes and behaviors that its proponents hope to achieve.

The workable design does not, however, preclude all problems. In practice, free exercise and establishment tensions emerge. Staff and volunteers will have questions about what they may or may not do, about what constitutes inducements, and about how much effort needs to be expended on locating and accommodating a wide range of faith and community groups. Throughout the implementation, we may expect pressures toward proselytizing; after all, many participants get involved because of their faith. FCBDTI staff and volunteers are willing to sacrifice proselytizing because they are committed to what they do. Such commitment will be necessary for success but may also push the boundaries of the law. DJJ's active involvement, training, and monitoring probably will need to be ongoing lest slippage occurs and First Amendment standards be compromised.

The members of the university evaluation team are not of like mind when it comes to their orientations toward free exercise and anti-establishment, but we do concur that the DJJ and its FCBDTI staff have picked a careful path to advance the pilot. We note that Florida's DJJ began its journey by putting together a task force that also included diverse voices. The different viewpoints contributed to a process of modifying and refining the operational plan so that it could work. The FCBDTI remains a work in progress, and it continues to be reflexive, learning from successes and failures. The way it has dealt with the First Amendment to this point is a success. The FDBDTI has shown that faith components can be incorporated in ways that fit with constitutional values and that tensions can be managed. Its solutions to the competing First Amendment demands and standards provide real-world lessons for others to follow.

NOTES

1. This analysis grows out of research being conducted under contract with the Florida Department of Juvenile Justice pursuant to its grant from the federal Office of Juvenile Justice and Delinquency Prevention. We wish to acknowledge the contributions of others, especially John Milla, who was the primary author of the Department's *Chaplaincy Guidelines,* and the members of our research team. The analysis and arguments presented in the paper, however, are those of the authors.

2. See Lipsey & Wilson, 1993.

3. See the review in Sumter & Clear, 2005.

4. Pollack, 2006, p. 242, emphasis in the original.

5. A concurring opinion by Justice Stewart noted the potential for tension between the establishment and free exercise clauses, which came to a head when Congress passed the Religious Freedom Restoration Act of 1993 (RFRA) to protect an individual's freedom to exercise religion by reinstating the compelling government interest standard announced in Sherbert in 1963. Congress acted after

the Supreme Court appeared to retreat from the compelling interest test generally in *Employment Division v. Smith* (1990), a case involving workers seeking unemployment after dismissal as drug and alcohol counselors because of their religious use of peyote in their Native American ceremonies. Congress's broad and far-reaching effort to override the Supreme Court through the RFRA was rejected by the Supreme Court in *City of Boerne v. Flores* (1997) because of concerns about separation of powers and federalism.

6. King, 2005.

7. *O'Lone v. Shabazz*, 1987, p. 343.

8. Pollock, 2006, p. 244.

9. Florida Department of Juvenile Justice, hereafter DJJ, 2005, p. 4.

10. *Cutter v. Wilkinson*, 2005.

11. E.g., security; see King, 2005.

12. *Everson v. Board of Education of Ewing Township*, 1947.

13. See for example, *Wolman v. Walter* (1977) in which states could provide funds to religious schools for secular textbooks and diagnostic testing of students but not for such instructional aids as maps or globes or for transportation to field trips.

14. Feinman, 2000, p. 74.

15. For more on viewpoint discrimination, see *Lamb's Chapel v. Center Moriches Union Free School District* (1993).

16. DJJ, 2005, p. 4, emphasis in the original.

17. See DJJ, 2005.

18. Champion, 2005, p. 394.

19. 45 CFR 46.301, et seq.

20. 45 CFR 46.401, et seq.

21. Foster, 2006, pp. 396–397.

22. See Operational Plan, 2004, pp. 61–62; the job descriptions are posted at www.djj.state.fl.us/faith/Staffing_Design.html.

23. Citing McConnell, 1986, p. 161, and *Benning v. Georgia*, 2004.

24. DJJ, 2005, pp. 2–3, emphasis in the original.

25. DJJ, 2005, p. 3.

26. Field notes, December 2004.

27. Field notes, December 2004.

28. DJJ, 2005, p. 9, emphasis in the original.

29. DJJ, 2005, p. 4, emphasis in the original.

30. DJJ, 2005, p. 4, emphasis in the original.

31. DJJ, 2005, p. 4, emphasis in the original.

32. Clear, Hardyman, Stout, Lucken, & Dammer, 2006.

33. Clear et al., 2006.

34. Mentor Training Manual, 2005, p. 69.

35. Amachi Training Workshop, January 28, 2005.

36. DJJ, p. 9, emphasis in the original.

37. DJJ, p. 9.

REFERENCES

Champion, D. J. (2005). *Corrections in the United States* (4th ed.). Upper Saddle River, NJ: Prentice Hall.

Clear, T. R., Hardyman, P. L., Stout, B., Lucken, K., & Dammer, H. R. (2006). The value of religion in prison. In R. Tewksbury (Ed.), *Behind bars: Readings on prison culture* (pp. 329–347). Upper Saddle River, NJ: Prentice Hall.

Feinman, J. M. (2000). *Law 101*. New York: Oxford University.

Florida Department of Juvenile Justice. (2005, March). *Chaplaincy guidelines*. Tallahassee, FL: Florida Department of Juvenile Justice, Office of General Counsel.

Foster, B. (2006). *Corrections. The fundamentals*. Upper Saddle River, NJ: Prentice Hall.

King, K. (2005). Prisoners' constitutional rights. In R. Muraskin (Ed.), *Key correctional issues* (pp. 149–160). Upper Saddle River, NJ: Prentice Hall.

Lipsey, M. W., & Wilson, D. B. (1993). The efficacy of psychological, educational, and behavioral treatment. Confirmation from meta-analysis. *American Psychologist, 48*, 1181–1209.

McConnell, M. W. (1986). Neutrality under the religion clauses. *Northwestern Law Review, 81*, 146–167.

Mentor Training Manual. (2005). Florida Department of Juvenile Justice. Tallahassee, FL.

Operational Plan. (2004, April). Florida Department of Juvenile Justice, Faith Based Corrections Initiative. Tallahassee, FL.

Pollack, J. M. (2006). Prisoners' rights. *Prisons today and tomorrow*. Sudbury, MA: Jones and Bartlett.

Sumter, M. J., & Clear, T. R. (2005). Religion in the correctional setting. In R. Muraskin (Ed.), *Key correctional issues* (pp. 86–119). Upper Saddle River, NJ: Prentice Hall.

CASES CITED

Benning v. Georgia, 391 F.3d 1299 (11th Cir. 2004).

City of Boerne v. Flores, 521 U.S. 507 (1997).

Cruz v. Beto, 405 U.S. 319 (1972).

Cutter v. Wilkinson, 544 U.S. 709 (2005).

Employment Division v. Smith, 494 U.S. 872 (1990).

Everson v. Board of Education of Ewing Township, 330 U.S. 1 (1947).

Lamb's Chapel v. Center Moriches Union Free School District, 508 U.S. 384 (1993).

Lemon v. Krutzman, 403 U.S. 602 (1971).

O'Lone v. Estate of Shabazz, 482 U.S. 342 (1987).

Rosenberger v. University of Virginia, 515 U.S. 819 (1995).

Sherbert v. Verner, 374 U.S. 398 (1963).

Turner v. Safley, 482 U.S. 78 (1987).

Wolman v. Walter, 433 U.S. 229 (1977).

CHAPTER 10

Cops in the Classroom: Assessing the Appropriateness of Search and Seizure Case Law in Schools

David Mueller and Richard Lawrence

During the 1999–2000 school year, more than one million serious disciplinary actions were taken against students, involving about 54 percent of public schools in the United States. A majority (83 percent) of the disciplinary actions were suspensions of five days or more; 11 percent were expulsions from school; and 7 percent were transfers to specialized schools. About 20 percent of schools took disciplinary actions for possession of drugs or alcohol in school; 4 percent for possession of a firearm and 19 percent for weapons other than firearms; 35 percent for fights, 22 percent for threats, and 18 percent for insubordination.[1] Lack of discipline and control ranked just behind lack of financial support in a national survey that asked respondents what were the biggest problems facing public schools; use of drugs, fighting, violence, and gangs were also listed among the top five problems.[2] Some believe that school discipline problems such as these are the result of an overemphasis on students' rights.[3]

Despite court decisions that have recognized students' rights in school disciplinary matters, teachers and principals have been given wide authority and power to supervise students and regulate their conduct.[4] Most school districts have regulations and discipline policies that are clearly spelled out to teachers, parents, and students in handbooks and policy manuals. Yet, some teachers still choose to ignore discipline problems and fail to intervene in student disruptions and rule violations because they believe their disciplinary actions will not be supported by school administrators or they will face litigation by students and their parents.[5] Most school administrators and many teachers will at some time in their career be involved in a lawsuit or legal challenge.[6] These educators, however, often lack sufficient knowledge of Supreme Court decisions that affect them with regard to maintaining discipline and order.[7]

The purpose of this chapter is to review the issues of students' rights versus the need for school administrators and teachers to maintain an orderly and safe school environment. We review case law and court decisions that have addressed the issue of students' Fourth Amendment rights, and discuss whether the exclusionary rule should apply to school disciplinary policies and practices. We review the disciplinary procedures and sanctions that have been upheld by the courts as acceptable for schools to use in enforcing rules. We conclude with a proposal that attempts to strike a balance between students' rights and school safety.

STUDENTS' RIGHTS IN SCHOOL

The U.S. Supreme Court in *Tinker v. Des Moines Independent Community School District* reminded educators and school boards that students do have rights and that school officials may not enforce discipline policies as if they have absolute authority over students. Students do not, in the words of Justice Abe Fortas, "shed their rights at the schoolhouse gate."

> It can hardly be argued that either students or teachers shed their constitutional rights ... at the schoolhouse gate.... School officials do not possess absolute authority over their students. Students in school as well as out of school are "persons" under our Constitution. They are possessed of fundamental rights which the State must respect....[8]

The Court in *Tinker* appeared to weigh in favor of students' constitutional rights over the need to maintain safe and orderly schools. This issue of student rights versus administrative responsibility to maintain order has become more significant in light of a perceived increase in the amount of drugs and weapons in schools.[9] A number of recent court decisions have attempted to address these disciplinary problems in schools, and much of the case law related to drugs and weapons in school has focused on the issue of search and seizure.

Search and Seizure

The Fourth Amendment to the U.S. Constitution provides for "the right of people to be secure in their persons, houses, papers, and effects" and offers protections "against unreasonable searches and seizures." School officials are frequently confronted with the question of whether to search a student's pockets, book bag, purse, locker, or automobile. The Fourth Amendment as applied to people conducting searches generally pertains to law enforcement, court, and security officers. The right of school officials to search students depends on whether any illegal evidence seized may be turned over to law enforcement officers and be used as evidence in juvenile or criminal prosecution.

There are three parts to the Fourth Amendment that apply to students' rights in school.[10] First, students have a right to privacy ("to be secure in their persons, papers, and effects"); second, they have a right against unreasonable searches and seizures; and, third, any search must be specific as to the location of the search and what is being sought. The courts have not required school officials to show probable cause for a search or to obtain a search warrant from a judge before initiating a search. Instead, school officials must have "reasonable suspicion" that the student has violated or is violating either the law or the rules of the school before conducting a search. "Reasonable suspicion" means that school officials must have some facts or knowledge that provide reasonable grounds to search, and a school search may only be conducted if it is necessary to fulfill educational objectives. A student's freedom from unreasonable search and seizure therefore must be weighed against the need for school officials to maintain order and discipline, protect the health and welfare of students, and provide a safe learning environment.

New Jersey v. T.L.O.

In the case of *New Jersey v. T.L.O.*[11] the U.S. Supreme Court defined students' Fourth Amendment rights and provided guidelines for officials in conducting school searches. T.L.O., a 14-year-old freshman, was caught smoking in the school restroom along with another girl. A search of her purse produced a pack of cigarettes, some marijuana, a pipe, plastic bags, a substantial amount of money, an index card containing a list of students who apparently owed her money, and two letters that implicated her in marijuana dealing. The evidence was subsequently turned over to the police and she was charged as a delinquent. The juvenile court denied her motion to suppress the evidence found in her purse, held that the search was reasonable, and adjudged her delinquent. The state appellate court affirmed the juvenile court's finding, but the New Jersey supreme court reversed, ordered that the evidence found in her purse be suppressed, and held that the search was unreasonable. On appeal, the U.S. Supreme Court ruled that the Fourth Amendment prohibition against unreasonable searches and seizures does apply to school officials, who are acting as representatives of the state. Students do have expectations of privacy when they bring to school a variety of legitimate, noncontraband items; but the Court noted that school officials have an equally important need to maintain a safe and orderly learning environment. In balancing students' Fourth Amendment rights and school officials' responsibilities, the Court ruled that school officials do not need to obtain a warrant before searching a student because such a requirement would prevent "the maintenance of the swift and informal disciplinary procedures needed in schools."[12]

A "Reasonable" Search

The Court in *T.L.O.* cited two considerations in determining whether a warrantless search was "reasonable." First, "one must consider whether the ... action was justified at its inception"; and second, "one must determine whether the search ... was reasonably related in scope to the circumstances which justified the interference in the first place."[13] The first involves justification or grounds for initiating the search, while the second relates to the intrusiveness of the search.[14] In a later case, a school administrator had heard reports that a student was involved in drugs. A search of the student's locker and car revealed drugs and was found reasonable and constitutional.[15] In another case, a student's car was searched and cocaine was found, after the assistant principal noticed that the student smelled of alcohol, walked unsteadily, and had slurred speech, glassy eyes, and a flushed face. The court found that these observations were sufficient to support reasonable suspicion.[16] School officials must also be able to justify the extensiveness and intrusiveness of searches, and show that there was reasonable suspicion. In one case in which money went missing from a schoolroom, a teacher searched the books of two students and then required them to remove their shoes. The court found the search to be reasonable and not excessively intrusive, because the two students had been alone in the room where the stolen money disappeared.[17]

EXPANDING SEARCH POWERS BEYOND *T.L.O.*

The U.S. Supreme Court expanded school search powers 10 years after *T.L.O.* in *Vernonia School District 47J v. Acton*.[18] The Court allowed the consideration of special circumstances to give school officials the right to conduct random searches without reasonable individualized suspicion. After experiencing several instances of drug possession and use at school, the Vernonia School District instituted a policy that required students who wanted to participate in extracurricular sports to sign a form consenting to random urinalyses to search for drug use among student athletes. The Court upheld the policy, resting the decision on three factors: (1) school officials may determine that "special needs" exist to conduct random searches for the use of drugs that place students at risk of personal harm; (2) students in sports programs have a lower expectation of privacy than students who do not participate (the Court also noted in *Acton* that student athletes dress and undress in uniforms, and shower together); and (3) the Court ruled that the method of the search, collecting urinalyses, was not overly intrusive, because the samples were collected by the students themselves in the privacy of enclosed stalls.

The Court used similar reasoning of *Acton* in a 2002 case, once again upholding random, suspicionless drug testing of students. The School District of Tecumseh, Oklahoma, adopted a drug-testing policy that required all students who wanted to participate in any extracurricular school activities to consent to random urinalysis tests. The student plaintiffs in this case were not student athletes, but members of the choir, marching band, and academic team. Writing for the Court majority opinion in *Board of Education of Independent School District No. 92 of Pottawatomie County v. Earls*,[19] Justice Clarence Thomas argued that "special needs" may justify the searches among students in activities beyond those required of all students; second, students in extracurricular activities have a lower expectation of privacy; third, the method of the search was minimally intrusive on students' privacy; and, fourth, the designation of "special needs" does not require the school district to show a pervasive drug problem to justify random suspicionless drug testing. Student safety is the important factor, for both athletes and nonathletes.[20]

Search Guidelines for Principals

The courts have recognized the need for school officials to maintain a positive and safe learning environment in schools, and therefore have required only "reasonable suspicion" rather than the more stringent standard of "probable cause" required for student searches. Courts nevertheless hold firmly to the need for officials to show that reasonable grounds existed to justify a search. Alexander and Alexander have offered some guidelines for school officials in determining whether a search is justified:

- Students do have a right to privacy of their persons, papers, and effects.
- The courts will consider the seriousness of the offense and the extent to which a search intrudes on a student's privacy.
- Reasonable suspicion requires that the school official have some evidence regarding the particular situation, including the background of the student, to justify a search for items that are in violation of school rules.
- Although a warrant is not required, a school official must have knowledge of the alleged violation, where illegal contraband is presumably located, and the identity of the student alleged to be in violation.[21]

Rulings on Types of School Searches

It is an accepted fact that locker searches are permissible at any time, for any locker, without any reasonable suspicion and without a warrant. Students do not have an expectation of privacy in their lockers. The lockers are the property of the school and may be searched for any reason at any time.[22] Other searches in the school are not so clear-cut, and the courts thus have laid out particular principles regarding the constitutionality of canine searches, metal detector searches, and strip searches.

Canine Searches

Court decisions regarding canine searches precede the *T.L.O.* decision. In general, individual suspicion or a risk to the health and safety of students are required for school officials to justify a canine search.

- *Zamora v. Pomeroy.* The Tenth Circuit Court of Appeals upheld the use of dogs in the exploratory sniffing of lockers.[23]

- *Doe v. Renfrow*: The Seventh Circuit held that school officials stand *in loco parentis* and have a right to use dogs to seek out drugs because of the diminished expectations of privacy in public schools.[24]
- *Jones v. Latexo Independent School District*:[25] The decision differs from *Zamora* and *Renfrow* because the school district in *Jones* used dogs to sniff both students and automobiles. The Court ruled against both: without individual suspicion, sniffing of students is too intrusive; and because students did not have access to their cars during the school day, sniffing them was unreasonable.
- *Horton v. Goose Creek Independent School District*:[26] The Court basically upheld the *Renfrow* decision, determining that if they have reasonable suspicion, school officials may search students; but canine searches of students were held to be unconstitutional when there is no individualized suspicion, because of the "intrusion on dignity and personal security."[27]
- *Illinois v. Cabelles*: In *Cabelles* the Court ruled that a vehicle pulled over during a lawful traffic stop may be subject to a suspicionless sniff test by a drug dog without the driver's consent. Although not directly related to the case law above, *Cabelles* seems to nullify the *Jones* ruling by opening the door to suspicionless canine searches of vehicles parked on or off campus.[28]

Metal Detector Searches

According to Garcia, some 15 percent of large urban schools in the United States have resorted to using metal detectors to curb the presence of weapons and to provide a safe learning environment.[29] Detection of weapons entering schools is more than just a school rule violation and may subject the student to arrest and judicial action. Courts have generally upheld the constitutionality of random metal detector searches based on the need for a safe school environment.

- *In the Interest of F.B.*: The Court upheld a metal detector search of a student entering a Philadelphia school who was carrying a folding knife. The search was deemed reasonable and justified in light of the high rate of violence in the Philadelphia schools.[30]
- *People v. Pruit*: The Court upheld the metal detector search in a Chicago high school that revealed a loaded 0.38-caliber revolver in a student's pants.[31]
- *People v. Dukes*: The New York City Board of Education established guidelines for using metal detectors in a high school. All students were subject to a search by police officers in the main lobby; but officers could limit the search by a random formula if the line became too long. In the process of conducting such a search, a student was found to be carrying a switchblade knife, and she was charged with criminal possession of a weapon. The Court denied the legal challenge, and upheld the search, based on the school's need to maintain safety and security.[32]

Strip Searches

In cases dating back to the 1980s, courts have generally ruled that strip searches are overly intrusive and therefore violate students' Fourth Amendment rights. Basically, a search that is more intrusive increases the need to show probable cause. In many cases, the strip searches were conducted to recover stolen money or contraband that did not endanger the health or safety of students or teachers.

- *Bellnier v. Lund*: A New York court held that school officials violated students' constitutional rights when they conducted a strip search of 5th-grade students following classroom thefts. There was no individual suspicion to suggest that the searched students had taken the money.[33]
- *Oliver v. McClung*: The Court ruled that a strip search of a class of 7th-grade girls to recover $4.50 was unreasonable.[34]
- *Doe v. Renfrow*: Commenting on the nude search of a 13-year-old student, the Court ruled that it was—

   an invasion of constitutional rights of some magnitude. More than that: it is a violation of any known principle of human decency. Apart from any constitutional readings and rulings, simple common sense would indicate that the conduct of the school officials in permitting such a nude search was not only unlawful but outrageous under "settled indisputable principles of law."[35]

THE EXCLUSIONARY RULE AND SCHOOL SEARCHES

School officials are concerned with enforcing school rules and policies that aim to assure students and staff of a safe school environment. The objective of the policies is not primarily the criminal prosecution of students. A discussion of the exclusionary rule is appropriate here because illegal substances or weapons that have been seized in public schools may be turned over to law enforcement officials. In *Weeks v. United States*, the Supreme Court ruled that evidence seized without a warrant could not be used in federal courts for prosecution.[36] In *Mapp v. Ohio*, the exclusionary rule was extended to ban illegally seized evidence in state courts.[37] Several cases have addressed the application of the exclusionary rule to public schools, but the courts generally have not applied the rule, thus allowing materials seized by school officials to be used in a criminal or juvenile court prosecution.[38]

However, in *Thompson v. Carthage School District*, the Eighth Circuit Court of Appeals found that the exclusionary rule did apply to an illegal search conducted by school officials.[39] In *Thompson*, a 9th-grade student, Ramone Lea, was patted down by the school principal on suspicion that he was carrying a firearm on school grounds. Although the search did not produce a gun, it did turn up a small quantity of crack cocaine. Following a disciplinary hearing, Lea was expelled for the remainder of the school year. In its decision, the circuit court not only deemed Lea's expulsion to be "wrongful," but also awarded him $10,000 in damages for the illegal search under U.S.C. 42, section 1983. Although the court expressed concern that application of the exclusionary rule in schools might "deter educators from undertaking disciplinary proceedings that are needed to keep the schools safe," it went on to assert that the impact of the exclusionary rule is mitigated by the fact that "*school officials are not law enforcement officers*, and thus do not occupy a role whose mission is closely analogous to that of police officers."[40]

The *Thompson* decision appears to make a clear distinction between the roles of school officials and law enforcement officers. But some researchers believe that this distinction is not so clear-cut.[41] It may be factually correct to assert that school officials are not law enforcement officers, but a number of recent court decisions have recognized school resource officers as "school officials" rather than police officers. Although this may seem like a minor semantic difference, it has significant implications for the issue of search and seizure in public schools.

When Is a Cop a Cop?

Among the first cases to address the distinctions between school resource officers and school officials was *People v. Dilworth*. In *Dilworth*, a school liaison officer confiscated a flashlight from a student, searched it, and discovered a powdery substance that was later determined to be cocaine. At trial, the student moved to suppress the cocaine evidence arguing that the search was a violation of the Fourth and Fourteenth Amendments. In its ruling, the court outlined three basic categories of school searches that involve police officers: (1) those in which school officials initiate the search and act with minimal officer involvement; (2) those involving a school police or liaison officer acting on his/her own authority; and (3) those in which outside police (e.g., patrol officers or detectives not assigned to the school) initiate a search on their own, independent of school officials. The court reasoned that the first two types of searches typically permit the lesser search standard of reasonable suspicion, while the third typically requires probable cause.[42]

In its decision, the court upheld the officer's search based on reasonable suspicion. In fact, it relied heavily on the Supreme Court's own language in *T.L.O.*, which permits reasonable suspicion searches of students by "a teacher or other school official." Because the officer in this case was assigned to the school on a full-time basis, he was recognized as a "school official."

However, a dissenting opinion in this case argues that the officer in question should not have been construed as a school official for Fourth Amendment purposes because his primary responsibility (as a police officer) was to investigate and prevent criminal activity. According to the opinion, (1) he arrested the offender and took him to the police station; (2) he was not a member of the school's security staff (which the school did have); (3) although he was listed in the school handbook as a member of the support staff, he was in fact a police officer assigned to patrol an area and investigate and prevent criminal activity; and (4) he acted as a police officer in this case: chasing, detaining, searching, arresting, and interrogating the suspect (with Miranda protections).

Because the *Dilworth* case raises more questions than it answers, courts have looked to other criteria such as employment issues and duties to clarify the officer's status—for example, is the officer employed by the school or the police department? Unfortunately, this line of inquiry also has not proved fruitful, for as Pinard points out, "[E]ven where the officers assigned to the school are ultimately responsible to a law enforcement agency, some courts have declared them to be more aligned with school officials and therefore allowed to search students based on reasonable suspicion."[43]

Another factor that courts have considered when determining the appropriate level of suspicion required for searches involving school resource officers is the underlying purpose of the search. If the purpose is to uncover evidence that the student has violated school rules, courts typically employ the lesser standard of reasonable suspicion.[44] If, however, the purpose is to investigate a criminal violation, courts will often require probable cause. Of course, criminal and school rule violations are not mutually exclusive. By and large, criminal law violations violate school rules; however, school rule violations do not necessarily constitute violations of the criminal law.

Another issue courts have considered is the level and extent of the officer's involvement in the search. For example, did the officer initiate the search on his or her own without the knowledge or consent of school administrators? If a school administrator, in the presence of an officer, conducts a search, what role did the officer play during the search? Rulings in this area generally indicate that as the officer's involvement and participation in the search increases, so too does the likelihood that courts will require the higher standard of probable cause.[45] Conversely, when the officer's participation is minimal, the reasonable suspicion standard will often suffice.[46]

Safety concerns also factor into such decisions. That is, courts seem willing to grant school officials "a certain degree of flexibility" to seek the assistance of law enforcement officers when faced with potentially dangerous situations without sacrificing the more lenient and flexible reasonable suspicion standard. For example, in the case of *In re Alexander B.*, the California appellate court upheld a police search based on reasonable suspicion when the school's dean directed officers to search a group of students after receiving a report that one of them had a weapon.[47] Here, the court defended its ruling by pointing to the California state constitution, which reads in part that "[a]ll students and staff of public ... schools have the inalienable right to attend campuses which are safe, secure and peaceful."[48] In a similar case, a Wisconsin court held that "[s]chool officials not only educate students ... but they have a responsibility to protect those students and their teachers from behavior that threatens their safety and the integrity of the learning process."[49]

In the absence of further clarification on this issue from the U.S. Supreme Court, various state courts have found it appropriate to apply the reasonable suspicion standard to searches conducted by school resource officers when the search in question is undertaken at the behest of a school official. This may be an appropriate standard given that (1) such searches may involve students in possession of weapons at school, and (2) school officials are not presumed to have the requisite skills and training necessary to deal with such dangerous situations. But zero-tolerance policies toward weapons in school are often applied blindly, discount individual circumstances, and have resulted in suspensions and expulsions (or worse) without considering the age of the student, the kind of weapon possessed, and whether or not the student intended to harm others with it.

One such example is the case of *Shade v. City of Farmington* in which a group of students was transported by bus from their technical/alternative school to an auto body repair shop in an adjoining community. Along the way, appellant Shade attempted to open an orange juice container with a knife he borrowed from a friend. The bus driver observed Shade with the knife and telephoned the school resource office. The officer subsequently searched all the males on the bus; the knife was located (on its owner— not Shade) and it was confiscated. However, Shade was the one charged with possessing a dangerous weapon on school property and he was expelled. The U.S. Court of Appeals upheld the expulsion even though Shade made no threatening gestures with the knife and had no intent of harming anyone on the bus. More important, for our purposes, the search was deemed constitutional even though it had been (1) carried out by a police officer, (2) based on reasonable suspicion, and (3) conducted *off* school grounds.[50]

"SPECIAL NEEDS" SEARCHES AND CRIMINAL SANCTIONS

School searches typically fall into a category known as administrative or "special needs" searches. These searches are generally characterized by a reduction in the traditional requirements for a search; typically, the court engages in a balancing test, weighing the rights of the searched against the needs of the person or institution conducting the search. These searches implicate some form of public safety issue that would be cumbersome or virtually impossible to address using the traditional rules of search and seizure. Another particular characteristic of special needs searches is that they are noncriminal in nature.

The case law in administrative and special needs searches provides strong support for the idea that these searches generally are not used for purposes of uncovering criminal wrongdoing but rather for the purpose of enhancing public safety. In *National Treasury Employees Union v. Von Raab*, the Court approved the drug testing of employees who met particular criteria in their jobs, including the carrying of firearms or the interdiction of illegal drugs. The Court reasoned that officers who intercept drugs being smuggled into the United States are a first line of defense in the fight against drugs, and the use of narcotics by these officers could seriously compromise their ability to perform their jobs. In addition, if an officer must use a firearm in the line of duty, the influence of drugs could impair their ability to do so properly and could potentially endanger the public.[51] In *Skinner v. Railway Labor Executives' Association*, the Court found that the mandatory drug testing of railroad workers was constitutional. The Court reasoned that individuals operating and working on and around trains perform tasks that, if not done properly, could endanger the public. Because of this, the Court saw a special need to conduct drug tests on railroad employees as a check against drug usage, which could hinder their ability to perform their work safely.[52]

Two noteworthy special needs rulings that focus on schools are *Vernonia School District 47 v. Acton*, and *Board of Education of Independent School District No. 92 of Pottawatomie County v. Earls*.[53] In *Acton*, the Court determined that the suspicionless drug testing of high school athletes was constitutional; the Court later extended this decision in *Earls* to include all students who participate in extracurricular school activities. The Court reasoned that students who engage in extracurricular activities while under the influence of drugs could jeopardize their health and safety. One of the key aspects of both *Acton* and *Earls* is that evidence of student drug use would not be used for purposes of criminal prosecution; it would simply disqualify them from participating in extracurricular activities. Additionally, drug-testing results would not be handed over to law enforcement for purposes of criminal prosecution; they would stay within the school. Clearly, the *Acton* and *Earls* cases demonstrate that the intent of the special needs search is not to gather evidence for later use in a criminal prosecution.

Likewise, the *T.L.O.* ruling was crafted to disencumber school officials from the more stringent and demanding search and seizure standard applied to police officers. Reducing the search and seizure standard for school officials was deemed appropriate because schools have a special need to maintain order and discipline in an environment conducive to learning. School officials were granted this flexibility to provide "an immediate response to behavior that threatens either the safety of schoolchildren and teachers or the educational process itself."[54] But within the school context, this flexibility was granted exclusively to school officials, not police officers. By limiting this power to school officials, the *T.L.O.* decision is consistent with the idea that "*the mission of teachers is to educate,* unlike that of police, who are trained to use the fruits of a search to bring a criminal prosecution."[55] So, how is it that today's state courts are interpreting the special needs doctrine to justify (1) reasonable suspicion searches conducted by police and school resource officers in schools, and (2) allowing items seized by these officers in school to be used in a criminal prosecution?

Extending the special needs doctrine to police officers in schools seems to be a blatant misinterpretation of both the Supreme Court's expressed and implied intent in the *T.L.O.* decision. As noted earlier, one of the primary motivations in granting school officials the power to search students under the reasonable suspicion standard was to free them from the search warrant requirement and the onerous standard of probable cause. The decision may also have been a more subtle recognition of the fact that if the Court applied the reasonable suspicion standard too broadly—to school officials and police officers alike—then public schools could quickly spiral into a pseudo–police state. Perhaps this is why, as Jones suggests, the lower search and seizure standard was reserved exclusively for school officials; because "school officials are not law enforcement officers, and ... do not occupy a role whose mission is closely analogous to that of police officers."[56]

Clearly, school officials have a special relationship with their students, and one of their primary duties is to educate young people about the difference between right and wrong. But recent court decisions that blur the distinction between the police and school officials would seem to undermine this relationship, casting teachers and other school personnel in the role of law enforcement officers. Granted, there will always be a need to discipline unruly students. But when this need arises, the disciplinary process should further the goals and objectives of the broader educational process. Rarely do school disciplinary problems require the full force of the criminal law.

Additionally, permitting the introduction of evidence seized by police in schools under the reasonable suspicion standard for the purpose of criminal prosecution seems to violate the Court's expressed desire to enhance public safety without resorting to criminal sanctions. This again would seem to be an obvious misinterpretation of the Supreme Court's later rulings in both *Acton* and *Earls*.

No Small Issue

In the 20 years since the *T.L.O.* ruling, police officers and security personnel have become regular fixtures in many public schools throughout the nation.[57] The Office of Community Oriented Policing Services (COPS) recently claimed to have awarded almost $748 million to more than 3,000 law enforcement agencies to train and fund more than 6,500 school resource officers through the Cops in Schools Program.[58] Estimates suggest that as many as 14,000 dedicated school resource officers work in public schools across the country.[59] Although these officers perform a variety of beneficial functions for schools (e.g., order maintenance, crime prevention, public relations, and so on), it is important to remember that they do not occupy the same role as educators. Their primary duty is to detect and apprehend law violators and gather evidence for criminal prosecution. What is particularly disconcerting about today's new search and seizure standards for police in schools is that America's institutions of public education seem to be drifting toward what Mello has referred to as a constitutional "free zone." Judges may pay lip service to the idea of the Fourth Amendment, "but the reality is that virtually any search and seizure ... will be upheld as reasonable and therefore constitutional."[60]

DISCUSSION

Our argument here should not be interpreted as a call to abolish all police officers from the school setting. Indeed, neighborhoods situated around middle schools and high schools invariably represent "hot spots" for crime and disorder that require a visible police presence. Additionally, police-sponsored initiatives such as the Drug Abuse Resistance Education (D.A.R.E.) and the Gang Resistance Education and Training (GREAT) programs offer hope of proactively preventing some of the most vexing forms of juvenile delinquency. In fact, our concerns about the proliferation of police officers in schools lies not so much with the police per se, but with the way teachers and school administrators have come to rely on these officers to handle problematic situations.

As police officers have become more embedded in American schools (largely in reaction to high-profile school shooting incidents), teachers and school administrators appear increasingly willing to relinquish their traditional responsibility for discipline and rule enforcement to the police and other security personnel. As noted earlier, school administrators may wish to avoid confrontation with problematic students because of fear of being sued.[61] Another reason to defer to law enforcement experts is that school officials may lack sufficient knowledge about Supreme Court decisions regarding school discipline and order maintenance.[62] But a third explanation strikes us as more telling—that is, the explanation that schools have become somewhat rule-bound in their approach to handling incidents of student misconduct and education policies have taken on a get-tough philosophy. Following this approach, problem students are removed from school for arguably trivial offenses without considering the legitimacy or the long-term ramifications of such action.

Even a cursory review of the academic literature from the fields of education and criminal justice suggests that "getting rid of the troublemakers" is an increasingly popular solution to dealing with problem students.[63] Zero-tolerance policies regarding student misconduct have become pervasive in school districts throughout the nation. These policies, initially created in response to student drug use, have been extended to address a wide range of disciplinary matters, including weapons-carrying, violence, and perceived acts of violence by students. Students who violate the school's zero-tolerance policy typically are suspended from school or, in more extreme cases, are expelled from school for up to a year.

Although we can all agree that drugs have no place in our public schools, excluding a student from school for a first-time drug offense denies them the opportunity to learn from a "teachable moment." Even more disintegrative is the policy that permits the student to be simultaneously expelled from school and then arrested and prosecuted. It is possible to debate the merits of prosecution and its long-term benefits for secondary crime prevention, but we believe it is better, if the student is to be prosecuted, to have them sentenced to a period of probation with the stipulations that they (1) refrain from further criminal activity, and (2) attend school (perhaps an alternative school) regularly. Prior research clearly shows that forced removal from school is a strong predictor of dropout[64] and dropping out of school is closely associated with a host of negative outcomes for youth, including increased likelihood of arrest,[65] welfare reliance,[66] and incarceration in later adulthood.[67] Logic dictates that keeping kids in school—perhaps an alternative school and under probation supervision—is better than banishing them from school altogether.

A similar approach could be taken with students who carry weapons to school. In spite of the extensive media coverage of the 1999 attack on Columbine High School, research suggests that students rarely carry guns to school.[68] Schiraldi and Ziedenberg highlighted a few of the more trivial examples for which students have been expelled for "weapons-carrying" at school.[69] Space limitations do not permit a review of those incidents here; suffice it to say that it is not beyond the realm of possibilities for educators to at least inquire into the nature of the offense: Why was the student motivated to carry the weapon to school in the first place? Was the weapon so dangerous as to warrant expulsion? Did they actually intend to harm someone with it? If so, then expulsion and prosecution is warranted. But Sheley and Wright report that students who carry guns (to school and elsewhere) typically do so in reaction to a perceived threat, for self-protection, or out of fear of attack.[70] Expelling and prosecuting a student under these circumstances is akin to punishing the victim while ignoring a potentially ongoing threat to the safety of others.

Policy makers should consider taking a closer look at the long-term utility of expelling or prosecuting students for participating in acts of violence at school. The *Indicators of School Crime and Safety* report shows that violence in schools is rare, and public schools are among the safest locations in any given community.[71] Incidents of serious juvenile violence in school are even more rare and tend to take place *away* from school, out in the community.[72] That said, of all the disciplinary actions taken by school administrators, mutually combative fights (e.g., simple assaults) between students are by the far the leading cause of suspensions. But here again, unless the problem is persistent, banishing a student from the school setting is likely to severely diminish his or her life chance and opportunity to learn the boundaries of acceptable behavior. There is no question that school administrators must "do something" to communicate that violence in school will not be tolerated, but it is hard to accept the claim that "society must be permitted to give up on students who are threatening the educational opportunities of their classmates."[73] Researchers like Zimring vehemently disagree with this claim by arguing that violence is, unfortunately, a "normal" aspect of adolescence.[74] Zimring writes elsewhere that for kids to develop social competence and become well-adjusted adults, policy makers and the public must learn to be more patient with adolescent offenders when they make mistakes. He writes,

> In blackjack, an "ideal" career is never to lose a hand. In the game of learning to make free choices, winning every hand is poor preparation for the modern world ... We want adolescents to make mistakes, but we hope they make the right kinds of mistakes ... An important part of cutting our losses

during this period of development is minimizing the harm young persons do [to] themselves, and keeping to a minimum the harm we inflict on them....[75]

By denying juveniles the opportunity to make and learn from their mistakes, and treating them as social pariah when they fail, it is easy to forget that most will eventually grow up to become productive, law-abiding citizens.

CONCLUSION

This chapter has shown, through numerous case law examples, that the legal trend in school discipline today is to establish safe schools through a punitive approach that is underlined by a heavy and arguably unfettered police presence in schools. We contend that an informal educational approach to school discipline would be not only more consistent with the constitutionality of student rights, but also more humane. The best social control is a good education, a fact that is in the slogan, if not the intent, of the *No Child Left Behind Act*.

We all agree that weapons and illegal drugs have no place in schools. Violation of school rules (and violations of the juvenile law) must be sanctioned. However, compulsory school attendance laws were developed for a reason, and the positive effects of regular school attendance (e.g., higher learning, improved social bonds, behavior modification, positive commitment, and attachment to a conventional lifestyle) are well documented. Given that, does it not make more sense to sanction inappropriate student conduct informally through the traditional educational process with an eye toward keeping kids *in* school rather than kicking them out?

For more serious offenses, it makes sense to sanction the behavior through the formal justice system, resulting perhaps in a probation sentence with special conditions and requirements to "attend school regularly and obey all school regulations." But widespread deployment of police into public schools, coupled with a lowered standard for search and seizure, will almost assuredly lead to a greater number of arrests and prosecutions. Durable sanctions like these should be used sparingly.

ACKNOWLEDGMENT

The authors appreciate the research assistance of Cody Stoddard in the preparation of this chapter.

NOTES

1. DeVoe et al., 2004, p. 28.
2. Rose & Gallup, 2004, p. 44.
3. Devine, 1996.
4. Lawrence, 1998.
5. Devine, 1996.

6. Chandler, 1992.

7. Reglin, 1992.

8. Justice Abe Fortas, *Tinker v. Des Moines Independent Community School District*, 1969, pp. 506, 511.

9. Brown & Benedict, 2004; National Center on Addiction and Substance Abuse at Columbia University, 2001.

10. Alexander & Alexander, 2005, p. 398.

11. *New Jersey v. T.L.O.*, 1985.

12. *New Jersey v. T.L.O.*, 1985, p. 340.

13. *New Jersey v. T.L.O*, 105 S. Ct. 733 (1985), p. 744.

14. See Alexander & Alexander, 2005, p. 399.

15. *State v. Slattery*, 56 Wn.App. 820, 787 P.2d 932 (1990).

16. *Shamberg v. State*, 1988.

17. *Wynn v. Board of Education of Vestabia Hills*, 1987.

18. *Vernonia School District 47J v. Acton*, 1995.

19. *Board of Education of Independent School District No. 92 of Pottawatomie County v. Earls*, 2002.

20. See also Alexander & Alexander, 2005, p. 400.

21. Alexander & Alexander, 2005, p. 401.

22. *In re Patrick Y.*, 2000.

23. *Zamora v. Pomeroy*, 1981.

24. *Doe v. Renfrow*, 475 F. Supp. 1012 (N.D. Ind. 1979); 631 R.2d 91 (7th Cir.1980); 635 F.2d 582; 451 U.S. 1022 (1981).

25. *Jones v. Latexo Independent School District*, 1980.

26. *Horton v. Goose Creek Independent School District*, 1982.

27. Alexander & Alexander, 2005, pp. 401–402.

28. *Illinois v. Cabelles*, 2005.

29. Garcia, 2003.

30. *In the Interest of F.B.*, 1995.

31. *People v. Pruit*, 1996.

32. *People v. Dukes*, 1992.

32. *Bellnier v. Lund*, 1977.

34. *Oliver v. McClung*, 1995.

35. *Doe v. Renfrow*, 631 F.2d 91 (7th Cir.1980); 635 F.2d 582; 451 U.S. 1022 (1981).

36. *Weeks v. United States*, 232 U.S. 383, 34 S.Ct. 341 (1914).

37. *Mapp v. Ohio*, 367 U.S. 643, 81 S. Ct. 1684 (1961).

38. Alexander & Alexander, 2005, p. 403.

39. *Thompson v. Carthage School District*, 1996.

40. Jones, 1997, p. 390, emphasis added.

41. Beger, 2002; Jones, 1997; Kagan, 2004; Pinard, 2003.

42. *People v. Dilworth*, 1996.

43. Pinard, 2003, p. 1084; see also, e.g., the case of *In re Ana*, 2002.

44. Stefkovich & Miller, 1999.

45. See *F.P. v. State*, 1998; *State v. Twayne H.*, 1997.

46. *State v. N.G.B.*, 2002.

47. *In re Alexander B.*, 1990.

48. See also *People v. Butler*, 2001.

49. *In re Angelia D.B.*, 1997.

50. *Shade v. City of Farmington*, 2002.

51. *National Treasury Employees Union v. Von Raab*, 1989.

52. *Skinner v. Railway Labor Executives' Association*, 1989.

53. *Board of Education of Independent School District No. 92 of Pottawatomie County v. Earls*, 2002; *Vernonia School District 47 v. Acton*, 1995.
54. *New Jersey v. T.L.O.*, 1985, p. 353.
55. Beger, 2003, p. 337, emphasis added.
56. Jones, 1997, p. 390.
57. Beger, 2002; Kagan, 2004.
58. U.S. Department of Justice, 2004.
59. Siegel, Welsh, & Senna, 2006, p. 410.
60. Mello, 2002, p. 377.
61. Devine, 1996.
62. Reglin, 1992.
63. Bowditch, 1993.
64. De Ridder, 1990.
65. Thornberry, Moore, & Christensen, 1985.
66. Rumberger, 1987.
67. Arum & Beattie, 1999.
68. DeVoe et al., 2004.
69. Schiraldi & Ziedenberg, 2001.
70. Sheley & Wright, 1998.
71. DeVoe et al., 2004.
72. Lawrence & Mueller, 2003.
73. Toby, 1980, p. 38.
74. Zimring, 1998, p. 27.
75. Zimring, 2005, p. 18.

REFERENCES

Alexander, K., & Alexander, M. D. (2005). *American public school law* (6th ed.). St. Paul, MN: West.

Arum, R., & Beattie, I. (1999). High school experiences and the risk of adult incarceration. *Criminology, 37*(3), 515–540.

Beger, R. R. (2002). Expansion of police power in public schools and the vanishing rights of students. *Social Justice, 29*(1–2), 119–130.

Beger, R. R. (2003). The "worst of both worlds": School security and the disappearing Fourth Amendment rights of students. *Criminal Justice Review, 28*(3), 336–354.

Bowditch, C. (1993). Getting rid of the troublemakers: High school disciplinary procedures and the production of dropouts. *Social Problems, 40*, 491–509.

Brown, B., & Benedict, W. R. (2004). Bullets, blades, and being afraid in Hispanic high schools: An exploratory study of the presence of weapons and fear of weapon associated victimization among high school students in a border town. *Crime and Delinquency, 50*, 372–395.

Chandler, G. L. (1992). Due process rights of high school students. *High School Journal, 75*(3), 137–143.

De Ridder, L. M. (1990). How suspension and expulsion contribute to dropping out. *Educational Horizons, 68*(Spring), 153–157.

Devine, J. (1996). *Maximum security: The culture of violence in inner-city schools.* Chicago: The University of Chicago Press.

DeVoe, J., Peter, I., Kaufman, P., Miller, A., Noonan, M., Snyder, T. D., & Baum, K. (2004). *Indicators of school crime and safety: 2004.* Washington, D.C.: U.S. Departments of Education and Justice.

Garcia, C. A. (2003). School Safety technology in America: Current use and perceived effectiveness. *Criminal Justice Policy Review, 14*(1), 30–54.

Jones, D. S. (1997). Application of the exclusionary rule to bar use of illegally seized evidence in civil school disciplinary proceedings. *Washington University Journal of Urban and Contemporary Law, 52,* 375–397.

Kagan, J. (2004). Reappraising T.L.O.'s "special needs" doctrine in an era of school-law enforcement entanglement. *Journal of Law and Education, 33*(3), 291–325.

Lawrence, R. (1998). *School crime and juvenile justice.* New York: Oxford University Press.

Lawrence, R., & Mueller, D. (2003). School shootings and the man-bites-dog criterion on "newsworthiness." *Youth Violence and Juvenile Justice, 1*(4), 330–345.

Mello, M. (2002). Friendly fire: Privacy vs. security after September 11. *Criminal Law Bulletin, 38,* 367–395.

National Center on Addiction and Substance Abuse at Columbia University. (2001, September). *Malign neglect substance abuse and America's schools.* New York: National Center on Addiction and Substance Abuse at Columbia University.

Pinard, M. (2003). From the classroom to the courtroom: Reassessing Fourth Amendment standards in public school searches involving law enforcement authorities. *Arizona Law Review, 45,* 1067–1125.

Reglin, G. L. (1992). Public school educators' knowledge of selected Supreme Court decisions affecting daily public school operations. *Journal of Educational Administration, 30*(2), 26–31.

Rose, L. C., & Gallup, A. M. (2004). The 36th annual Phi Delta Kappa/Gallup Poll of the public's attitudes toward the public schools. *Phi Delta Kappan.* Retrieved February 19, 2005, from www.pdkintl.org/kappan/K0409 pol.htm.

Rumberger, R. W. (1987). High school dropouts: A review of issues and evidence. *Review of Educational Research, 57,* 101–122.

Schiraldi, V., & Ziedenberg, J. (2001, September). Schools and suspensions: Self-reported crime and the growing use of suspensions. *Policy Brief.* Washington, D.C.: Justice Policy Institute. Retrieved February 16, 2005, from www.cjcj.org.

Sheley, J. F., & Wright, J.D. (1998, October). High school youths, weapons, and violence: A national survey. *Research in Brief.* Washington, D.C.: U.S. Department of Justice, Office of Justice Programs.

Siegel, L. J., Welsh, B. C., & Senna, J. J. (2006). *Juvenile delinquency: Theory, practice, and law* (9th ed.). Belmont, CA: Thomson/Wadsworth.

Stefkovich, J. A., & Miller, J. A. (1999). Law enforcement officers in public schools: Student citizens in safe havens. *BYU Education and Law Journal, 1999*(1), 25–69.

Thornberry, T. P., Moore, M., & Christensen, R. L. (1985). The effect of dropping out of high school on subsequent criminal behavior. *Criminology, 23,* 3–18.

Toby, J. (1980). Crime in American schools. *Public Interest, 58,* 18–42.

U.S. Department of Justice. (2004, September). COPS in schools: The COPS commitment to school safety. *COPS Fact Sheet.* Retrieved February 3, 2005, from www.cops.usdoj.gov.

Zimring, F. (1998). *American youth violence.* New York: Oxford University Press.

Zimring, F. (2005). *American juvenile justice.* New York: Oxford University Press.

CASES CITED

Bellnier v. *Lund*, 438 F.Supp. 47, N.D.N.Y. (1977).

Board of Education of Independent School District No. 92 of Pottawatomie County v. Earls, 536 U.S. 822 (2002).

Doe v. Renfrow, 451 U.S. 1022 (1981).

F.P. v. State, 528 So. 3d 1253 (Fla. Dist Ct. App. 1998).

Horton v. Goose Creek Independent School District, 690 F.2d 470, 5th Cir. (1982).

Illinois v. Cabelles, 543 U.S. 405 (2005).

In re Alexander B., 220 Cal. App. 3d. 1572 (1990).

In re Ana, No. D-10378/01, 2002 N.Y. Mics. LEXIS 53 (N.Y. Fam. Ct., Jan 14, 2002).

In re Angelia D.B., 564 N.W. 2d 685 (Wis. 1997).

In re Patrick Y., 746 A.2d 405 [Md 2000].

In the Interest of F.B., 658 A.2d 1378, S.Ct PA (1995).

Jones v. Latexo Independent School District, 499 F. Supp. 223, E.D. Tex. (1980).

Mapp v. Ohio, 367 U.S. 643 (1961).

National Treasury Employees Union v. Von Raab, 489 U.S. 656 (1989).

New Jersey v. T.L.O., 469 U.S. 325 (1985).

Oliver v. McClung, 919 F. Supp. 1206, N.D. Ind. (1995).

People v. Butler, 725 N.Y.S. 2d 534 (N.Y. Sup. Ct. 2001).

People v. Dilworth, 661 N.E. 2d310, Ill (1996).

People v. Dukes, 580 NY2d 850, NY Crim. Ct. (1992).

People v. Pruit, 662 N.E.2d 540, Ill. App. Ct. (1996).

Shade v. City of Farmington, 309 F.3d 1054 (8th Cir., 2002).

Shamberg v. State, 762 P.2d 486, Alaska App. (1988).

Skinner v. Railway Labor Executives' Association, 489 U.S. 602 (1989).

State v. N.G.B., 806 So. 2d 567 (Fla. Dist. Ct. App. 2002).

State v. Slattery, 56 Wash. App. 820, Wash. Ct. App. (1990).

State v. Twayne H., 933 P.2d 251 (N.M. Ct App. 1997).

Thompson v. Carthage School District, 87 F.3d 979 (8th Cir., 1996).

Tinker v. Des Moines Independent Community School District, 393 U.S. 503 (1969).

Vernonia School District 47J v. Acton, 515 U.S. 646 (1995).

Weeks v. United States, 232 U.S. 383 (1914).

Wynn v. Board of Education of Vestavia Hills, 508 So. 2d 1170, Ala. (1987).

Zamora v. Pomeroy, 639 F.2d 662, 10th Cir. (1981).

CHAPTER 11

The Death Penalty for Juveniles in the United States: An Obituary

Robert M. Bohm

T he death penalty for juveniles in the United States is dead. This is its obituary. On March 1, 2005, in the case of *Roper* v. *Simmons*,[1] the U.S. Supreme Court, by a vote of five to four, ruled that the U.S. Constitution's Eighth and Fourteenth Amendments prohibit the execution of offenders who were under the age of 18 at the time they committed their capital crimes. It thus ended a practice that began in America during the seventeenth century and that currently is used in only a handful of countries.

HISTORICAL BACKGROUND

Throughout the history of the United States, the death penalty has been reserved almost entirely for the crimes committed by adult men. Fewer than 3 percent of the approximately 20,000 people executed under legal authority in the United States have been women and fewer than 2 percent were juveniles. Most of the juveniles executed (about 70 percent) were black, nearly 90 percent of their victims were white, and approximately 65 percent of them were executed in the South. The first juvenile executed in America was Thomas Graunger in the Plymouth colony in 1642 for the crime of bestiality. He was 16 at the time of his crime and execution. The youngest nonslave executed in the United States was Ocuish Hannah. On December 20, 1786, she was hanged at the age of twelve for a murder she had committed in New London County, Connecticut. At the time the Bill of Rights was ratified in 1791, American law only prohibited the execution of children under the age of seven. Besides murder, juveniles in America have been executed for sodomy with animals, arson, robbery, assault, and rape.

Before the 1980s, the age of a capital offender received little public or legal scrutiny, probably in part because death sentences were rarely imposed on juveniles. Most death penalty states had death penalty statutes that established a minimum age eligibility requirement at the time of the crime. Indiana's death penalty statute allowed juveniles as young as 10 years of age at the time of their crime to be executed. Montana's statute provided the death penalty for juveniles as young as 12 years old. Mississippi's minimum age was 13. Other states had minimum age limits ranging from 14 to 18. Some death penalty states set no statutory minimum age limits.

Eddings and the First Post-*Furman* Executions of Juveniles

The U.S. Supreme Court first considered the issue of age in capital cases in *Eddings v. Oklahoma*.[2] Monty Eddings was sentenced to death for killing a highway patrol officer. He was 16 at the time of the crime. Although on appeal Eddings challenged the constitutionality of the death penalty for juveniles, the Court vacated his death sentence on narrower grounds. The key issue for the Court was not his age, which was presented as a mitigating circumstance at trial, but the trial court's failure to consider two other mitigating factors—his unstable family life and emotional disturbances. Even though the Supreme Court sidestepped the broader constitutional question in *Eddings*, it did stress that chronological age was an important mitigating factor that must be considered during the sentencing phase of a capital trial.

Between 1983 and 1986, the Supreme Court had five more opportunities to rule on the constitutionality of the death penalty for juveniles but declined in each case. Also, during that period, three juveniles were executed. They were the first post–*Furman v. Georgia*[3] executions of juveniles, and the first juveniles executed in more than two decades. *Furman* was the landmark decision in which the Supreme Court held for the first time in American history that the death penalty, as administered, was unconstitutional. The three juveniles were Charles Rumbaugh, who was executed in Texas on September 11, 1985; James Terry Roach, who was executed in South Carolina on January 10, 1986; and Jay Pinkerton, who was executed in Texas on May 15, 1986. They were all 17 years old at the time of their crimes. (At the time of their executions, Rumbaugh was 28, Roach was 25, and Pinkerton was 24.) By the end of the decade the Court finally agreed to consider the constitutionality of the death penalty for juveniles in *Thompson v. Oklahoma*.[4]

Thompson, Stanford, and *Wilkins*

William Thompson was one of four people convicted and sentenced to death for the brutal murder of his former brother-in-law. Thompson was

15 years old at the time of the murder and was certified to stand trial as an adult. In *Thompson*, the Court held that the Constitution prohibited the execution of a person who was under 16 years of age at the time of his or her offense. The Court reasoned that (1) besides the special certification (as an adult) process used in the *Thompson* case, Oklahoma had no statutes, either criminal or civil, that treated anyone under 16 years of age as anything but a child; (2) although states varied in the line they drew demarcating childhood from adulthood, they were near unanimity in treating a person under 16 years of age as a minor for several important purposes; (3) of the 18 death penalty states that had established by statute a minimum age for death eligibility, none of them allowed the death penalty for anyone under 16 years of age; (4) respected professional organizations and peer nations had expressed the view that the execution of people younger than 16 years of age at the time of their offense offended civilized standards of decency; (5) the evidence of thousands of murder trials showed that jurors, as representatives of the conscience of their communities, had generally found it abhorrent to impose the death penalty on a 15 year old; and (6) the imposition of the death penalty on people under 16 years of age had not made, nor could be expected to make, any measurable contribution to the goals of capital punishment, especially the principal goals of retribution and general deterrence. The Court stipulated, however, that the decision applied only when a state had not specifically legislated a minimum age for its death penalty, as was the case in Oklahoma at the time.

The next year, in the cases of *Stanford v. Kentucky* and *Wilkins v. Missouri*,[5] the Court determined that the Eighth Amendment did not prohibit the execution of people who were 17 (in *Stanford*) or 16 (in *Wilkins*) years of age at the time of their offense. Kevin Stanford was convicted and sentenced to death for raping, sodomizing, and murdering a female service-station clerk in Jefferson County, Kentucky, on January 7, 1981. Heath Wilkins was certified to stand trial as an adult and was convicted and sentenced to die for stabbing to death a young female liquor store clerk in Avondale, Missouri, on July 27, 1985. Together, the three decisions in *Thompson*, *Stanford*, and *Wilkins* suggested that the Supreme Court would not allow the execution of people under 16 years of age at the time of their offense.

Following the Court's decisions in *Thompson*, *Stanford*, and *Wilkins*, death penalty jurisdictions began amending their death penalty statutes to conform to the Court's age rulings. By 2001, 23 states and the U.S. military allowed by law the execution of people who were younger than 18 years of age at the time of their crime. Five states had a minimum age of 17, and 18 states and the U.S. military had a minimum age of 16. No death penalty state allowed by statute the execution of a person younger than 16 years of age at the time of the crime. Thus, the amended death penalty statutes institutionalized a long-standing American tradition. Historically, fewer than 20 percent of all juveniles executed in the United States were younger than 16 years of age at the time they committed the offense for which they were executed.

The Last Executions of Juveniles in the United States

After the execution of the three 17 year olds in the 1980s, 19 or 20 more young men were executed in seven states. (Whether the number is 19 or 20 depends on whether Jose High is included. High was executed in Georgia on November 6, 2001. His age was in dispute, but it is generally believed that he was 17 at the time he committed his crime. He is counted here.) The last juvenile executed in the United States was Scott Allen Hain in Oklahoma on April 3, 2003. Of the 23 juveniles executed, 10 were white, 12 were black, and 1 was Hispanic. More than half of the 23 executions took place in Texas and about 70 percent of them in Texas and Virginia. The others were executed in Georgia (2), Louisiana (1), Missouri (1), Oklahoma (2), and South Carolina (1). All but 1 of the 23 juveniles executed were 17 years of age at the time of their crimes. The other juvenile, Sean Sellars, who was executed in Oklahoma on February 4, 1999, was 16 years old at the time of his crime. The last 16 year old (at the time of his crime) executed in the United States was Leonard Shockley. Shockley was executed in Maryland on April 10, 1959.

Between 1990 and Hain's execution in 2003, the United States was one of only eight countries that executed anyone under 18 years of age at the time of the crime; the others were Iran, Pakistan, Saudi Arabia, the Republic of Yemen, Nigeria, the Democratic Republic of Congo, and China. The Court found this fact instructive but not controlling in its landmark decision in *Roper v. Simmons* (discussed later).

JUVENILES ON DEATH ROW

On December 31, 2004, 72 people who committed crimes before their 18th birthdays sat on death rows throughout the United States awaiting their executions. That represented about 2 percent of the total death row population. The typical juvenile on death row was a 17-year-old minority male who killed a white adult female, after robbing or raping her. Of the total number of juvenile death row inmates, 46 percent were black, 33 percent were white, and 21 percent were Hispanic. Although all of the juvenile death row inmates were either 16 or 17 at the time they committed their crimes, by the end of 2004, their ages ranged from 18 to 43. They had been on death row from 4 months to 24 years. No juvenile females were on death row as of December 31, 2004. Only five females who were younger than 18 years of age at the time of their crimes have been sentenced to death since 1973 (following the landmark *Furman v. Georgia* decision and the beginning of the modern death penalty era), and none of them were executed. Four of them had their sentences reversed, and one had her sentence commuted. The 72 juvenile death row inmates as of December 31, 2004, were on death rows in 12 of the 21 states that at the time authorized the death penalty for juvenile offenders. Texas, by far, had the largest number of juvenile death row inmates, 29, or 40 percent.

A study of 14 juvenile death row inmates conducted in the mid-1980s revealed that (1) 14 of them had head injuries as children; (2) 12 had been brutally abused physically, sexually, or both; (3) nine had major neuropsychological disorders; (4) seven had psychotic disorders since childhood; (5) seven had serious psychiatric disturbances; (6) five had been sodomized as children; (7) only three had at least average reading ability; and (8) only two had intelligence scores above 90 (90–100 is considered average).[6]

Sentencing Juveniles to Death

Between 1973 and December 31, 2004, jurisdictions in the United States had imposed death sentences on 228 offenders under the age of 18 at the time of their crime, which represented about 3 percent of the 7,528 death sentences imposed for offenders of all ages during the period. Three states—Texas (58), Florida (32), and Alabama (25)—accounted for about half of the death sentences imposed on juveniles. As noted above, only 72 of those death sentences remained in force at the end of 2004. Even before the *Simmons* decision, however, the chances of any juvenile on death row being executed was remote. Since 1973, the reversal rate for juveniles sentenced to death was about 90 percent.

Public Opinion Following *Thompson*, *Stanford*, and *Wilkins*

After the Court's decisions in *Thompson*, *Stanford*, and *Wilkins*, the question of whether or not juveniles should be subjected to capital punishment received more attention. In a 1994 Gallup Poll,[7] for example, 60 percent of Americans thought that when a teenager committed a murder and was found guilty by a jury, he (the survey item did not address female teenage killers) should get the death penalty (compared with 80 percent who favored the death penalty for adults), 30 percent opposed the death penalty for teenagers, and 10 percent had no opinion. Among those who favored the death penalty for adults, 72 percent favored the death penalty for teenage killers. When asked whether juveniles convicted of their first crime should be given the same punishment as adults convicted of their first crime, 50 percent of Americans believed juveniles should be treated the same as adults, 40 percent believed they should be treated less harshly, 9 percent responded that it depends, and 1 percent had no opinion. When asked whether juveniles convicted of their second or third crimes should be given the same punishment as adults convicted of their second or third crimes, 83 percent of Americans believed juveniles should be treated the same as adults, only 12 percent believed they should be treated less harshly, 4 percent thought it depends, and 1 percent had no opinion. As for how juveniles who committed the same crimes as adults should be treated, 52 percent of Americans believed they should receive the same punishment, 31 percent believed that juveniles should be rehabilitated, 13 percent responded that it depends on the circumstances, 3 percent chose another sanction, and 1 percent had no opinion. One problem with alternatives to capital punishment was that Americans had little confidence in the rehabilitative programs available to juveniles. Only 25 percent of Americans believed that rehabilitation programs for juveniles were even moderately successful. However, nearly half (48 percent) of the respondents also believed that the rehabilitation programs for juveniles had not been given the necessary money and support to be successful.

THE DEBATE

As the death penalty for juveniles was being debated, both sides mounted strong arguments for their positions. Among the reasons given for not subjecting juveniles to capital punishment were the following:

- Our society, as represented by legislatures, prosecutors, judges, and juries, had rejected the juvenile death penalty.
- Other nations had rejected the juvenile death penalty. (The United States and Somalia were the only two countries in the United Nations not to ratify Article 37(a) of the U.N. Convention on the Rights of the Child, which bans capital punishment for anyone less than 18 years of age.)
- The threat of the death penalty did not deter potential juvenile murderers, because juveniles often did not consider the possible consequences before committing their murderous acts and because, even if they did consider these consequences, they would realize that few juveniles actually received the death penalty.
- Juveniles were especially likely to be rehabilitated or reformed while in prison, thus rendering the juvenile death penalty especially inappropriate.
- The juvenile death penalty did not serve a legitimate retributive purpose, because juveniles were generally less mature and responsible than adults, and should therefore be viewed as less culpable than adults who committed the same crimes.

An additional reason for treating juveniles different than adults in the administration of justice was that juveniles were already treated legally different than adults in other areas of life, such as driving, voting, gambling, marriage, and jury service.

Conversely, some of the reasons for subjecting juveniles to capital punishment were as follows:

- The evidence of a societal consensus against the juvenile death penalty was nonexistent, or at least too weak to justify a constitutional ban.
- The views of other nations were irrelevant to the proper interpretation of our Constitution, at least absent a consensus within our own society.
- The threat of the death penalty could deter potential juvenile murderers, or at least the judgments of legislatures and prosecutors to that effect deserved deference.
- The most heinous juvenile murderers, who were the only ones likely to receive the death penalty, were not good candidates for rehabilitation or reform.

- Some juvenile murderers were sufficiently mature and responsible to deserve the death penalty for their crimes, and thus the juvenile death penalty served a legitimate retributive purpose.

As for other areas of the law that distinguished between adults and juveniles, proponents of capital punishment for juvenile offenders stressed that, although juveniles may not vote conscientiously or drive safely, they did know that killing other human beings was wrong.

Another reason for supporting the death penalty for at least some juvenile capital offenders—and one that, for some people, made the practice of excluding most death-eligible juveniles from the death penalty discriminatory—was that the designation of "juvenile" was arbitrary and only a proxy for more relevant social characteristics. In the first place, it was not until the sixteenth and seventeenth centuries that the young began to be viewed as anything other than miniature adults or property. Before that time, juveniles as young as five or six years old were expected to assume the responsibilities of adults and, when they violated the law, were subjected to the same criminal sanctions as adults. Moreover, it is debatable whether significant differences exist on any relevant social characteristic between a 17 and 18 year old, other than what has been created by law. Given that, is it really meaningful to consider a 17 year old a juvenile and an 18 year old an adult?

In considering whether a person deserved the death penalty from a retributive standpoint, it had been argued that age was largely irrelevant. It was used because it served as an imperfect proxy for more relevant social characteristics. Whether a murderer, regardless of age, deserved the death penalty depended, not on age, in this view, but on maturity, judgment, responsibility, and the capability to assess the possible consequences of his or her actions. In some cases, juveniles possessed those characteristics in greater quantity than some adults did, or in sufficient quantities to be death-eligible; in other cases, they did not. According to the argument, because age was an imperfect proxy for the more relevant characteristics, the use of age as a basis for determining who was or was not death-eligible was discriminatory. Regardless of one's position on the subject of the death penalty for juveniles, it remained a controversial issue.

A NATIONAL CONSENSUS

By 2002, it appeared that a national consensus had developed about the desirability of executing juveniles. In a 2002 Gallup Poll,[8] for example, only 26 percent of respondents favored the death penalty for juveniles, 69 percent opposed it, and 5 percent didn't know or refused to answer. Among subgroups, only 31 percent of males, 21 percent of females, 25 percent of whites, and 29 percent of nonwhites favored the death penalty for juveniles. This was a dramatic change from the results of the 1994 Gallup Poll in which 60 percent of respondents favored the death penalty for juveniles. The Supreme Court was slow to move, however, perhaps because the Justices generally do not consider the results of public opinion polls probative. Toward the end of 2002, the Court by a five to four vote declined to hear another appeal by Kevin Stanford (the appellate in *Stan-ford v. Kentucky*). Stanford's execution date was set for January 7, 2003, but the Kentucky governor refused to sign the death warrant, giving the reason of Stanford's age at the time of the crime. On December 8, 2003, the Kentucky governor commuted Stanford's death sentence to life in prison without opportunity of parole.

By 2005, 18 death penalty states prohibited the death penalty for juve-niles, and the 20 death penalty states that had not prohibited it, infre-quently imposed it. A majority of the Court found these indications probative of a national consensus. The dissenters did not, noting that only 47 percent of death penalty states prohibited the execution of those less than 18 years of age. (At the time *Stanford* was decided, 42 percent of death penalty states prohibited the execution of those less than 18 years of age, which the Court concluded was insufficient as evidence of a national consensus.) More important, by 2005, Justice Anthony Kennedy had changed his mind on the issue.

Simmons and the End of the Death Penalty for Juveniles

Based on the aforementioned developments, the Court, in *Roper v. Simmons*,[9] affirmed by a five to four vote the decision of the Missouri Supreme Court and ruled that the Eighth and Fourteenth Amendments forbid the imposition of the death penalty on offenders who were under the age of 18 at the time their crimes were committed. Justices Kennedy, Stevens, Souter, Ginsburg, and Breyer formed the majority; Justices O'Connor, Scalia, Rehnquist, and Thomas dissented. The Missouri Supreme Court had set aside Simmons' death sentence in favor of "life imprisonment without eligibility for probation, parole, or release except by act of the Governor." It should be noted that the dissenters in the recent *Simmons* decision were particularly incensed by the Missouri Supreme Court's flagrant disregard of the Court's controlling precedent in *Stan-ford*. Before the Simmons' decision by the Missouri Supreme Court, it was understood that it was the Court's sole prerogative to overrule one of its own precedents. According to Justice Scalia,

> To allow lower courts to behave as we do, "updating" the Eighth Amend-ment as needed, destroys stability and makes our case law an unreliable basis for the designing of laws by citizens and their representatives, and for action by public officials. The result will be to crown arbitrariness with chaos.[10]

Christopher Simmons, seven months shy of his 18th birthday at the time of the crime, and a 15-year-old companion broke into a home near St. Louis early one morning in 1993 to commit a burglary. A woman, alone in the house, awoke and recognized the two boys. Simmons and his partner bound the woman and drove her to the river, where they threw her off a bridge. She subsequently drowned. Simmons, who had no previ-ous criminal record, had repeatedly told his friends that he wanted to mur-der someone and bragged that, because he was a minor, he could "get away with it." Simmons confessed to the crime, and about nine months later, he was convicted of the murder and sentenced to death. Under Missouri law, he was tried as an adult. In 1997, the Missouri Supreme Court affirmed Simmons' conviction and death sentence, and, in 2001, the federal courts denied his petition for a writ of habeas corpus.

Following these proceedings, in 2002, the U.S. Supreme Court decided *Atkins v. Virginia*,[11] after which Simmons filed a new petition for state postconviction relief. Simmons argued that the reasoning of *Atkins* established that the Constitution prohibited the execution of a juvenile who was under 18 at the time the crime was committed. In 2003, the Missouri Supreme Court accepted Simmons' claim, and, in 2004, the U.S. Supreme Court granted certiorari.

In *Atkins*, the Court ruled six to three that it is cruel and unusual punishment to execute the mentally retarded. The Court reasoned that the death penalty's two social purposes—(1) retribution, that is, "just deserts," and (2) deterrence of capital crimes by prospective offenders— are not served by the execution of mentally retarded capital offenders. Regarding retribution, the Court believed the lesser culpability of mentally retarded offenders by virtue of their cognitive and behavioral impairments did not merit that form of retribution; as for deterrence, the Court averred that those impairments made it less likely that they could process the information of execution as a possible penalty and, therefore, control their behavior based on that information. The Court surmised that exempting the mentally retarded from execution would not lessen the death penalty's deterrent effect for offenders who are not mentally retarded. The Court was especially concerned that mentally retarded offenders faced a special risk of wrongful execution because they might unwittingly confess to crimes they did not commit, be less able to meaningfully assist their attorneys, be poor witnesses, and possess demeanor that may create an unwarranted impression that they lacked remorse for their crimes. The debatable question, of course, was whether a 17-year-old offender was in the same class as, or equivalent to, a mentally retarded offender with regard to culpability and susceptibility to deterrence.

In *Simmons*, the Court identified three differences between juvenile offenders and adult offenders that diminished the former's culpability. First, "[j]uveniles' susceptibility to immature and irresponsible behavior means 'their irresponsible conduct is not as morally reprehensible as that of an adult.'" Second, "[t]heir own vulnerability and comparative lack of control over their immediate surroundings mean juveniles have a greater claim than adults to be forgiven for failing to escape negative influences in their whole environment." Third, "[t]he reality that juveniles still struggle to define their identity means it is less supportable to conclude that even a heinous crime committed by a juvenile is evidence of irretrievably depraved character."[12]

In support of his position, the petitioner in *Simmons* (Donald P. Roper, superintendent, Potosi Correctional Center) claimed that, "given the Court's own insistence on individualized consideration in capital sentencing, it is arbitrary and unnecessary to adopt a categorical rule barring the imposition of the death penalty on an offender under 18." The petitioner argued that jurors "should be allowed to consider mitigating arguments related to youth on a case-by-case basis, and in some cases to impose the death penalty if justified."[13]

The Court's majority, however, was not willing to take that risk. It noted that in the very case before it, the prosecutor had argued that Simmons' youth was aggravating rather than mitigating. Thus, in response to the petitioner's argument, the Court opined,

> An unacceptable likelihood exists that the brutality or cold-blooded nature of any particular crime would overpower mitigating arguments based on youth as a matter of course, even where the juvenile offender's objective immaturity, vulnerability, and lack of true depravity should require a sentence less severe than death.[14]

The Court concluded,

> When a juvenile commits a heinous crime, the State can exact forfeiture of some of the most basic liberties, but the State cannot extinguish his life and his potential to attain a mature understanding of his own humanity. While drawing the line at 18 is subject to the objections always raised against categorical rules, that is the point where society draws the line for many purposes between childhood and adulthood and the age at which the line for death eligibility ought to rest.[15]

With those words the Supreme Court brought an end to a more than 350-year-old practice in the United States. Years from now, will we ask ourselves how a society could have executed juveniles, or will we ask whether the decision not to execute juveniles was a wise one? The natural experiment has begun.

NOTES

1. *Roper* v. *Simmons*, 2005.
2. *Eddings v. Oklahoma*, 1982.
3. *Furman v. Georgia*, 1972.
4. *Thompson v. Oklahoma*, 1988.
5. *Stanford v. Kentucky* and *Wilkins v. Missouri*, 1989.
6. Lewis, D. O., Pincus, J. H., Bard, B., Richardson, E., Prichep, L., Feldman, M. & Yeager, C. (1988). Neuropsychiatric, psychoeducational, and family characteristics of 14 juveniles condemned to death in the United States. *American Journal of Psychiatry*, 145, 584–589.
7. Moore, 1994.
8. Jones, 2002.
9. *Roper v. Simmons*, 2005.
10. *Roper v. Simmons*, 2005, p. 630.
11. *Atkins v. Virginia*, 2002.
12. *Roper v. Simmons*, 2005, pp. 569–570.
13. *Roper v. Simmons*, 2005, p. 572.
14. *Roper v. Simmons*, 2005, p. 573.
15. *Roper v. Simmons*, 2005, p. 574.

REFERENCES

Bohm, R. M. (2003). *Deathquest II: An introduction to the theory and practice of capital punishment in the United States* (2nd ed.). Cincinnati, OH: Anderson.

Bright, S. B. (1997). *Capital punishment on the 25ᵗʰ anniversary of Furman v. Georgia*. Atlanta, GA: Southern Center for Human Rights.

Cothern, L. (2000, November). Juveniles and the death penalty. Washington, D.C.: U.S. Department of Justice, Coordinating Council on Juvenile Justice and Delinquency Prevention.

The Death Penalty Information Center. (n.d.). *Juveniles.* Retrieved August 1, 2006, from www.deathpenaltyinfo.org.

Hoffmann, J. L. (1993). On the perils of line-drawing: Juveniles and the death penalty. In V. L. Streib (Ed.), *A capital punishment anthology* (pp. 117–32). Cincinnati, OH: Anderson.

Jones, J. M. (2002). *Slim majority of Americans say death penalty applied fairly.* The Gallup Organization. Retrieved August 1, 2006, from www.gallup.com/poll/releases/pr020520.asp.

McCaffrey, S. (2002, October 12). Justices refuse to review execution of juveniles. *The Orlando Sentinel*, p. A3.

Moore, D. W. (1994, September). Majority advocate death penalty for teenage killers. *The Gallup Poll Monthly*, 2–5.

Schneider, V., & Smykla, J. O. (1991). A summary analysis of executions in the United States, 1608–1987: The Espy file. In R. M. Bohm (Ed.), *The death penalty in America: Current research* (pp. 1–19). Cincinnati, OH: Anderson.

Streib, V. L. (1988). Imposing the death penalty on children. In K. C. Haas & J. A. Inciardi (Eds.), *Challenging capital punishment: Legal and social science approaches* (pp. 245–267). Newbury Park, CA: Sage Publications.

Streib, V. L. (1989). Juveniles' attitudes toward their impending executions. In M. L. Radelet (Ed.), *Facing the death penalty: Essays on a cruel and unusual punishment* (pp. 38–59). Philadelphia, PA: Temple University Press.

Streib, V. L. (2003). Executing women, children, and the mentally retarded: Second class citizens in capital punishment. In J. R. Acker, R. M. Bohm, & C. Lanier (Eds.), *America's experiment with capital punishment: Reflections on the past, present and future of the ultimate penal sanction* (2nd ed., pp. 301–323). Durham, NC: Carolina Academic Press.

Streib, V. L. (2005). *The juvenile death penalty today: Death sentences and executions for juvenile crimes, January 1, 1973–December 31, 2004.* Retrieved August 1, 2006, from www.law.onu.edu/faculty/streib.

CASES CITED

Atkins v. Virginia, 536 U.S. 304 (2002).

Eddings v. Oklahoma, 455 U.S. 104 (1982).

Furman v. Georgia, 408 U.S. 238 (1972).

Roper v. Simmons, 543 U.S. 551 (2005).

Stanford v. Kentucky and *Wilkins v. Missouri,* consolidated under 492 U.S. 361 (1989).

Thompson v. Oklahoma, 487 U.S. 815 (1988).

Index

About the Editors and Contributors

Marilyn D. McShane is a trustee-at-large member of the executive board to the Academy of Criminal Justice Sciences. She and Frank Williams have recently published the textbook *Step By Step Through the Thesis Process: A Resource Guide*. Their *Criminological Theory* book is in its fourth edition with the same publisher.

Frank P. Williams III is professor emeritus at California State University. He is author of *Imagining Criminology* and coauthor of four editions of *Criminological Theory*. He also is coauthor of the soon-to-be-released textbook *Step by Step Through the Thesis Process: A Resource Guide*.

Victoria Simpson Beck is an assistant professor of criminal justice at Indiana University East. Her published works have appeared in the *Journal of Criminal Justice, Juvenile and Family Court Journal*, the *Journal of Psychiatry and Law,* and the journal of *Violence and Victims*. Her research interests include juvenile diversion court programs, sex-offender notification policies, and corrections.

Peter J. Benekos is professor of criminal justice and sociology at Mercyhurst College. His research interests include juvenile justice, corrections, and public policy. Most recently he completed the second edition of *Crime Control, Politics, and Policy* (coauthored with Alida V. Merlo).

Robert M. Bohm is professor of criminal justice and legal studies at the University of Central Florida. He has published widely on the topics of criminal justice, criminological theory, and capital punishment. His most recent article entitled "'McJustice': On the McDonaldization of Criminal Justice" appeared in *Justice Quarterly*.

Michael P. Brown has been at Ball State University since 1993. He earned a doctorate in sociology from Western Michigan University. His research interests include juvenile delinquency, community corrections, and pedagogy.

Jill M. D'Angelo is an assistant professor of criminal justice and criminology at Ball State University. Her primary research specialty is juvenile court judges' decision making. She is, however, broadening her research agenda to include the study of women in prison.

Jon R. Farrar is the chief staff attorney for the U.S. District Court for the Eastern District of Texas. He earned a Juris Doctor from the University of Houston and a doctorate in criminal justice from Sam Houston State University. His prior experience includes being the administrator of Inmate Legal Services for the Texas prison system; an assistant district attorney for Orange County, Texas; and a criminal justice instructor for University of Texas at Tyler.

Wesley A. Krause is a retired deputy chief probation officer of San Bernardino County Probation, California. He has more than 30 years of experience in juvenile justice and community corrections and currently is an adjunct lecturer at the California State University San Bernadino.

Attapol Kuanliang is a doctoral candidate in the Justice Studies Department at Prairie View A&M University. His main areas of interest are juvenile justice, evaluation research, and correction. He has participated in multiple research projects involving the Texas Juvenile Crime Prevention Center and other agencies.

Jodi Lane is associate professor of criminology, law, and society at the University of Florida. She earned her doctorate in social ecology from the University of California, Irvine. Her interests and publications focus on fear of crime, juvenile justice, corrections, crime policy, and program evaluation.

Lonn Lanza-Kaduce is professor of sociology and criminology, and chairperson of the Department of Criminology, Law, and Society at the University of Florida. He is a 2004 ICARE (Institute for Child and Adolescent Research and Evaluation) Development Grant recipient. His research interests include social learning in crime and deviance, criminological theory, drug and alcohol behavior, delinquency, sociology of law, and deviant behavior.

Richard Lawrence is professor of criminal justice at St. Cloud State University in Minnesota. He is the author of several book chapters and journal articles. His most recent publication is *School Crime and Juvenile Justice* (in its second edition).

Alida V. Merlo is professor of criminology at Indiana University of Pennsylvania. Previously, she was a faculty member in the Criminal Justice Department at Westfield State College in Westfield, Massachusetts. She has conducted research and published in the areas of criminal justice policy, juvenile justice, and women and the law. In the last three years, she has coauthored or coedited three books, including the second edition of *Crime Control, Politics, and Policy* (coauthored with Peter J. Benekos), the second edition of *Women, Law and Social Control* (coedited with Joycelyn M. Pollock), and *Controversies in Juvenile Justice and Delinquency* (coedited with Peter J. Benekos).

John K. Mooradian is an assistant professor in the School of Social Work at Michigan State University, where he coordinates the Certificate in Clinical Social Work with Families. He holds a doctorate in social work from Michigan State University, and is a certified social worker, licensed master social worker, and a licensed master and family therapist. His research focuses on issues that affect oppressed and marginalized populations. He is author of *Disproportionate Confinement of African-American Delinquents.*

David Mueller is associate professor of criminal justice at Boise State University. He has written several articles and book chapters on school crime issues, including a recent article entitled "School Shootings and the Man Bites Dog Criterion of Newsworthiness" (coauthored with Richard Lawrence).

David Myers is the doctoral program coordinator at Indiana University Pennsylvania. He is author of *Boys Among Men: Trying and Sentencing Juveniles as Adults* and *Excluding Violent Youths from Juvenile Court: The Effectiveness of Legislative Waiver.*

Robert J. Ramsey is director of the criminal justice program and an assistant professor of criminal justice at Indiana University East. His published works have appeared in the *Juvenile and Family Court Journal,* the *Salem Press,* and *The Journal of Psychiatry and Law.* His research interests include wrongful conviction, juvenile justice, and corrections.

Jon Sorensen is professor of justice studies at Prairie View A&M University. He has published numerous articles on prison violence and capital punishment, and he is coauthor of *Lethal Injection: Capital Punishment in Texas during the Modern Era.*

Lawrence F. Travis III is a professor of criminal justice at the University of Cincinnati. He has directed a number of local, state, and national research projects, including a national study of the role of law enforcement in public schools. Dr. Travis has published five books and monographs and more than 70 articles and book chapters on a range of criminal justice topics.